The Water Doctor's Daughters

Pauline Conolly

ROBERT HALE • LONDON

© Pauline Conolly 2013
First published in Great Britain 2013

ISBN 978-0-7198-0570-7

Robert Hale Limited
Clerkenwell House
Clerkenwell Green
London EC1R 0HT

www.halebooks.com

A catalogue record for this book is available from the British Library

2 4 6 8 10 9 7 5 3 1

Typeset by e-type, Liverpool
Printed by Imprint Digital Limited, India

This book is dedicated to the memory of my mother Myra, whose spirit, humour and love of history had a very positive effect on my life.

It has been well and wittily said, 'The body and the mind are like a jerkin and a jerkin's lining – rumple the one, and you rumple the other.' I may add, ill-use one and you ill-use the other; injure the one and you injure the other.

James Loftus Marsden, *The Action of the Mind on the Body*, 1859.

Contents

Acknowledgements   9

Prologue 11

  1. WET SHEETS AND SHOWER BATHS 13

  2. A CONVERT TO THE CURE 19

  3. THE PENALTY OF MARRIAGE 26

  4. AVUNCULAR AFFECTION 37

  5. VISITORS AT THE VICARAGE 44

  6. THE GOVERNESS 53

  7. SEXUAL MORALITY 59

  8. BANISHMENT 66

  9. A STRANGE LETTER FROM PARIS 78

10. INTERMEDDLING 87

11. A COMPLAINT IS LAID 95

12. THE ENGLISH ENQUIRY 101

13. THE COURT OF ASSIZES 108

14. ALL THIS IS FALSE 122

15. A FÊTE OF THE HEART 132

16. HYMNS OF PRAISE 143

17. THE CHILL WIND OF DEFEAT 153

18. EVERYONE HERE IS RUINED 160

19. A FAMILY BREACH 175

20. DISGRACE AND EXILE 184

21. DANGEROUS LIAISONS 197

22. BURGUNDY AND MRS COX 204

23. REDUCED CIRCUMSTANCES 213

24. AS EASY AS ABC 219

25. A BROKEN BOTTLE 223

26. MAKE HER GRAVE STRAIGHT 234

27. ELLEN AMY 238

28. BEQUESTS AND LEGACIES 247

Epilogue 254

Notes 258

Further Reading 268

Index 269

Acknowledgements

I would like to express my appreciation to the following:

At Robert Hale – my patient editor Nikki Edwards.

The staff at the Bodleian Library, Oxford. It was a special privilege to read the Reverend John Rashdall's diaries in the ancient Duke Humphrey Room.

The Worcestershire Records Office
The Worcestershire History Centre
Malvern Library
Hastings Library
The staff at Montmartre Cemetery, Paris

Individuals – Robert Dudley, Timothy Stunt, Cora Weaver, Randal Keynes, Carlton Tarr, David Force, Derek Wain, Brian Iles, Errol Fuller, plus the many other people who took the time to answer my countless emails and letters. A special thanks to family and friends in Australia and the UK for their support and encouragement. Above all, I would like to thank my partner, Rob. This book could never have been written without his love and faith, not to mention his skills as photographer, chauffeur, proofreader, computer technician, coffee maker etc. etc.

Prologue

Within the churchyard of the beautiful old Priory Church at Great Malvern in Worcestershire are the graves of two young girls. Once playmates, they died less than three years apart. Flowers have been planted around the smaller grave and visitors often leave tributes below its curved headstone. There is a loving dedication:

ANNE ELIZABETH DARWIN
BORN MARCH 2 1841
DIED APRIL 23 1851
A Dear and Good Child.

Several metres away is a flat, weathered stone covering the remains of Lucy Marsden. The iron railings once enclosing the plot were removed to provide scrap metal during the Second World War. Few people seek out the grave, or pause to decipher its inscription:

LUCY HARRIET MARSDEN
DIED SEPT 1853 AGED 14

It could be said that Lucy died because, unlike Annie Darwin, she was *not* viewed as 'dear and good'.

Neither of the girls had been born at Great Malvern. It was the town's reputation as a health spa that attracted the attention of their respective fathers. The famous naturalist Charles Darwin first visited Malvern as a 'water-cure' patient in 1849. Doctor James Loftus Marsden arrived in 1846, an ambitious young physician specializing in the unorthodox therapies of hydropathy and homeopathy.

Inside the Priory Church is an honour board of past vicars. The Reverend John Rashdall is listed as serving from 1850 until 1856. It was John Rashdall who delivered the sermon at Annie Darwin's funeral. He also sat by the bedside of the dying Lucy Marsden, but although he attended her burial service he was too distraught to take his place in the pulpit.

1. Wet Sheets and Shower Baths

❧

The village of Great Malvern grew up on the eastern slopes of Worcestershire's Malvern Hills, following the establishment of a Benedictine monastery in 1085. In the wake of Henry VIII's dissolution of the monasteries, the Priory Church was purchased by the local community. Dedicated to St Mary the Virgin, it still serves as the town's parish church. St Mary's medieval stained glass windows are acknowledged as some of the largest and finest in England. Other treasures include a collection of 1,200 medieval tiles, handmade by the monks, and elaborately carved misericords or 'mercy seats', dating from the fifteenth century.

Overlooking St Mary's Priory Church and the town of Great Malvern

Malvern quickly became known for its healing wells, fed by crystal-clear springs filtering through the surrounding granite and limestone hills. In 1756 Dr John Wall famously proclaimed that Malvern water was so pure it contained 'just nothing at all!' By the turn of the century the spa centre had become fashionable, and more than a little snobbish. When the novelist Catherine Hutton visited in 1802 she was almost turned away from the Well House Hotel until making it clear she was a gentlewoman:

> I entered the Well House alone, and without attendants, having walked up the hill. The master of the house seemed doubtful whether he should let me in – he would 'Enquire of the chambermaid whether there was a vacant bedroom.' 'I have a chaise, a horse, and a servant with me,' I said. This settled the point, and I was conducted to the vacant bedroom.[1]

During the early 1820s a pump and commercial baths were established, a development followed several years later by the social coup of royal patronage. In the summer of 1830 the *Worcester Journal* proudly announced that the Duchess of Kent and the Princess Victoria, 12-year-old heir presumptive to the British throne, were to visit Malvern for six weeks: 'The presence of the Duchess and her interesting daughter will no doubt attract numerous visitors…'. However, it was not until the introduction of Vincent Priessnitz's famous 'water-cure' in 1842 that Malvern really began to capitalize on its natural gifts.

Priessnitz (1799–1851) was a peasant farmer from the village of Graefenberg in Austrian Silesia, now part of the Czech Republic. It was said that after watching a fawn heal itself by bathing in a mountain spring he wrapped wet bandages around his own ribs, which had been fractured in a cart accident. Several months later Priessnitz declared himself cured and began treating neighbours and their livestock. Word spread and in 1822 he opened a small clinic. By 1839 it had evolved into a sanatorium treating some 1,500 patients per year. The regime was rigorous to say the least. Patients were housed in rough, army-style barracks and awakened by attendants at first light to be swaddled in wet sheets. This was followed by therapeutic baths, douches and cold compresses plus the drinking of vast quantities of spring water. Long walks, a plain diet and strict abstention from alcohol and tobacco formed an integral part of the 'cure'.

THE ASCENDING DOUCHE.—"NOW SIR,—DO SIT STILL".

The unorthodox therapies involved in the water-cure provided
an easy target for cartoonists

In 1842 Englishman R.T. Claridge wrote a glowing account of the treatment at Graefenberg in *Hydropathy or the cold-water cure as practised by Vincent Priessnitz*. However, not everyone was impressed. Shortly afterwards a humorous review appeared in an English magazine. The writer joked that damp sheets were already well known to the chambermaids of England's inns, and that while the water used in the cure may have been ice cold, Priessnitz had made himself 'warm' to the extent that he was already worth £50,000. Dismissing hydropathy as 'pure quackery', the article continued:

It has been our good fortune, since reading Claridge on Hydropathy, to see a sick drake avail himself of the 'Cold Water Cure' at the dispensary in St James Park. First in waddling in, he took a Fuss-Bad; then he took a Sitz-Bad, and then, turning his curly tail up into the air, he took a Kopf-Bad. Lastly, he rose almost upright on his latter end, and made such a triumphant flapping with his wings, that we expected he was going to shout 'Priessnitz for ever!' But no such thing. He only cried, 'Quack! quack! quack!'[2]

15

Others, including some members of the orthodox medical profession, were more receptive to the novel, water-based therapy. It at least offered an alternative to the use of poisonous compounds containing arsenic and mercury and to the Victorian panacea of laudanum, which was opium based and highly addictive.

Two of Vincent Priessnitz's earliest disciples in England were doctors James Wilson and James Manby Gully. In 1841 Dr Wilson had spent eight months at Graefenburg, observing Priessnitz's techniques and undergoing the treatment himself to alleviate neuralgia and a persistent skin complaint. He returned to England an enthusiastic convert and convinced his friend Gully to join him in establishing a practice at Great Malvern, chosen for its pure water, fresh air and romantic scenery. By coincidence, an ancient grave in the Priory churchyard carried an epitaph the partners could have chosen as their mantra:

> *Pain was my portion – physic my food*
> *Groans my devotion – drugs done me no good.*

James Gully was born in Jamaica, the son of a successful coffee grower. He had been taken to England as a young child and later studied medicine at Edinburgh University. His first wife died in 1838, leaving him with three young children. On 14 October 1840 Dr Gully married Francis Kibble, a wealthy widow seventeen years his senior. The relationship failed after just eighteen months and the couple separated. This crisis in Gully's personal life almost certainly influenced his decision to join forces with James Wilson at Great Malvern. In the summer of 1842 he set up home there with his children and his two spinster sisters, Anne and Helen.

Drs Wilson and Gully were both forceful and strong-minded characters, but while Wilson was inclined to be brusque and autocratic, Gully was urbane and personable. Dr Wilson arrived at Malvern slightly ahead of his partner, setting up at the Crown Hotel. His first patient was an elderly local called Probert, a hopeless drunkard with a range of complaints such as gout and heart disease. Naturally enough, a wholesome diet and the replacement of alcohol by water worked wonders. Wilson later wrote, 'He was only a fortnight under my care and his improvement in every respect was so great that it made a sensation in the village and neighbourhood.'³ The canny Dr Wilson had treated Mr Probert free of charge, but before long he and Gully were attracting well-heeled patients from all over the country.

One of the earliest and most outspoken opponents of the water-cure was Dr Charles Hastings from Worcester. In an article published in November 1842, Hastings dismissed those flocking to Malvern for treatment as '...old Indians from Cheltenham, hypochondriacal ladies, and dyspeptics'. He suggested that within a year the therapy would vanish like St John Long (an infamous quack doctor convicted of manslaughter).⁴ Gully and Wilson countered by co-authoring a book comparing the drug-free water-cure with the dangers of conventional medicine. Nevertheless, a chapter titled 'Ridicule of the Water-Cure' revealed that the taunts of men like Hastings had hit their mark:

A few short months ago it [the water-cure] was met by the laughter of the great and small among the medical profession. We remember well the cachinnatory explosions that followed the announcement that wet sheets were excellent in fever, so excellent as to preclude the necessity of drugs in that disease. There was no end to the smart things emitted and the guffaws which ensued upon them, when sitz-baths were mentioned as effective in constipated bowels. We have a distinct recollection of a little priggish surgeon-apothecary, who told us that if we continued to talk in such strain, 'we should convert his eyes into a shower bath, for he must laugh until he cried'.⁵

Twelve months later Dr Wilson published a pamphlet claiming that hydropathy could cure virtually every scourge of the day, including leprosy, tubercular consumption and syphilis. The next part of his treatise, he said, would be co-authored with Dr Gully. However, the men quarrelled and their partnership was acrimoniously dissolved. In 1846 it was Dr Gully alone who published *The Water Cure in Chronic Disease*. The book met with immediate success and eventually ran to nine editions. Despite Dr Wilson having served his long apprenticeship with Priessnitz, it was the charismatic James Gully whose star now shone the brightest. He was soon looking about for a new partner and the most

THE DOUCHE.
" Oh! Oh! Oh! Oh! "

Cause for more humour at the expense of the water-cure
doctors; the shock of the Descending Douche!

obvious choice was a young doctor by the name of James Loftus Marsden,
who had visited Graefenberg and embraced the new therapy. Dr Marsden
was then practising in Devon, but had a strong family connection with
Worcestershire.

2. A Convert to the Cure

James Marsden was born in Dublin in 1815. He was the second son of British army officer Captain James Marsden of the 7th Dragoon Guards, whose family had originated in Derbyshire. His mother Harriet was the daughter of Wakeman Long, an attorney from the village of Upton-upon-Severn, just a few miles from Great Malvern. Captain and Mrs Marsden returned to Worcestershire around 1820, settling in Kempsey, close to Harriet's family. Their house was called The Palace, which sounds pretentious, although the name had probably been inspired by Kempsey's thirteenth-century Bishop's Palace. The Marsden residence was comfortable, though certainly not grand. It was set on an acre of land with a walled garden, stables, a coach house, a worker's cottage and an orchard.

Little is known of Dr Marsden's childhood, but evidence suggests his home life was stable and happy. Among the friends from his university days was Scots-born William Hewitson (1812–50). Hewitson spent part of 1838 in England and in a letter to Marsden, dated 11 October of that year, he wrote, 'Having left Malvern on Monday morning of last week, I reached Worcester before eight o'clock. I strained my eyes in the direction of Kempsey, if perchance, I might discover some object in it round which I might assemble the recollections of happy hours spent with your family.'[1]

James's brothers, Frederick and John, followed their father into the army. Both served in India, with Frederick eventually achieving the rank of Lieutenant Colonel. However, young James was academically gifted and it was decided he should study medicine. He graduated from Edinburgh University in August 1836. While his fellow students presented final dissertations on conditions such as cholera, tetanus and apoplexy, James Marsden's chosen topic was ennui, defined by the *Oxford Dictionary* as 'a feeling of listlessness and dissatisfaction from a lack of occupation or excitement'. It was an early indication of his lifelong interest in the human mind and its effects on physical health.

On 14 June 1838 James married 27-year-old Lucy Rashdall, whose family were minor landed gentry from Spilsby in Lincolnshire. Lucy's father Robert died in April 1812 when Lucy was still a babe-in-arms: 'at Louth co. Lincoln, aged 33, Robert Rashdall … has left a widow and four small children to mourn him'.[2] There were actually five young Rashdalls. Lucy had two brothers, John and Robert (who became Anglican clergymen), and two older sisters, Frances (known as Fanny) and Elizabeth. By 1838 the widowed Mrs Rashdall and Lucy's unmarried sisters had moved from Lincolnshire to the Gloucestershire spa town of Cheltenham. It was here that Lucy and James exchanged vows at medieval St Mary's church. That same day, James's older brother Frederick, home on leave from army service in India, married Sidney Jane Hughes at St Mary-de-Crypt church in Gloucester. Miss Hughes was the youngest daughter of a Welsh peer.

On 28 June, 19-year-old Queen Victoria was crowned at Westminster Abbey. She had acceded to the throne the previous year following the death of her uncle, William IV. Her long reign would not only define a nation, but an empire encompassing a quarter of the world's land mass. At a more human level it would profoundly affect the lives of James Marsden and his children.

The newly qualified Dr Marsden set himself up in general practice at Melcombe Regis, on the south Dorset coast. As a physician he would have been interested to know that in 1348 the port had been the point of entry for the bubonic plague, brought ashore by flea-infested rats on a ship arriving from the Continent. In the late eighteenth century Melcombe Regis (now part of Weymouth) became a fashionable seaside resort due to the patronage of King George III. It is possible that Dr Marsden chose to practise in the town due to its proximity to France. He and Lucy spent the next few summers in Paris, where Dr Marsden studied under French physicians at a large hospital on the outskirts of the city. Their first child, Lucy Harriet, was christened in Paris on 31 May 1839. The couple were also in Paris when their second daughter, Emily Frances, arrived in 1840, the year Queen Victoria married her first cousin, Prince Albert. A third daughter, Marian Theodosia (affectionately known as Poppy), was born in England in June the following year, while Lucy was staying with her family at Cheltenham.

On 18 August 1841, the *Gentleman's Magazine* reported the death of Dr Marsden's father in Hanover Square, London. Captain Marsden was buried in Kensal Green Cemetery. Harriet Marsden subsequently let The

Palace, moving with her unmarried daughter Theodosia to Claremont Cottage in Winchcombe Street, Cheltenham.

Early in 1842 Dr Marsden moved his own young family to Devon, purchasing a fourteen-year lease on a property in fashionable Dix's Field, in the city of Exeter. Approached via an impressive carriage drive, the house was one of a double row of Georgian terraces built on opposite sides of a central green. Its five levels included two drawing rooms, two sitting rooms, a library, four bedrooms and four large attics. To Lucy's joy there was also a private rear garden for the children. The move represented a step up the ladder both socially and professionally for Dr Marsden, but was also prompted by the fact that Lucy's bachelor brother John Rashdall was curate of Exeter's Bedford Chapel. The Reverend John Rashdall became godfather to the Marsdens' first and only son, James Rashdall Jr, who arrived at Dix's Field on 7 April 1842, during the family's first spring in their new home. There was little rest for Lucy as her fourth daughter, Rosa Sidney, came into the world on 14 October 1843.

© PETER D. THOMAS, EXETER

The Georgian terraces of Dix's Field, Exeter, became home to the enterprising Dr Marsden and his growing family

James Marsden was ambitious and intellectually curious. He read widely and experimented with the patent medical devices so eagerly embraced by the Victorians. In 1844 he travelled to Plymouth for a medical conference, where he demonstrated a dry-cupping device invented by a Frenchman called Tunod: 'It was made of copper, in the shape of a boot, and is applied as one, having an India rubber top to tie around the thigh and render it air tight. The air is then exhausted with a syringe. By the application of this apparatus, the leg may be distended to double its normal size.'[3] Marsden had witnessed this alarming contraption being used during his summers in Paris. He claimed it could be applied up to sixty times within two or three days without ill-effect and that it was effective in cases ranging from deafness to sore throat and croup, without recourse to drugs.

Like Drs Wilson and Gully, James Marsden had been forming the view that conventional drug therapy was dangerous and ineffective. It was around this time that a medical friend visited Exeter and offered to treat the doctor's head cold using the holistic system of homeopathy. Marsden later wrote that after abstaining from tea and wine and taking what appeared to be 'small sugar plums', he was cured within twenty-four hours. Impressed, he began to experiment with homeopathic remedies himself, though in secret for fear of being dubbed a quack. The fear was well founded as homeopathic practitioners were often catagorized as little better than snake oil salesmen. A contemporary essay by American doctor Oliver Wendell Holmes began, 'Homeopathy has proved lucrative, and so long as it continues to be so will surely exist, as surely as astrology, palmistry, and other methods of getting a living out of the weakness and credulity of mankind and womankind.' Holmes was aware that the treatment would have its champions: 'So long as the body is affected through the mind, no audacious device, even of the most manifestly dishonest character, can fail of producing occasional good to those who yield it an implicit or even a partial faith.'[4]

In one of Dr Marsden's first experiments he claimed to have cured a lung abscess in his horse, using extract of the highly toxic plant belladonna. Intense and obsessive by nature, he would soon embrace alternative medicine with religious fervour.

Meanwhile, Lucy Marsden did her best to keep her young brood quiet while her husband prepared his potions and pored over medical tracts. She was not always successful and the doctor became increasingly irritated and frustrated with the distractions of family life. Perhaps due to stress, his health deteriorated and in the autumn of 1844 he announced that it was necessary for him to spend the winter in a warmer climate. Lucy was to accompany him, but to her great distress she was informed that the children were to remain at home, including baby Rosa who was just twelve months old. Since a Victorian wife's first duty was to attend to her husband's comfort, Lucy could only grieve silently and accept the decision. John Rashdall's diary indicates that he too was part of Dr Marsden's grand plan:

> A remarkable change seems imminent in my domestic arrangements by the decision of Dr Marsden to spend the winter at either Malta or Egypt for his own health, in danger from pulmonary disease. The plan is to board the children & Lucy & he to go alone. I to keep house at No. 3…he will, I feel persuaded, not return. Lucy is very sad at the thought.[5]

There is no record of who cared for the children, although the mention of 'board' implies a foster family rather than relatives.

Despite the veiled criticism of Dr Marsden in John Rashdall's comments, he meekly acquiesced to his brother-in-law's wishes, something he would do constantly in the years ahead. The minister was wrong in assuming that his sister and her husband would not return to Exeter, but correct in sensing Dr Marsden was unsettled and planning major changes in his professional life.

Malta was chosen over Egypt as the Marsdens' winter base and they left Exeter at the end of October. Soon afterwards Lucy fell pregnant for the sixth time. She expected to be back in England well before her confinement but, instead of returning home in the spring, the couple moved on to Austria. The doctor would later explain, 'Though time was on the wing, I thought there would be profit and pleasure in seeking health in famous places, and people, and things I had not yet had an opportunity of seeing.'[6] First stop on his pilgrimage was Vienna, where he spent several months observing the work of renowned homeopathist Dr Fleishmann, at the Hospital of Grey Sisters. Lucy's baby, a daughter they named Alice, was born in Vienna in mid-July 1845 and christened there on 26 August. Interestingly, Marsden's health now failed again. It is tempting to connect his malaise with the fact that he no longer had his wife's undivided attention!

By autumn, the couple had been away from England for nine months. The situation must have been unbearable for Lucy, but incredibly they now moved on to Graefenberg, where Dr Marsden studied Vincent Priessnitz's water-cure treatment for a further five months. It was early in 1846 before they returned to Exeter and Lucy was finally reunited with her children. After such a prolonged absence, the younger ones would have had no memory of their parents.

The Reverend John Rashdall, following his extended stint of 'house sitting', stayed on with the family at Dix's Field and was soon converted to homeopathy by his brother-in-law.

Dr Marsden was fairly bursting with information gathered on his travels. He was the star turn at the annual gathering of West Country medical men, held that year in Exeter. Proving he had done more than just rest and recuperate on Malta, he demonstrated an extendable catheter invented on the island by a Dr Stillon. Before the meeting ended he was on his feet again, lecturing on his experiences at Vincent Priessnitz's water-cure establishment. At his Dix's Field practice, Marsden moved further away from orthodox medicine, prescribing drug-free, homeopathic remedies and claiming almost miraculous cures. He would applaud the system as having a remarkable effect on the emotional well-being of his patients, particularly the young. For a man who had so selfishly deprived his children of their mother's love and comfort, the doctor's praise of homeopathy in the nursery was ironic:

> What tears and distress, and nausea from nauseous drugs, does it spare the poor little invalids. 'He shan't then Darling; he shan't touch it', still rings grating in my ears. Thank heaven! I am no more the terror of the nursery. Sickness has lost half its misery, and more than half its bitterness.[7]

Dr Marsden's interest in the water-cure also continued, despite a torrent of adverse publicity following the death in January 1844 of the respected politician Sir Francis Burdett. *The Provincial Medical Journal* published an article on the subject, damning both homeopathy and hydropathy: 'The death of this kind-hearted old man tempts us to make one or two observations on the inconsistencies displayed by those who desert the rational and well-educated physician and place implicit confidence in the delusions of quackery.' Sir Francis had consulted a London hydropathist in the hope of curing his painful gout and such was his faith in the 'cure' that he even rode his horse while wrapped in wet sheets. Not surprisingly, he fell dangerously ill. His family urged him to seek orthodox medical help, but the old man refused: 'Two invaluable days were wasted; for Sir Francis insisted on seeing a homeopath, whose silly inanities usurped the place of active invigorative treatment. After this the efforts of medicine were fruitless.'[8]

It was a measure of James Marsden's self-belief that he was willing to risk the antagonism and ridicule of his colleagues by embracing not one, but two, highly controversial therapies. But it was Great Malvern, not Exeter, that was the most lucrative place to practise alternative medicine. Since returning home, Dr Marsden had been communicating with the Malvern water doctors, exchanging case notes, supporting their campaign against the 'drug men' and letting them know he had spent considerable time with Vincent Priessnitz. The strategy paid dividends and in 1846 he was approached by James Gully: 'Dr Gully, whose views of practical medicine coincided with my own, proposed our forming a partnership for a limited time. Not only was the relaxing climate [of Devon] beginning again to undermine my health, but the proposition was agreeable, and was accepted.'[9] Poor Lucy Marsden was forced to uproot herself yet again.

The contents of Dix's Field were packed up and the house was auctioned in June 1846. Most of the staff were let go, but at least three members of the household accompanied the family to Great Malvern: the children's governess Maria Hayne, Devon-born housekeeper Eliza Burnell, and Eliza's younger sister, Adelaide. Although Adelaide would replace Maria as governess two years later, the women remained good friends. Miss Hayne continued to take a fond interest in the Marsden children.

News that his sister and her family were to leave Devon prompted the Reverend John Rashdall to review his own situation. In February 1847 he moved to London. At Exeter he had spent much of his time ministering to the underprivileged, and in lieu of a farewell gift his Bedford Chapel congregation raised money for the starving Irish and Scots (victims of the potato famine) to be donated in his name. John Rashdall now became the incumbent of Eaton Chapel in exclusive Belgravia, having purchased the lease of the building. There would be few needy souls among his new flock.

3. The Penalty of Marriage

❧

Although Lucy Marsden had been reluctant to leave Exeter, Great Malvern had its compensations. The 36-year-old was pregnant with her seventh child, and as the town was within a few miles of Cheltenham she was able to call on the support of her mother and sisters, as well as her mother-in-law, Harriet Marsden. Perhaps Lucy felt she could make a new start here, sheltered below the Malvern Hills with her children around her as she waited to give birth. In Radclyffe Hall's novel *The Well of Loneliness*, the pregnant Lady Anna Gordon looked across to those same

First on the left – No. 21 Lansdowne Terrace, Cheltenham; home of the young Marsdens' Granny Rashdall and their doting maternal aunts

hills, taking comfort in their beauty: 'From her favourite seat underneath an old cedar, she would see these Malvern Hills in their beauty...their swelling slopes seemed to hold new meaning. They were like pregnant women, full-bosomed, courageous, great green-girdled mothers of splendid sons.'[1]

The young Marsdens were able to establish close relationships with their aunts and grandmothers at Cheltenham, spending time with Harriet Marsden at Claremont Cottage and at Granny Rashdall's impressive five-storey home at No. 21 Lansdowne Terrace. While under construction in 1838, the terraces were described as being '...unrivalled for elegance of exterior by any similar row of private houses in the kingdom'.[2] Built of glowing Cotswold stone, their first-floor balconies were flanked by twin pairs of Ionic columns. Today, Lansdowne Terrace is cherished as part of Cheltenham's rich architectural heritage.

At Great Malvern, Dr Marsden moved his family into one-half of a substantial four-storey Georgian property on the Worcester Road called Abberley House. It was located a few minutes' walk from the town centre

Today, Cotswold House in Worcester Road, Great Malvern, is externally unchanged but it has reverted to its original name of Abberley House

and owned by the local Candler family: William Candler, who lived at nearby Malvern Link, and his three unmarried sisters. The Misses Candler continued to live in one side of the divided property. To avoid confusion, Dr Marsden renamed his section Cotswold House. From the rear, the property enjoyed a spectacular view overlooking the Severn Valley. A terraced lawn provided a safe playing area for the children.

The timing of Dr Marsden's move to Malvern was perfect. His partner James Gully's best-selling book had come to be regarded as the 'bible' of hydropathy and was attracting a large clientele. Gully had also begun co-editing a journal on the cold water cure and Dr Marsden contributed to its first issue with an essay on his pilgrimage to Graefenberg. He promised a second instalment would appear in the following issue, but owing to a family tragedy the piece would never be written.

On 23 June 1847 Lucy Marsden haemorrhaged after giving birth to a stillborn baby. For the children, hushed and anxious voices brought a frightening awareness that something terrible was happening to their mother. Dr Marsden had witnessed the treatment of a similar case at the homeopathic hospital in Vienna: 'A woman had been given up as lost for haemorrhage. A few drops of the millionth part of aconite, of ipecacuanha, of china, of secale carnatum, of nux vomita and pulsatilla, given each at a time in due succession, stopped completely the uterine bleeding, and these medicines given in the course of treatment completely restored her.'[3] If Lucy Marsden received the same potion, then the outcome was very different. Maria Hayne, the children's governess, sat by her mistress over the next nine hours as she slowly bled to death.

Coincidentally, one of Dr Marsden's fellow water-cure physicians would compose a touching but bitter epitaph for Lucy and so many women like her. Mary Gove Nichols was then living in America, but would later set up a water-cure practice in Malvern with her husband. In 1854 she wrote:

Our graveyards are filled with the corpses of women who have died at from thirty to thirty-five years of age, victims of the marriage institution. The children are, from the laws of heredity descent, ill-tempered, sick, and often short-lived. The cares, the responsibilities, the monotony, the perpetual struggle between inclination and duty, make life a burthen and death a welcome relief.[4]

Even the happily married Queen Victoria lamented the lot of perennially pregnant young wives, as a letter to her daughter Vicky reveals: '...the poor woman is bodily and morally the husband's slave. That always sticks in my throat. When I think of a merry, happy, free young girl – and look at the ailing aching state a young wife generally is doomed to – which you can't deny is the penalty of marriage'.[5]

Lucy was buried in the churchyard of the Priory Church. Her heartbroken brother John Rashdall noted in his diary that Dr Gully and various other medical men attended the funeral. The emotional impact on the six young Marsdens must have been enormous. Their sense of security had been badly shaken during the long and painful separation from their mother beginning in 1844, and now they had lost her forever. The older girls, Lucy and Emily, became loving 'little mothers', especially to the baby of the family, Alice, who was yet to celebrate her second birthday.

Soon afterwards, during an epidemic of typhoid fever, James Jr and Marian fell ill and almost followed their mother to the grave. It was the prospect of losing his son and heir that had the greatest impact on Dr Marsden and he would later use his son's recovery to enhance his professional reputation:

> I have passed through the favourite ordeal – the greatest test by which faith can be tried...I have but one son. Eighteen months ago typhus fever broke out in the house. He was one of those who suffered from it...he recovered completely under homeopathy. No case could be more severe. It was one to test the utmost my confidence in our therapies. For a long and weary time I hoped against hope, and when his convalescence was assured, I could only, with a humbled yet thankful heart, acknowledge the goodness of the Healer, who had blessed the means for his recovery.[6]

Next door, the three middle-aged Candler sisters took a kindly interest in the motherless young Marsdens, as did the women's yardman, Thomas Trehearn. Trehearn could be relied upon when the children needed someone to fix a toy or to supply materials for their playhouses. Meanwhile, Dr Marsden found distraction from grief and worry in his work. The water-cure was beginning to attract the most eminent and well-to-do members of Victorian society.

In September 1848 the poet Alfred Lord Tennyson placed himself under the care of James Gully. As Gully's partner, Dr Marsden also had the opportunity of attending Tennyson. Writing from his mother's house in St James Square in Cheltenham a few weeks earlier, the poet told Gully he had called to ask advice about a 'hydropathical crisis' on his arm, but on finding Gully out, 'I showed it to Dr Marsden who likewise was ready to give me his advice gratis, so that really Malvern seemed to be the headquarters of all that is liberal & openhanded in your profession; & your heathen veneration for the poetical attribute comes out as a most practical Christian virtue.'[7] As it happened, James Marsden was already acquainted with Alfred Tennyson, who was a close friend of the Reverend John Rashdall.

Other visitors to Malvern that autumn were Florence Nightingale and her mother Fanny, who both underwent treatment at Dr Gully's establishment. In a letter to the poet Richard Monckton Milnes, Miss Nightingale wrote: 'Your friend Tennyson was there, with a skin so tender he walked backwards whenever the wind was north or east and that was generally. He was sadly contumacious, smoking vile tobacco in [a] long pipe till Dr Gully told him it coarsened his imagination and made him write bad poetry.' Florence Nightingale was an early witness to Gully's magnetic appeal to women, despite the fact that he was short, plump and balding: 'Mama was so taken in by him that I was obliged to tell him I had a father living.'[8]

In March 1849 the chronically unwell Charles Darwin arrived for treatment: 'Having heard accidently of two persons who had received much benefit from the water-cure, I got Dr Gully's book and made further enquiries, and at last started here, with wife, children, and all our servants…I feel certain that the water-cure is no quackery.'[9] The family moved into a large house called The Lodge, located not far from Cotswold House in Worcester Road. It was owned by the elderly Miss Mary Hind, a good friend of Dr Marsden, who may well have recommended the property. Charles Darwin got along famously with Dr Gully and considered the water-cure so beneficial that the family's intended stay of six weeks extended to four months. Darwin's older children, William, George, Annie and Etty, were around the same age as the young Marsdens and they were soon in and out of each other's houses and gardens, having great fun and no doubt trying the patience of their elders. Charles Darwin would return to Malvern in 1851 with two of his children, but unfortunately the outcome would not be so positive.

On 14 June 1849, while the Marsden children were still acting as unofficial hosts to the young Darwins, their father officially but amicably dissolved his partnership with Dr Gully.[10] The growing popularity of the cold-water-cure had convinced Marsden to establish his own practice, combining hydropathy with homeopathy. Perhaps to humour his fervent young colleague, Dr Gully had also embraced homeopathy, although he would never be *totally* convinced of its efficacy. Nevertheless, both he and Dr Marsden would serve on the council of London's first homeopathic hospital, which opened its doors at Golden Square, Soho, in April 1850. It was an indication of the pair's continued close association.

Soon after Dr Marsden had gone his own way, the water-cure treatment at Malvern received some unwelcome publicity involving the son of Andrew Henderson, one of the bath attendants that Dr Marsden had worked with at Dr Gully's establishment. In April 1850, 2-year-old James Henderson fell against a fireplace and, although it seemed he was only slightly injured, he developed a fever several days later. His family packed him with wet towels, a treatment continued by Dr Gully when he was belatedly called in. At the inquest, local surgeon William West commented pointedly that the water-cure treatment was unlikely to have provided the child with any relief.

With a large family and a full complement of household staff, space was at a premium for Dr Marsden at Cotswold House, particularly as he provided accommodation for favoured patients. It was a lucrative arrangement, with board and lodging charged separately to medical fees. In-house treatment also allowed doctors tighter control over their patients. Describing the purpose-built clinic of Dr James Wilson after a stay of three weeks, Bristol journalist Joseph Leech commented:

There was something in fact about the establishment, the order, its regularity, and the control exercised over the inmates, which might be said to partake equally of the boarding-house and the boarding-school, and under the mastering glance and preceptorial authority of Wilson and his assistants, grown-up and even grey-headed people, imperceptibly succumbed to the influence of the man and the place with a juvenile deference, which was almost puerile.[11]

One incidence of Dr Wilson exerting his authority entered the realms of Malvern folklore. The doctor spotted one of his patients, the eminent politician and author Sir Edward Bulwer-Lytton, walking along Church Street with a suspicious bulge under his coat. When challenged, an abashed Bulwer-Lytton admitted to having purchased a bag of tarts from the local baker. Hoping to escape a tongue lashing, he said he had been asked to buy them for a lady friend. Dr Wilson did not care who they were for, roaring, 'Poison! Throw them down in the gutter at once, and have more respect for her inside!'[12]

Dr Marsden ran an equally tight ship at Cotswold House, and for his children the atmosphere was far more oppressive than for temporary, fee-paying clients. They were now sharing their home with invalids, and the old adage that children should be seen and not heard was magnified a thousand-fold. Disturbingly, Dr Marsden's medical theories were beginning to affect all aspects of the youngsters' lives. The restricted diet prescribed for patients was also enforced in the nursery. No doubt the doctor was influenced by the views of men like the American hydropathist Russell Thacher Trall, who called pastry an abomination, and plum cake indigestible trash. He described the Victorians' beloved suet pudding as one of the most pernicious compounds ever invented. Trall would later publish *The Water-cure Cook Book*. It included a cheerless recipe for Snow-ball Puddings, in which peeled apples were packed in cooked rice then wrapped in cloths and boiled for another hour. Unhappily for the little Marsdens, ships biscuits and water crackers were among the few foods to receive Mr Trall's blessing.

The children were also being subjected to strict intellectual control. On the subject of infant development, their father would write:

> ... the mind grows by what it feeds on – that impressions and images (and these include every kind of learning) are the food of the mind, is the reason of the importance that good thoughts and impressions should be received, whilst the mind is ductible, as in infancy and youth: channels of feeling and thought are then formed.[13]

It is interesting to note that while Charles Darwin agreed young minds were impressionable, he also recognized an attendant danger. In his book *The Descent of Man*, Darwin observed:

How so many absurd rules of conduct, as well as so many absurd religious beliefs, have originated, we do not know; nor how it is that they have become, in all quarters of the world, so deeply impressed on the minds of men; but it is worthy of remark that a belief deeply inculcated during the early years of life, while the brain is impressible, appears to acquire almost the nature of an instinct, and the very essence of an instinct is that it is followed independently of reason.[14]

Although Dr Marsden may have been well-intentioned, to impair a child's independence of thought can prove fatal if he or she should fall under a malevolent outside influence.

The doctor had visions of producing six young models of physical and mental health, a glowing tribute to homeopathy and the perfect advertisement for his burgeoning water-cure practice. He was bitterly disappointed when the children failed to meet his expectations. Both his eldest child Lucy and young James Jr were struggling in the schoolroom. Lucy was barely literate and Marsden feared she might actually be slow-witted. Emily was bright and spirited, but her father considered her headstrong and wilful, setting a bad example for her siblings.

When he was not tending to his patients or upbraiding his offspring, Dr Marsden was busy completing a book on homeopathy that he had begun writing while in Exeter. It was published to coincide with the establishment of his new medical practice. In the preface he stated that it would soon be followed by a second volume, covering Malvern and the water-cure. The book was dedicated to the Reverend John Rashdall:

My dear Rashdall

I beg leave to dedicate these 'Notes on Homeopathy' to you, because we were living together when the circumstances and cases related took place, and because they tended to make you, as well as myself, a convert to the new practise. Dedications are made for patronage, for compliment, for esteem-sake. While I value friendship and kindness, you know I think every man is his own best patron. Compliments are out of the question; but I hope you will accept this, as a token of affectionate regard from your brother-in-law,

The Author
June 10 1849

Although Dr Marsden claimed the dedication had nothing to do with patronage, he was well aware that his brother-in-law's long friendship with Alfred Tennyson could prove advantageous. A few well-chosen words from Rashdall might persuade the famous poet that his next experience of the water-cure should be at Cotswold House rather than at Dr Gully's establishment.

Malvern's water-doctors were now vying for prestigious clients and, as Joseph Leech noted with amusement, their efforts at self-promotion knew no bounds:

> The three hydropathic doctors, who are more to Malvern than the three kings were to Brentford, have each had their portraits lithographed, and from the windows of the bookshop and the bazaar, and even from the walls of the inns, they seem to bid for the possession and management of the visitor's body on his arrival. With whiskers silkily curled, sitting by a table, and severely musing, the 'Great Original', Wilson, seems intrepidly to assure the invalid and hypochondriac of a cure. Standing up with arms a-kimbo, pert and pragmatic Dr Gully appears to push himself forward and say, 'I'm your man – try me': while Marsden, who unites homoeopathy with hydrotherapy, may be said to have a mezzotint manner between both, and looks from his frame upon you as if he were listening to your case.[15]

The description of James Marsden's portrait matches a lithograph by B. Smith (1849), now held in the library of London's Wellcome Trust. Seated at his desk surrounded by textbooks, he appears entirely self-assured. He is immaculately turned out in cravat and wide-cuffed, cutaway-coat. His long side-whiskers may have been grown to compensate for a receding hairline.

LITHOGRAPH BY B. SMITH, 1849. WELLCOME LIBRARY, LONDON

Dr James Loftus Marsden established himself as one of Great Malvern's successful water-cure doctors but his motherless children were repressed and unhappy

Dr Marsden knew that if he hoped to compete with the more prominent Gully and Wilson, he would require a much larger and grander establishment than Cotswold House. Although some clients were content to reside in Malvern's boarding houses as out-patients, Dr Wilson had built a seventy-room spa hotel, complete with ballroom. Following their bland dinners of mutton, vegetables and copious amounts of water, his clients could enjoy music and even a little dancing before being ushered to their early beds.

Dr Gully was able to offer his clients luxurious accommodation at Tudor House in Wells Street, although he preferred to separate the sexes, explaining:

... it appears an arrangement of very doubtful propriety to place male and female patients in the same establishments. By means of the bath attendants (and the uneducated *will* babble) the infirmities of females are liable to become known to everybody with whom they sit at table...What would a parent or husband say to the presence of women of doubtful character in the same house with his wife or daughter?[16]

The male and female sections of Tudor House were connected by a elaborate, covered walkway. It was jokingly referred to as the 'Bridge of Sighs' and not only because of its resemblance to the famous seventeenth-century Ponte dei Sospire in Venice.

For some time, Dr Marsden had been purchasing parcels of land in Malvern from different vendors, finally consolidating them into a 5-acre site stretching from Abbey Road through to what is now College Road. But before he could begin drawing up plans for his state-of-the-art treatment centre, another quite different opportunity to enhance his social and professional standing arose.

4. Avuncular Affection

D r Marsden had been in sole practice for about twelve months when he discovered the living of the Priory Church was about to become vacant. Great Malvern's wealthy water-cure patients filled the pews of the old church every Sunday and Marsden realized what a coup it would be if his brother-in-law John Rashdall became St Mary's next vicar.

A chance to push this idea presented itself in the summer of 1850. On 24 June Dr Marsden stayed overnight with the Reverend John Rashdall after delivering his six children and their governess Adelaide Burnell to the minister's home in London. Rashdall and his elderly mother had generously agreed to take the youngsters on holiday to Dunkerque, on the north coast of France. It was quite an undertaking and a measure of the Rashdall family's affection for the children. The Victorians were indefatigable travellers but, as a contemporary guidebook warned, the small steamboats crossing the Channel were often uncomfortably overcrowded. In rough weather many passengers were soaked to the skin by rain or sea spray. Passengers, especially ladies, were warned to take 'a small change of raiment in a hand bag'. Large swells could also make the twelve-hour journey a nightmare for those prone to seasickness. One remedy with echoes of the water-cure advocated swathing the body in bandages from thighs to neck, requiring an estimated twelve yards of linen. Fortunately for Rashdall, the young Marsdens proved to be good sailors, though apparently the same could not be said for poor Granny Rashdall.

The resort of Dunkerque was popular among English travellers for its twin benefits of fresh air and sea-bathing, but ironically all six children fell seriously ill, most likely from cholera. The bacterial infection was rife throughout Europe at the time and at its height during the summer months. Alice was the worst affected, and for a while it was feared she might not recover. It was early October before the children were well enough to return home. Such a frightening experience in unfamiliar surroundings strengthened Rashdall's already strong bond with his nieces and nephew, but nevertheless he agonized over the suggestion of a move to Malvern, aware it would be a huge personal sacrifice.

Since leaving Exeter, Rashdall had thoroughly enjoyed his ministry at Eaton Chapel. He mixed with politicians and the fashionable clergy, and his connection with the poet Tennyson had led to other friendships within the literary world. He was regarded as a stimulating conversationalist and his sermons drew appreciative crowds. But James Marsden's insistence that his children would benefit from avuncular affection and spiritual guidance left the minister in a moral dilemma. Was it selfish to want to stay in the capital? What would God want him to do?

John Rashdall was born on 19 December 1810. He grew up with a bad stammer, possibly an emotional reaction to the early death of his father. He was an intelligent child but the speech impediment, which he never fully overcame, persuaded his mother to have him educated at home rather than expose him to the rigours of public school. His friendship with Alfred Tennyson had begun during their shared childhood in country Lincolnshire. The boys were almost exactly the same age and their families were close neighbours. Tennyson's father was the rector in the village of Somersby, 6 miles south of the Rashdall home at Spilsby. As young men they became contemporaries at Cambridge University, where Tennyson attended Trinity College and Rashdall Corpus Christi.

After obtaining his BA in 1833, Rashdall was ordained an Anglican minister by the Bishop of Lincoln. He served as curate at Orby in Lincolnshire and then at Cheltenham before being appointed incumbent of Exeter's Bedford Chapel in 1840. As a passionate, evangelical preacher he preferred to address the chapel's congregation without a written sermon. Like Dr Gully at Malvern, he was besieged by female admirers and reputedly accumulated a cupboardful of lovingly embroidered slippers. He developed a close friendship with the deeply religious Leakey family of Exeter. James Leakey (1775–1865) was an artist, and he painted Rashdall in clerical robes in 1846. A mezzotint of the portrait engraved

The Reverend John Rashdall, circa 1846, depicted here by Samuel Cousins. Following his sister Lucy's death in 1847 Rashdall maintained close bonds with his Marsden nieces and nephew

by Samuel Cousins bears the inscription 'To the Congregation of Bedford Chapel, Exeter. This Plate is respectfully dedicated by their obedient servant, James Leakey'.

From the year of his ordination until his death, John Rashdall kept a journal, which he described as 'a diary of the soul'. Its entries reveal a man whose inner life was so tortured by guilt and self-reproach that it is easy to imagine him donning a hair shirt, or flailing himself with a medieval scourge. He was forever striving to achieve a state of godliness but, at least in his own eyes, failing miserably: 'I am now in the state of the most desperate sinner, only that my lot is the worse from a knowledge of the excellence of the state from which I have driven myself. Satan is fearfully successful against me.'[1] Rashdall constantly wrestled with the twin sins of pride and ambition, triumphing over them only to accuse himself of taking pride in his humility. His constant self-analysis and spiritual angst were in direct contrast to the assured and forceful personality of Dr James Marsden.

The minister may have interpreted the children's recovery at Dunkerque as a sign from above, although his ultimate decision to apply for the vacancy at Malvern no doubt had more to do with pleasing his brother-in-law than the Almighty.

When Rashdall returned from France an approach was made to Lady Emily Foley, Malvern's Lady of the Manor and patroness of the Priory Church. By mid-August he had received her seal of approval. On 23 October 1850, he travelled to Worcester to see the Bishop and was officially granted the living of Great Malvern. The next day he preached at St Mary's Priory Church for the first time, referring to the occasion as 'a great day at Malvern'.

John Rashdall soon settled into St Mary's vicarage, located close to the junction of Church Street and Abbey Road. It was an impressive, multi-chimneyed Georgian building, with dozens of lancet windows proclaiming its ecclesiastical connection. The young Marsdens would have been delighted to see more of their Uncle John. Despite constantly reminding them to pray and to be good children for God, he was a kindly figure, who had much more time for them than their busy father. On Guy Fawkes's night in 1850, Rashdall's diary records that his nephew and nieces took tea at the vicarage, staying overnight after watching the local firework display on Worcester Beacon, the highest point of the Malvern Hills.

With John Rashdall installed as vicar, the Priory Church became a more personal and familiar place to the children. One suspects they did not always behave as reverently as their uncle might have hoped. It is easy

St Mary's Vicarage, nestled under the tower of the Priory Church

to imagine them running up and down the aisles, giggling over the strange carvings on the misericords and frightening little Alice with stories of mythical beasts. How they must have enjoyed the occasions when their uncle's eccentrically grand patron attended Sunday service. The bells in the church's battlemented tower rang out as Lady Foley arrived like royalty in a canary-yellow landau driven by four white horses. If her servants turned heads in their scarlet livery trimmed with gold lace, their mistress's costume was just as spectacular. In a book on Malvern titled *A Little City Set on a Hill* (1948), author C.F. Severn Burrow mentioned that his father had been a church warden whose duty it was to escort Lady Foley to her reserved seat in the monks' stalls. One outfit in particular made a deep impression on the warden: 'A rich silk be-bustled gown with short train, and a bugled purple mantle surmounted by the most amazing bonnet covered with flowers and high ostrich tips with broad mauve strings tied to one side.'[2]

Revealing an inflated sense of his own importance, the children's father adopted a scaled-down version of Lady Foley's equipage, riding around the township escorted by a uniformed manservant on a white horse. Presumably the servant carried Dr Marsden's medical bag, allowing his master to cut a more elegant figure. The doctor habitually rode at full gallop, 'as if intent upon overtaking the course of time that had gone too fast for his numerous engagements'.[3] It is impossible to imagine him having the time or inclination to rein in his steed, scoop up one of his offspring, and deliver the child to Mr Need the confectioner for a treat of hydropathic gingerbread.

In April 1851 Charles Darwin made a return visit to Malvern, though not on account of his own chronic ill-health. His eldest daughter and special favourite Annie had been unwell for some time. Darwin's suggestion that she may have shared his 'wretched digestion' was merely an attempt to quell his true fears about the seriousness of her condition. Annie was to be treated by Dr Gully, in whom Darwin had great faith. The patient was settled into Montreal House in Worcester Road, with her nurse Jessie Brodie, and later her governess, in attendance. Etty Darwin was taken along as company for her older sister. After the little girls had been on a shopping trip together, Etty wrote to her mother wistfully, 'We saw the Marsdens' playing in a garden.'[4]

Sadly, before the Darwin and Marsden children could properly renew their friendship, Annie's condition deteriorated and Dr Gully wrote to Darwin, asking him to come. By the middle of the month she was beyond hope. Her father kept vigil at her bedside, sending heartbreaking reports to his wife Emma, who was in the final stages of pregnancy and unable to travel.

Annie died on 23 April. She was farewelled with great dignity. In keeping with the conventions of the time, there were paid mourners or 'mutes'. Ostrich-plumed black horses drew the hearse to the Priory Church, where John Rashdall conducted the funeral service. The child's aunt and uncle represented the family, her father being too grief-stricken to attend. Rashdall was a gifted preacher, but no words could have matched those Darwin himself would compose in memory of his daughter a few days later:

> From whatever point I look back at her, the main feature in her disposition, which at once rises before me is her buoyant joyousness... Her whole mind was pure and transparent... We have lost the joy of the household and the solace of our old age: she must have known how we loved her; oh that she could know how deeply, how tenderly we do still and shall ever love her dear joyous face.[5]

Rashdall's college friend Alfred Tennyson was also grieving. Three days earlier, on Easter Sunday, his wife Emily had given birth to their first child, a stillborn son: 'My poor little boy got strangled in being born: I would not send the notice of my misfortune to the Times and I have had to write some 60 letters.'[6]

The death of Annie Darwin is a reminder that Malvern did not only attract bored, over-indulging hypochondriacs. Gravely ill people were brought to the town as a last resort, their families hoping against hope for a miraculous cure. In the midst of his humorous account of the 'cure', Joseph Leech commented on the many sad cases at watering-places. He noted that the most distressing sight of all was young people upon whom tuberculosis had left its 'hectic and hopeless mark'. It is now believed Annie was consumptive, although Dr Gully described her illness as a typhoid-like fever. For Dr Marsden's children the passing of someone

Annie Darwin's much-visited grave in the Priory Churchyard, Great Malvern.

ANNE ELIZABETH
DARWIN
BORN MARCH 2 1841.
DIED APRIL 23. 1851.
A DEAR AND GOOD CHILD

their own age, especially a child they had played with so happily, would have been very difficult to cope with. Annie was buried close to their own mother's grave in the Priory churchyard.

5. Visitors at the Vicarage

❧

The 1851 English census was held on the night of 30 April. Dr Marsden's 70-year-old mother Harriet was recorded as a visitor at Cotswold House. Her name was followed by the six little Marsden 'steps': Lucy, twelve; Emily, eleven; Marian, ten; James, eight; Rosa, seven; and Alice, six. The household staff consisted of the Burnell sisters in their roles of housekeeper and governess plus a cook, a nursery maid, a parlourmaid, a general servant and a groom.

At St Mary's vicarage, the Reverend John Rashdall was already missing his friends and the intellectual stimulation of life in the capital. His brother-in-law was preoccupied with his medical practice and ambitious building project, and Rashdall found himself battling boredom. On 31 March 1851 he had written, 'This wk. precisely spent as the last so unvarying is my Malvern life – & such a contrast with that in London.' Nevertheless, his days were full. In his ministry at Malvern he was faced with a challenging dual role: delivering high-minded sermons to the town's wealthy and often famous water-cure clients on the one hand, and attending to the day-to-day pastoral duties of a local vicar on the other. With the town's high proportion of invalids, there were constant visits to the sick, plus the sombre task of conducting burial services for those the doctors could not save.

Presiding over the more joyful ceremonies of christenings and weddings must have raised the Reverend's flagging spirits. On Sunday 5 October 1851 he married young labourer James Jervis Welch to local girl Mary Ann Foster. The couple already had a year-old son, and Rashdall may have gently shepherded them to the altar. The following year Mary Welch gave birth to a daughter, Sabina Amanda. Sabina would grow up to form a connection with the Marsden family that neither John Rashdall nor the Marsdens themselves could ever have imagined.

During the spring of 1851 the much anticipated Great Exhibition opened in London's Hyde Park, housed in Joseph Paxton's extraordinary Crystal Palace. The event was conceived by Prince Albert to showcase the artistic and technological achievements of the vast British Empire. Grateful for the diversion, John Rashdall returned to London, and was on hand to watch Queen Victoria and her consort arrive in state for the official opening on 1 May. Victoria could barely contain herself when she described the occasion in a letter to her Uncle Leopold, the King of Belgium:

> My Dearest Uncle, – I wish you *could* have witnessed the 1st May 1851, the *greatest* day in our history, the *most beautiful* and *imposing* and *touching* spectacle ever seen, and the triumph of my beloved Albert. Truly it was astonishing, a fairy scene. Many cried, and all felt touched and impressed with devotional feelings. It was the *happiest*, *proudest* day in my life, and I can think of nothing else…[1]

John Rashdall's first look at the exhibits was on 8 May: 'It is very grand indeed: all that could have been anticipated.'[2] Tennyson, newly appointed Poet Laureate, was inspired to add the following stanza to his ode 'To the Queen':

> *She brought a vast design to pass,*
> *When Europe and the scatter'd ends*
> *Of our fierce world were mixt as friends*
> *And brethren in her halls of glass.*[3]

Like many people, Rashdall made multiple visits to the Crystal Palace, on one occasion with his brother-in-law James, who had particular reason to applaud the Prince's vision. The Exhibition presented the Malvern water-cure doctors with undreamed-of free publicity. The centre-piece of the main hall was a giant crystal fountain, 27-foot high and weighing 4 tons. Representing the fabled Fountain of Youth, it flowed with sparkling soda water drawn from Malvern's very own St Ann's Well. When a bottle of the healing water was presented to a beaming Victoria, Great Malvern suddenly became the most celebrated spa in the country, and subsequently dubbed 'the place of the golden fee'.

ARTIST UNKNOWN

Malvern water flows from the Crystal Palace Fountain at the Great Exhibition of 1851.
It was the perfect publicity for Dr Marsden and his water-cure colleagues

Everything was falling into place for Dr Marsden. The construction of his treatment centre in Abbey Road was now well underway, a five-storey building almost as grand as the Crystal Palace. It was called Hardwicke House, commemorating the village of Elmstone Hardwicke, 3 miles north-west of Cheltenham. In Kelly's 1843 Post Office Directory for Gloucestershire, James Marsden Esq. of Dicks (sic) Field, Exeter, is listed as

Dr Marsden's grand, purpose-built treatment complex, from left:
The Baths, Hardwicke House and Elmsdale

one of the chief landowners in the village. It seems likely that at least some of the property, perhaps inherited through his mother's people, was sold to fund Hardwicke House. Fortuitously, the Gothic revival style building had been designed by Samuel Teulon, a technically innovative architect championed by the hero of the hour, Prince Albert. Hardwicke House had a separate, four-room bathing pavilion, equipped with 'the most up-to-date hot, cold, electro-chemical, Turkish, vapour, and douche baths'.[4]

In the wake of the Exhibition and the huge increase in visitor numbers, an Improvement Commission was established at Malvern. Drs Gully and Marsden were among the twelve founding Town Commissioners, addressing issues such as building dust and debris, the mess created by donkeys carrying patients up to St Ann's Well, and the town's now heavily congested roads.

One of the visitors around this time was Charles Dickens. Though sceptical of the water-cure's benefits, the novelist brought his wife to Malvern for treatment under Dr Wilson. In an amusing letter to his future biographer John Forster, Dickens described the frenzied pedestrian traffic:

O Heaven, to meet the Cold Waterers (as I did this morning when I went out for a shower-bath) dashing down the hills, with severe expressions on their countenances, like men doing matches and not exactly winning! Then, a young lady in a grey polka going up the hills, regardless of legs; and meeting a young gentleman (a bad case, I should say) with a light black silk cap on under his hat, and the pimples of I don't know how many douches under that. Likewise an old man who ran over a milk-child, rather than stop! – with no neckcloth, on principle; and with his mouth open, to catch the morning air.[5]

A German band was employed to entertain the 'cold waterers' at St Ann's Well and enterprising stall holders sold contraband devilled kidneys to those weary of the prescribed diet of mutton and potatoes. Given his brother-in-law's position on the Improvement Committee it was probably no coincidence that the Reverend John Rashdall launched into the restoration of the Priory Church, organizing a parish grant of £2,000 for the repair of its ancient tower and battlements. The project relieved his boredom and earned the approval of Lady Foley, but in fairness to Rashdall he was acutely conscious of the building's long history and exquisite beauty.

Donkeys at St Ann's Well, Great Malvern

With the opening of Hardwicke House, Dr Marsden felt he might soon eclipse the success of James Wilson and perhaps even his friend Gully. He began to specialize in the treatment of women's complaints and in the autumn of 1851 Rashdall noted, 'James recd. a most flattering letter from Sir J Clark asking his opinion and advice on some difficult cases of feminine disease.'[6] The letter was particularly gratifying as the doctor mentioned was Sir James Clark, personal physician to the Queen. For Marsden it was akin to being granted a Royal Warrant. Flushed with success, he held a grand dinner at Cotswold House. The children crept on to the stairs to watch the ladies in their beautiful dresses move into the dining room. Marian, in her excitement, lost her balance and fell head first to the hallway below. She was quite badly hurt, but one suspects her father was more upset that she had disrupted the evening.

It was the following year that an opportunity came for the doctor to gain the patronage of the Tennysons. On 23 January the poet wrote to his wife Emily, '...John Rashdall wants us to spend three weeks with him at Malvern which I think will be nice when thou canst move.' Emily was then a few weeks pregnant with their son Hallam, and feeling unwell. The couple arrived at the vicarage in March, and Hallam Tennyson mentions their visit in a memoir of his father published in 1897:

> Early in 1852 my father and mother went on a visit to one of his old college friends, Mr Rashdall the clergyman of Malvern... Rashdall was a man so beloved by his parishioners, and so simple and direct in his language from the pulpit, that he had emptied the Dissenting Chapels for miles around. He would often hold his Church services in the fields. A flowery record of Spring follows in my mother's journal, about the beauty of the daffodils, wood anemones, primroses, and violets; the pear trees throughout the country in bloom 'like springing and falling fountains'.[7]

If Rashdall's invitation had been extended at the prompting of his brother-in-law it was a clever move; Emily Tennyson was soon being attended at the vicarage by Dr Marsden.

The Tennysons thoroughly enjoyed their stay and it was a memorable experience for the young Marsdens. How exciting to be invited to tea with Uncle John to meet Queen Victoria's very own poet. With his bushy beard and straggly hair, Tennyson was so wonderfully untidy that the children must have half expected him to be rebuked by their father. In an 1842 letter to Ralph Waldo Emerson, Thomas Carlyle's description of the poet suggests he was the antithesis of the prim and proper Dr Marsden, in both appearance and personality:

> One of the finest-looking men in the world. A great shock of rough, dusky dark hair; bright, laughing, hazel eyes; massive aquiline face, most massive, yet most delicate; of sallow brown complexion, almost Indian-looking, clothes cynically loose, free and easy, smokes infinite tobacco. His voice is musical, metallic, fit for loud laughter and piercing wail, and all that may lie between; speech and speculation free and plenteous. I do not meet in these late decades such company over a pipe![8]

Alfred Lord Tennyson, lifelong friend of the Reverend John Rashdall

However, the men had one interest in common. Like many Victorians, Tennyson had an interest in mesmerism, a subject that also fascinated Dr Marsden. Given his belief that the power of the mind could affect physical health, it is not surprising that the doctor was excited by the idea of using the technique in his medical practice. While he was treating Emily Tennyson at the vicarage he took the opportunity of asking her husband to mesmerize another of his female patients. Years later Tennyson would relate the story to Hallam:

> Dr. Marsden was attending my wife and said to me, 'Instead of paying me my fee, I wish you would grant me a favour. Come and mesmerize a young lady who is very ill.' I said, 'I can't mesmerize, I never mesmerized anyone in my life.' But the doctor would take no refusal and said, 'Pooh! Look at your powerful frame!' So I mesmerized her according to the doctor's instructions. The first day it took me about an hour to send her to sleep; afterwards only a few seconds. Once she had a pain over her eye, and the doctor said, 'Breathe upon her eye!' I did so, then begged her pardon, saying I had forgotten I had been smoking. Dr Marsden said, 'She cannot hear you, that one breath has sent her off into the deepest of slumbers.' In a little while the lady grew better and we moved to Cheltenham. A week or so afterwards I returned to Malvern for a few hours, but I had not thought of telling anyone that I was coming. I met Dr. Marsden in the street, who at once went and told the lady. Before he had said more to her than, 'I have good news for you,' the lady said, 'I know what you have come to tell me, I have felt Mr Tennyson here for half an hour.'[9]

The poet's visit to Malvern coincided with an upheaval within Dr Marsden's domestic circle. In *Notes on Homeopathy* he had boasted that alternative medicine freed him from the burden of being perceived as the 'terror of the nursery', yet he remained a frightening presence in the lives of his own children, particularly in relation to their schoolwork. The two eldest girls were the most frequent targets of his anger: Lucy because of her general 'stupidity' and Emily because her father considered her intelligent enough to do better. However, the doctor suddenly found himself dealing with an infinitely more serious issue than blotted copybooks or mangled French grammar.

It seems the young governess Adelaide Burnell saw Emily touching herself in what she suspected may have been an 'impure way'. Too embarrassed to address such a delicate matter herself, she mentioned it to Dr Marsden, assuming that as a physician her employer would handle the situation appropriately. But to the horror of the household, the doctor flew into a violent rage. He thrashed his daughter with a stick until Adelaide's older sister Eliza intervened, saying she was sure the girl had simply been relieving the itch of a feminine complaint. This may well have been correct, although masturbation in childhood is often an expression of anxiety and insecurity.

Nothing more was said, but Dr Marsden remained convinced that Emily was 'tarnished' and ordered she be made to sleep separately to her sisters. That she may have been indulging in masturbation was contrary to his entire ethos, particularly his theory of instilling pure thoughts into young minds. It was an affront to him both professionally and personally. During the nineteenth century a hearty appetite in a female was linked to an excess of sexual energy and Marsden felt his children's meat-restricted diet alone should have prevented such behaviour. The incident contributed to his decision to look for a new governess, at least for the older ones. Since they were all hopelessly inadequate in French, he made enquiries within the English community in Paris and was given the name of Célestine Doudet, who was then living in Scotland. Mademoiselle Doudet's credentials were described as impeccable and she had been employed by aristocratic families in both France and Great Britain. An interview was duly arranged.

6. The Governess

Flore-Marguerite-Célestine Doudet was thirty-four years old, tall and distinguished, with a high forehead and dark, almost black, eyes. She was born in Rouen on 15 June 1817 to an English mother and a French father, Antoine Doudet. The couple had met when Captain Doudet was a prisoner of war in England during the Napoleonic wars. In September 1803 he had been serving as Lieutenant Commander aboard the *Wraak,* an eight-gun Dutch privateer schooner. Accompanied by the larger, more heavily armed *Faust,* the *Wraak* attacked the tiny British cutter *Princess Augusta,* whose captain, boatswain and gunner were killed. By 1805 Doudet had been given command of a twelve-gun Dutch vessel, the *Honneur.* On 11 April 1805 she was captured by the British after a dramatic chase in the North Sea. Three days later Rear-Admiral Thomas Russell conveyed the good news to William Marsden, Secretary to the Admiralty: 'Enclosed herewith you will receive the copy of a letter from Captain Carteret, of the Scorpion, informing me of his having, in company with the Providence armed ship, captured the Schooner l'Honneur, Captain Antoine Doudet.'[1]

It was a significant victory for Carteret. First, Doudet's ship was carrying arms and uniforms for 1,000 men, as well as cannons, military tents and other 'war-like' stores. Second, she had been entrusted with a cache of sensitive documents, which her crew tried unsuccessfully to destroy. And third, on board *Honneur* was Jean Saint-Faust, considered by Napoleon Bonaparte to be one of his most brave, able and enterprising officers.

Captain Doudet was imprisoned at Chatham in Kent.[2] However, like many commissioned officers, he was granted parole. This involved pledging his word that he would not escape or communicate with France. He was allowed to live relatively freely under the supervision of a government agent

THE WATER DOCTOR'S DAUGHTERS

and during this period he forged his own Anglo-French *détente* by marrying a local woman. When he was released in 1814 he took his English bride back to Normandy. The following year he distinguished himself by leading a detachment of the National Guard of the lower Seine, successfully defending the town of d'Ardres in the Pas-de-Calais.[3] Hostilities finally came to an end with the British victory at Waterloo, and Captain Doudet and his wife settled in the cathedral city of Rouen, where Célestine was born. She had an older sister, Louise, and about ten years later the family was completed with the arrival of a third daughter, Zéphyrine.

When the captain retired from the navy the family returned to England. Célestine's father was most likely Captain Doudet of Watling Street, Canterbury, listed as a professor of languages in the 1826 edition of *Pigot's Directory*. It would not have been a highly remunerative occupation, and as his family had lost most of their money due to the war the captain found himself unable to provide decent dowries for his daughters. Instead, he ensured they were well educated and able to earn their own living. The girls were sent to a ladies academy in Paris run by a Madame de Chabaud-Latour and her daughter, who were French Protestants. It was the perfect choice for the Doudets; the young women would be exposed to their father's culture while living among adherents of their English mother's faith.

Following her husband's death on 18 January 1838,[4] Madame Doudet was forced to return to France herself, in order to continue receiving the Captain's service pension. Her daughters were still studying under Mademoiselle de Chabaud-Latour, a respected Protestant author and translator. Célestine in particular had excelled academically and was also a competent pianist and horsewoman. The de Chabaud-Latour family had connections within the highest ranks of French society, and through their recommendation Célestine became governess to the children of Count Löwenhielm, the Swedish ambassador in Paris. However, in 1841 Madame de Chabaud-Latour secured her protégé an even more prestigious position: wardrobe lady to the Queen of England, with special responsibility for Her Majesty's jewels. Although the placement lasted only a few months, Victoria provided the departing Célestine with a personal recommendation:

I consider Mademoiselle Doudet an excellent person, of mild disposition and amiable character, but her education has been too good for her situation of wardrobe woman with me, and I think that of governess would suit her better. I look on her as a person of the greatest probity and worthy of confidence.

Victoria
Buckingham Palace 8th April 1842[5]

The high-minded ex-wardrobe woman followed the Queen's advice, finding employment in the years that followed as governess to the children of the nobility, including a period with the Marquis of Hastings. However, her acceptance of the position at Cotswold House is an indication that her career was beginning to wane; Dr Marsden was a controversial provincial doctor, not an English lord. When she arrived in Malvern for her interview, Mademoiselle Doudet was understandably anxious about her future. At thirty-four, she was already considered 'old' within the profession.

In 1843 the Governesses' Benevolent Institution was established to provide at least some support for ill and impoverished governesses. Doudet's blood would have run cold at some of the case histories listed in the GBI's annual report of 1847:

Miss Amelia -------, aged sixty-one. Father a naval officer, died when she was an infant, and her mother when she was sixteen – compelling her to become a governess. Unable to save, on account of small salaries, ill health, and the want of a home. No income whatever, having only occasional assistance from an old friend who will have nothing to leave her at death.

Miss Dorothea -------, aged fifty-four. Father a surgeon in the army: governess chiefly in Scotch families for thirty years; was the chief support of her family from 1811 to 1838, when her mother died, leaving her with failing health through over-exertion, and only £5 a year from the Government Compassionate Fund.

For a governess, being of genteel birth was not always an asset. In a novel written by a Miss Ross in 1836, the lady of the house refers to her children's new governess while in conversation with her mother, Lady Lyster, 'I have not told you who I have engaged as their governess; she is a Miss Walcot, a daughter of the late Colonel Walcot. She was very highly recommended by Lady Jane Spencer, whose friend she is; she is very elegant, a most perfect gentlewomen.' Horrified, Lady Lyster replies, 'The very worst person in the world, Mrs Elphinstone. There is nothing so intolerable as a well-born, and what people call a lady-like governess; a sort of school-room princess, who will do literally nothing she is desired to do.'[6]

But fortunately for Mademoiselle Doudet, her links with the cream of French and English society greatly appealed to her prospective employer, who was even more impressed by her sojourn at Buckingham Palace. The country's post-Exhibition love affair with Victoria and Albert was at its height and for Dr Marsden the prospect of enhancing his social standing with another royal connection, however tenuous, was irresistible. On 2 March 1852, Célestine Doudet was engaged as governess to his three eldest children, Lucy, Emily and James.

After their years with the gentle Miss Adelaide, the young Marsdens would have been understandably nervous when their new teacher made her appearance in the nursery. Mademoiselle Doudet had a haughty manner and a severe appearance; the very thought of speaking French with her must have been even more terrifying than their father's examinations on the subject. Dr Marsden's elderly mother Harriet was again staying at Cotswold House and she too had reservations about Célestine Doudet, though for a different reason. Although many English families employed French governesses, centuries of conflict between the two nations had led to a strong prejudice against them:

> There was a general perception that [a French governess] was likely to be sexually aggressive in her dealings with the men of the house, to initiate her pupils into all sorts of unspecified 'sin', to dress too well, to lie and possibly to steal. Much of this was left at the level of implication, yet nonetheless a stock caricature soon emerged.[7]

One of the most vivid and stereotypical portraits of a French governess appears in the novel *Uncle Silas*, by the Victorian Anglo-Irish writer Joseph Le Fanu. The housekeeper provides young Maud Ruthyn with an alarming description of her new governess:

> You never saw such a sight. The great long nose and hollow cheek of her, and oogh! Such a mouth! I felt a'most like little Red Riding

Hood…I wonder why honest English girls won't answer the gentry for governesses, instead of them gaping, scheming, wicked furriners? Lord forgi'me, I think they're all alike.

Maud, too, judges the Frenchwoman harshly on first sight:

> Next morning I made acquaintance with Madame de la Rougierre. She was tall, masculine, a little ghastly perhaps, and draped in purple silk, with a lace cap and great bands of hair, too thick and black perhaps to correspond quite naturally with her bleached and sallow skin, her hollow jaws, and the fine but grim wrinkles traced about her brows and lids. She smiled, she nodded, and then for a good while she scanned me in silence with a steady, cunning eye and a stern smile.[8]

The governess lived up to her sinister image and was sacked after being caught rifling through a desk.

Harriet Marsden may have viewed Mademoiselle Doudet as a threat to her own status within the family – a predatory 'spider' aiming to catch her widowed son. However, she kept her own counsel, aware of the doctor's sensitivity to criticism and his intense dislike of having his decisions questioned. Perhaps she was also mollified by the knowledge that the governess had been brought up under the civilizing influence of an English mother.

During his initial interview with Mademoiselle Doudet, Dr Marsden had felt it necessary to broach the sensitive subject of Emily and the suspicion that she may have succumbed to a 'moral sin'. The governess's response was reassuring. She told him this sort of behaviour was something she was continually on guard against in her charges and that if detected she always dealt with it severely. She said a similar situation had occurred in her last placement.

In handing over her responsibility of the older children, Adelaide Burnell also felt obliged to warn her replacement that 7-year-old Rosa had been guilty of committing several small thefts. She was probably referring to something as inconsequential as stealing food which, given the children's restricted diet, must have been a temptation to them all. According to Hester Candler, on the days the young Marsdens were allowed meat they were forbidden an entrée or a pudding.

With the education of his children so satisfactorily settled, Dr Marsden was able to concentrate on his water-cure clients – one in particular. The young lady mesmerized by Alfred Tennyson was receiving far more care and attention than her fellow patients at Cotswold House. That Marsden had waived a fee on her behalf was a hint that his interest was more than professional. If Célestine Doudet had romantic designs upon her employer, they were destined to fail, because Dr Marsden had already fallen in love.

7. Sexual Morality

There was a strong undercurrent of sexual tension in the country's spa centres, as evidenced by the famous 'Bridge of Sighs' separating the male and female sections of Dr Gully's treatment centre at Malvern. Not surprisingly, the relationship between doctor and patient could also become highly charged. We might remember Florence Nightingale's comment about her mother's passion for Dr Gully, and of having been obliged to remind the doctor that she 'had a father living'. In a letter to her cousin Helen Welsh in 1851, Jane Carlyle wrote, with typical dry wit, that Gully was:

> dreadfully persecuted with the devotion of Ladies – all his female patients seeming to feel it their duty to fall in love with him – he has whole drawerfuls of purses, greekcaps, braces and other Ladies works – besides all the chairs sofas and tables in the house being covered with worsted work! – If the poor ladies only saw the fun that is made of their presents they would send them to any bazaar, rather![1]

Ironically, there would come a day when the tables were turned and Dr Gully began sighing over one of his young patients.

Though lacking the warmth and charisma of James Gully, the widowed Dr Marsden attracted his own share of admirers, particularly after he began specializing in the area of women's health. The lady who captured his heart was Scottish-born Mary Lyon Campbell, then aged thirty. Mary lived with her widowed mother in Edinburgh, but her late father, Colin Campbell, had been Laird of the Hebridean Isle of Jura and of the Craignish estate on mainland Argyllshire. Craignish, with its fortress-like castle, had just been sold by Mary's brother, Richard (the then Laird), for

£26,000. The sale reduced the Campbell family's influence, but provided much needed cash for the ancestral estates on Jura following the devastating potato famine.

In 1849 Mary almost lost her life after falling from a horse at full gallop and her recovery remained incomplete. Although doctors could find no permanent damage, the accident left her unable to walk. When all other treatment failed, her Edinburgh surgeon suggested she try the water-cure, and she arrived as a patient at Cotswold House in October 1851.[2] It is possible there was a psychological aspect to her condition. She was still unmarried in a society that considered a woman's only worthwhile role to be that of wife and mother. A romantically frail 'invalid' was viewed far more sympathetically than a despised spinster.

Among the female patients who travelled to spa towns such as Malvern were those seeking treatment for 'hysteria', a nineteenth-century euphemism for sexual frustration. Symptoms included loss of appetite, nervousness, insomnia and muscle spasm. The water-cure doctors employed novel therapies in the form of stimulating water jets, douches and sitz baths – said to increase the flow of blood to the pelvic regions and to help in achieving a 'release of tension', i.e. sexual orgasm. Their methods formed an alternative to vibrators, which were not only widely used in medical practice, but advertised openly for use in the home under headings such as 'Aids That Every Woman Appreciates' and 'Vibration Is Life'.

Whatever the cause of Mary Campbell's affliction, being courted at thirty by her doctor would have been a heady experience, not to mention having the Poet Laureate lay healing hands upon her brow. It was in this rarefied atmosphere that, surprise, surprise, she began to regain the use of her legs. By the time Dr Marsden enlisted Alfred Tennyson's help in treating Mary, the boundary between doctor and patient had well and truly been crossed. As a physician, Marsden was already in a position of power and there is something slightly sinister in his use of mesmerism on a woman he desired physically and who was, by his own description, seriously ill and therefore emotionally vulnerable.

The issue of improper conduct between doctors and their female patients was highlighted in a court case some years later which had an interesting connection to Malvern. A respectable spinster servant was being attended by a doctor for 'cataleptic hysteria' and ulcers in the womb.

Over a period of about a year the doctor treated her using a speculum, a medical tool used for examining body cavities. It was the patient's habit to lie with a handkerchief over her face during the procedure, but on one occasion she removed it and saw the doctor buttoning his trousers. Eventually her periods ceased, she suffered nausea, and her stomach began to swell. She was told she had an enlarged liver!

About to visit Malvern, her concerned mistress asked the doctor whether she should seek a second opinion, but was told it would be pointless. His advice was for the servant to drink copious amounts of wormwood tea (a herbal remedy for inducing miscarriage) and to walk on the steep Malvern Hills as much as possible. However, the woman's employer consulted Dr Gully, who diagnosed a tumour of the womb and put the patient through a complete course of the water-cure. The 'tumour' continued to grow and while at Malvern the woman gave birth to a baby boy. The original doctor was charged with improper conduct, but during the court case a medical expert for the defence, Dr Smith, stated that women suffering from hysteria were 'given to systematic lies and imposture'.[3] The doctor was acquitted and a subscription raised by his colleagues to cover his legal costs.

Meanwhile, Dr Gully had left himself and his water-cure colleagues open to ridicule through his bizarre diagnosis of a tumour. Smith later commented:

> Would any old petticoated nurse in the country have committed such an unpardonable blunder as not to recognize pregnancy in so well marked a case?... Dr Gully owns to having treated her hydropathically and homeopathically. It is only a pity for his sake that he had not recourse to other such means as mesmerism and spirit-rapping, to escape the droll errors of diagnostic and so-called treatment into which he fell.[4]

After five years as a widower, Dr Marsden was more than ready to remarry and a long courtship was out of the question. He was frantically busy, not only with his thriving practice and construction of his treatment centre, but in preparing to move from Cotswold House to a larger, detached property. There is no evidence that he made sexual advances towards Mary while she was under the influence of mesmerism, but certainly an increase in psychological control would have proved useful in dispelling any misgivings she may have had about leaving her family in Scotland to become stepmother to six young children.

In Dr Marsden's mind, his offspring became an even greater liability after Célestine Doudet, having been with the family for just a few weeks, told him that Emily was still indulging in masturbation. Worse still, the governesss reported that the habit had spread like a contagious disease, with all five of the Marsden girls, including 6-year-old Alice, now 'infected'. The doctor's shock and disgust was intensified by the thought that if Miss Campbell agreed to become his wife, she would inevitably discover that his children were morally perverted. He was unaware that his intended had a sexual skeleton in her own closet.

In 1841, 20-year-old Mary made an extended visit to her sister Isabella's home of Jarvisfield, on the Scottish Isle of Mull. Isabella's husband Lachlan Macquarie Jr had inherited the estate from his late father. In the early years of the century, Lachlan Macquarie Sr had been one of New South Wales' most highly respected colonial governors. Unfortunately, spoiled Lachlan Jr grew up to become a hopeless alcoholic, which may explain why, after five years of marriage, he and Isabella remained childless. It may also explain why a doctor was staying at the house on a professional basis.

Towards the end of that year stories began to circulate that Mary was sleeping with her brother-in-law. On 14 January 1842 Lachlan was forced to write a passionate letter of denial to his father-in-law, Colin Campbell, explaining the source of the rumours:

> The person who was brought here as my family medical adviser & who since he has been under my roof has been treated with the utmost kindness and respect has endeavored to destroy our happiness by the most diabolical report – Some weeks ago your daughter Mary…received an anonymous letter from Edin. advising that this was no place for her to be residing & that she should immediately return to your home.[5]

It transpired that the medical adviser (and author of the anonymous letter) had witnessed a maid returning a hair comb to Mary that had been found in Lachlan's bed. Despite this damning evidence, Macquarie continued to defend his sister-in-law's honour. The Campbell family closed ranks, but gossip travelled fast within the closely interconnected Highland clans, damaging Mary's reputation and her chances of marriage. Three years later Macquarie died from alcohol abuse, having bequeathed his estate to a friend, to whom he was deeply in debt. In November 1851 his cousins challenged the will, arguing that Macquarie had been of unsound mind. The action failed, but evidence regarding the dead man's dissipated lifestyle led the judge to describe him as 'morally insane'. Had the real reason Mary left Edinburgh immediately prior to the court case been fear of the old scandal being aired?

At Malvern, with no inkling of any stain on Miss Campbell's character, the lovesick Dr Marsden was going to great lengths to cure his daughters of their alleged sexual deviancy, including the use of corporal punishment. He also made further restrictions to their homeopathic diet, specifically banning red meat, which was thought to excite the passions. But the vigilant governess insisted they showed no signs of improvement. With the doctor's approval she began using physical restraints, tying the girls' hands and feet when they were in bed.

It was a setback for Dr Marsden when Mademoiselle Doudet, after being at Cotswold House for about five weeks, was forced to take leave. Her sisters had sent word from Paris that their mother was dying. Strangely enough, instead of Adelaide Burnell simply resuming charge of the older children for what was expected to be a brief period, the doctor employed a temporary governess, Miss Dowmann. Miss Burnell returned to Devonshire to stay with her family and while she was there Dr Marsden sent her a curt letter of dismissal. Perhaps he felt she had failed in the moral supervision of his daughters, although it may simply have been a cost-saving measure. Why waste money on a teacher for the little ones when the efficient new French governess was clearly capable of handling all six of his children?

Sadly, Madame Doudet died before her daughter reached Paris. After organizing the funeral, Célestine stayed on for a couple of weeks caring for her grieving sister, Zéphyrine. She then resumed her position at Cotswold House. Around the same time, Adelaide Burnell returned to Malvern to confront the doctor over her dismissal. However, if she received an explanation, it was never disclosed. Annabella Candler would later say that Mademoiselle Doudet described Dr Marsden's treatment of her predecessor as 'capricious', expressing regret over joining his household because, 'how would she know if she wouldn't be treated the same way as mademoiselle Adelaide Burnell?'[6] It may have been for this reason that an idea Doudet had conceived during her stay in Paris assumed fresh appeal.

The governess approached Dr Marsden and told him she was thinking of establishing a small school in her late mother's apartment. She proposed that the Marsden girls become her first pupils, aware that the arrangement would provide her with more security. As mistress of her own establishment she would also enjoy greater autonomy and prestige. And for a woman of Doudet's refined tastes, Paris offered a more congenial environment than the cultural backwater of Great Malvern. Naturally the idea was music to Dr Marsden's ears. His daughters would benefit from a little European polish, and of course the alternative meant revealing their sordid habits to Miss Dowmann or a replacement governess. Besides, for a man with marriage on his mind, a house full of children was an encumbrance. Here was the perfect opportunity to clear the field. He decided to enrol his son James at a private school in England and to send his daughters to Paris for an initial period of six months. William Candler would later say that he remonstrated with the doctor about handing the girls over to a virtual stranger, but that Dr Marsden insisted Mademoiselle Doudet was a woman of the highest character, in whom he had complete confidence.

The governess was to be paid the less than generous sum of 100 francs per month per child, to cover full board and tuition. However, fees for outside music, language and drawing masters were to be paid for separately by Dr Marsden. Mademoiselle Doudet also reserved the right to augment her income by providing lessons to day students. She was to be assisted in her venture by her younger sister Zéphyrine. Perhaps she dreamed that the school would grow, and that it might eventually be as highly regarded as Madame de Chabaud-Latour's academy.

As preparations for the journey to France were underway, a new and serious accusation was made by the governess against Rosa. Mademoiselle Doudet said the girl had crept into her bedroom and stolen a brooch. When Rosa pleaded her innocence she was branded a liar as well as a thief. Her father clearly viewed this as quite different to any previous offence. Rosa was given a severe beating and locked up, on a diet of bread and water, until she confessed. Harriet Marsden wept for her granddaughter, but did not feel she could intervene. Mary Campbell was so upset by the draconian punishment that she quietly slipped the child extra food. It was three days before the little girl was released, still insisting she had not taken the brooch. It was later found in the garden, hidden behind a pile of sticks. The incident confirmed Dr Marsden's belief that his daughters were incorrigible. He decided their only hope of salvation lay with Mademoiselle Doudet, and banishment to France.

For the children, school in Paris not only meant leaving the familiarity of Malvern but being separated from a close extended family. They would sorely miss their Marsden and Rashdall aunts, their grandmothers, and above all their devoted Uncle John. But in Dr Marsden's view, daughters who stole, neglected their lessons, and indulged in immoral habits had no right of complaint. Their insecurity was thus compounded by shame and a sense of rejection. A further anxiety was prompted by servant gossip about their father and Miss Campbell. Emily, if not her siblings, was perceptive enough to understand that by the time they returned home they might well have a stepmother.

8. Banishment

On 25 June Dr Marsden and his mother arrived at London's Euston Square railway station with Mademoiselle Doudet and the five girls. They booked into the Drummond Hotel, located on the western side of the busy terminus. John Rashdall was already in town with his brother Robert and Granny Rashdall, and the two families met at the Drummond at 8 p.m. to say goodbye. Rashdall then saw his nieces and their governess safely stowed aboard the Dunkerque steamer, accompanied by their many trunks and travelling boxes.[1] One of Mademoiselle Doudet's English cousins, Mr Frederick Baker, also arrived to wish Célestine well in her new venture. He and his wife were planning a visit to Paris and promised to call on their cousin and her young pupils.

Dr Marsden's farewell gifts to his daughters included a framed portrait of himself and a handsome, silver-cornered Bible which he hoped might improve their morals. For the rest, he hoped the zeal and perseverance of their governess would eventually change their behaviour. He instructed Doudet to maintain his daughters' strict homeopathic diet and to take whatever other corrective measures she deemed necessary.

There is a possibility that Dr Marsden's reaction to the girls' alleged vice was intensified by feelings of guilt. His first wife Lucy had been pregnant almost her entire married life and one of the prevailing water-cure theories was that sexual intercourse during pregnancy and breastfeeding had dire consequences. Dr Marsden's fellow physician Mary Gove Nichols wrote:

> I speak what I know, and testify what I have seen in a long and varied medical practice, when I assert that masturbation in children, and every evil of sensuality, spring from the polluted hot-bed of a sensual and unloving marriage, where a woman is subjected to a destroying sensualism during pregnancy and lactation...I have also

known cases where subsequent children, born in a second marriage which was loving and healthy, had no such tendency. They were pure from birth, as the first were impure.[2]

Having crossed the Channel, Paris-bound travellers and their baggage were transferred to a public stagecoach known as a *diligence* for the long, bone-shaking journey south. The vehicle was drawn by five or six horses and consisted of three compartments. Mademoiselle Doudet and the children would have taken up the whole of the middle carriage, known as the *intérieur*.

In Paris, the Doudet apartment was located on the first floor of No. 1 Cité Odiot, a private *allée* of terraced houses with a portered entrance leading off Rue Washington, a convenient and highly desirable location just a short walk from the Champs-Elysées. It was named in 1847 in honour of silversmith Jean-Baptiste-Claude Odiot (1763–1850), who once owned a mansion on the site. Monsieur Odiot was one of the finest craftsmen of his day, and a favourite of Emperor Napoleon Bonaparte. In 1852 Cité Odiot

© ROB CONOLLY, 2010

No. 1 Cité Odiot, Paris, with the Porter's Lodge on the right. Célestine Doudet's apartment was on the first floor

and the surrounding neighbourhood formed part of a close-knit community which included a number of genteel English ladies. Small cliques had formed, but Célestine Doudet was favoured with immediate *entrée* due to the friendships already formed by her mother and sisters. A few months after settling in, she realized she needed more space for her school. With Dr Marsden's approval she organized the lease of additional space on the ground floor of the building.

The introduction of five lively youngsters must have had quite an impact on the quiet, mainly middle-aged residents of Cité Odiot, but the French nation's love of children ensured Mademoiselle Doudet's pupils were embraced rather than resented. They would also enjoy a rich cultural environment. At No. 6 lived the inventor Monsieur Faulion, who was about to exhibit a wonderful model steamboat in New York. Occupying No. 1's third floor was the poet and lyricist Désirée Pacault, and in the apartment directly above Mademoiselle Doudet was a kindly, cultivated widow by the name of Madame Espert. This lady had recently witnessed a phenomenon guaranteed to leave the children wide-eyed with wonder. On an oppressively hot summer evening she looked out of her window at Cité Odiot and saw a giant golden balloon in the sky. As she watched, it exploded into jagged streaks of lightning. In an article published soon after the young Marsdens arrived she wrote, 'Paris resounded with this terrible thunderbolt, but perhaps I am the only person who happened actually to see it.'[3] Her cook collapsed, three men in the street were knocked down, and a governess in a nearby school was injured. One lightning bolt struck the wall of No. 4 Cité Odiot, leaving a crater the children were still able to inspect.

The girls found playmates in the local area and were soon sharing their lessons with Mademoiselle Doudet's day pupils. Through their Uncle John, they may also have befriended the daughters of William Thackeray. Rashdall was closely acquainted with the novelist's elderly mother, Mrs Carmichael-Smyth, then living in Paris with Thackeray's daughters Anny and Minny. Then, as now, the city was a magical place in the eyes of young girls. On 2 December 1852 15-year-old Anny wrote to her friend Laetitia Cole:

Today we walked out in the Champs Elysée & I can't tell you how charming it was there with the very blue sky & the splendid ladies and gentlemen who look as though they had stepped out of fashion prints…I wish you would come here & see us & Paris & my favourite Place de la Concorde. To get to it we walk down the Champs Elysées wh. are as broad as three Oxford Sts, & trees and shops of toys & gingerbread & nurses & turnabouts, beautiful carriages & horses trotting down the middle.

In the same letter Anny said her Granny liked to give small parties, adding '…there are some little girls coming this evening'.[4] Could these young guests have been the Marsden sisters?

While Anny and Minny Thackeray were able to enjoy all that Paris had to offer, Cité Odiot was becoming an unhappy place for the young Marsdens. Within weeks of their arrival, Mademoiselle Doudet was sending extremely negative reports to their father. The doctor responded by urging the governess to instil strict discipline:

It upsets me that Lucy has been so bad, she must be treated like a small girl. [Lucy was then fifteen years old.] As for Alice, make her obey you and the instant she refuses, put her over your knee and smack her hard. I assure you she will not refuse a second time…I am pleased to hear they are learning to jump rope like the little Parisiennes, but I beg of you not to forget that morals are above all else.[5]

What a relief it must have been for the girls to escape the slaps and rebukes of the schoolroom, swirling their rope in the courtyard as they skipped and jumped with their little French *amies*, reciting age-old rhymes instead of times tables, French verbs, and the dates of long forgotten battles:

Dis-moi oui,
Dis-moi non,
Dis-moi si tu m'aimes.
Dis-moi oui
Dis-moi non
Dis-moi oui au non.
Oui, non, oui, non.

Children in Paris enjoying their hoops and skipping ropes. Sadly, the
Marsden sisters would eventually lose their ability to play

John Rashdall was the first family member to visit the children, spending
ten days in Paris prior to embarking on a European tour in mid-September.
While there, he took his nieces shopping with their governess and on an
excursion to the Louvre. In 1852 the museum's star attraction was not Da
Vinci's *Mona Lisa*, but Murillo's painting of the Virgin Mary, *Immaculate
Conception*. It had been purchased by the French government in May that
year for the record price of 615,000 francs (about £24,000). The portrait
provided the perfect model of purity for the minister's impressionable
young nieces.

Rashdall's diary records a hint of concern regarding Célestine Doudet.
After examining the girls on their French he commented that she lacked
'the power of instruction'. When the children dutifully recited French
poetry and played the piano for their uncle, it was Emily alone who shone,
with Rashdall noting that she would clearly make a good musician. All
five girls appeared happy and healthy, but nevertheless he wrote:

> …had a conversation with Md. Doudet & on the whole am
> pleased, tho there is still a 'Je ne sait quoi' which one wd wish

otherwise. Her opinion of the children is certainly very chequered.
I hardly know what to think:– still she seems zealous & interested
for them...[6]

Mademoiselle Doudet's chequered opinion of her pupils included her
insistence that they were continuing to indulge in their unfortunate
sexual habits, which the pious Rashdall could not bring himself to
mention, even in his 'diary of the soul'. However, his comments convey
the feeling that he doubted the truth of the governess's claims. Presumably
he communicated his uneasiness to his brother-in-law, but by now Dr
Marsden was totally preoccupied with his love life and resistant to any
criticism of the person he hoped would 'cure' his daughters. On 15
October he wrote asking if Mademoiselle Doudet would allow Emily to
sleep with her as a means of increasing surveillance over the girl. His
request illustrates the then widespread disregard for a governess's privacy.
Mademoiselle Doudet was expected to relinquish the sanctity of her own
bed without a murmur.

By the time John Rashdall arrived home from Europe in mid-November
Dr Marsden had proposed to Mary Campbell, who was about to return
home to organize her wedding. On 17 November Rashdall suppressed the
painful memories of his dead sister and escorted the bride-to-be north as
far as Carlisle, from where Mary continued on to Edinburgh by train. The
minister's unfailing willingness to do his brother-in-law's bidding is
difficult to fathom. Certainly Marsden was overbearing, but Rashdall was
five years his senior, articulate, well educated, and highly respected within
the clergy. The most logical explanation is that he feared offending Dr
Marsden and becoming estranged from his nephew and nieces. At this
point Rashdall and his siblings were all over forty and unlikely to marry,
making their sister Lucy's children that much more precious.

Although Dr Marsden had been courting Mary Campbell since the
early months of 1852, John Rashdall made no mention of her in his diary
prior to the journey to Carlisle. The only inference that can be drawn
from this omission is that he resisted acknowledging the relationship
until there was no other option.

In Paris, the Marsden girls were told they were to have a stepmother.
The news could only have increased their anxiety, already sky high due to
their father's fury over Lucy's blotted, misspelled letters and Doudet's

continued reports of their collective 'bad habits'. It would later be alleged that the governess forced the girls to write letters of confession to their father:

> My dear father
> I am sorry to have to tell you that I am still a liar, a thief, and given to bad habits, of which I can't cure myself, in spite of the efforts of Mademoiselle Doudet...[7]

Dr Marsden said he burned the letters, not in disbelief but in disgust. It was widely believed in Victorian times, even by the medical profession, that masturbation led to emaciation and debility. On 6 August, two months after his daughters left Malvern, he had sent the following letter to Emily:

> I beg you in your own interest to make every effort to follow the advice and instructions I gave you before you left. If you have not done so, I shall be deeply disappointed when I see you again. Neither French nor music, nothing in a word will compensate if you neglect to do what I recommended in this matter. And illness – a goitrous neck, a crooked back, tender feet – as well as this moral illness, drying up all self-esteem, which will destroy every good quality you have, will cause you to feel personally, and oh how bitterly when you grow older, just how you have forced the laws of nature to your own destruction, and how you have disobeyed my wishes to your complete ruin.[8]

How different were the warmly humorous letters Thackeray sent to *his* daughters in Paris that same autumn. From on board ship in Nova Scotia he joked, 'I thought I would say good day to two young ladies: who are no doubt in their best bonnets walking in the Shomdeleesy: for Law bless you, its 4 o'clock where you are.'[9]

Emily was mature beyond her years, attractive and intelligent. However, Mademoiselle Doudet's allegations fuelled her father's paranoia and he was determined to crush the girl's spirit. In a letter to the governess dated 15 October 1852 he wrote:

Her composition is very nice but I beg you to look upon her as a child, treat her like a child, don't ask her opinion and don't speak to her as though she were a woman; if you do not follow my advice, she may seem pleasing enough, but she will become a most intolerable creature through impertinence and extravagance. There is no danger of overworking her. She is headstrong and it is necessary to prevent her misbehaving. I want Emily to see that conduct, goodness and unselfishness are on a higher plane than gifts of the mind, and I would rejoice to learn that she was cultivating these qualities.[10]

But letters of confession from the girls and bad reports from their teacher continued to arrive at Great Malvern. On 12 November Dr Marsden told Mademoiselle Doudet that he had reached the end of his tether and that if his daughters' conduct did not immediately change for the better his own conduct towards *them* would change. The governess was to impress upon her charges that he was sick of making personal sacrifices and would soon simply stop arguing and place them in a cheap boarding house where they could indulge their habits at their own risk.

The doctor also enlisted his brother-in-law's help in frightening the girls into changing their behaviour. One can almost feel the doctor's presence at Rashdall's elbow when the minister wrote to his nieces in December, threatening not to visit them again:

I do not know how to tell you how much all this has cooled the interest which I had in you. One of the main reasons I moved to Malvern was to be closer to all of you, but since then your conduct has demonstrated that I would be better off by being far away from nieces who give me so little satisfaction.[11]

After telling them to pray to God for forgiveness he increased their burden of guilt by chiding them for their ingratitude towards a father who had given them so much. The children, in a foreign country and at the complete mercy of their governess, had now been rejected by the two people closest to them.

Rashdall's habitual subservience to Dr Marsden did a grave disservice to his nieces. It was impossible for them to stand up to their father's emotional and intellectual bullying when their beloved Uncle John fell in with his wishes so meekly.

On 4 December 1852 John Rashdall and James Marsden travelled to Edinburgh together for the doctor's wedding. In the days before the ceremony they were entertained at Westcoates House, the home of Mary's widowed mother. They were introduced to legions of the bride's relatives and Rashdall betrayed the ingrained English prejudice against the Scots by commenting, 'Found Jura and his brother James much more companionable and gentlemanlike than we expected.'[12] Mary must have been thankful that Lachlan Macquarie Jr, the 'morally insane', alcoholic brother-in-law she had been accused of sleeping with was not alive to disrupt proceedings.

Prior to the wedding, a formal marriage settlement had been drawn up and signed, then common practice among well-to-do families. Mary's dowry of £6,500 was to be invested in a trust fund. Throughout her married life she would be at liberty to enjoy the annual dividends and interest for her 'sole and separate use', independent of her husband. The trust fund guaranteed her financial independence long before the Married Women's Property Act of 1870. The settlement also provided Mary with a life interest in her future husband's valuable real estate at Great Malvern. To protect the interests of the children from his first marriage, the doctor reserved the right to dispose of the properties as he saw fit in the event of Mary's death. John Rashdall agreed to become one of Mary's three trustees, a responsibility that would lead to awkwardness several years later.

It was of course the Reverend John Rashdall who performed the wedding service in the drawing room of Westcoates House on 8 December. The happy couple then drove off, en route to Italy for a two-month honeymoon. Celebrations continued in their absence, with the minister enjoying a 'splendid dinner' and 'diverse toasts', for which he was called on to reply for the bride and groom. Given the Scots' reputation for the consumption of whisky on such occasions, he did well to remain upright.

The newlyweds broke their journey in Paris, spending three days at the elegant Hotel Mirabeau in the Rue de la Paix. During this period Dr Marsden did not bother to visit Cité Odiot. He saw his daughters on only one occasion, when they were taken to the hotel for tea by Mademoiselle Doudet. It was not a happy meeting. The girls reacted very badly to their stepmother and by comparison appeared almost abnormally attached to the governess. Their attitude hurt Mary's feelings, increasing Dr Marsden's frustration and annoyance with them. The initial arrangement with Doudet was about to expire, but it was mutually agreed that it would be extended for another six months.

When Christmas came, the young Marsdens remained in Paris. In Malvern, their brother Jimmy spent the holiday at St Mary's vicarage with his Uncle John, Granny Rashdall and Aunt Elizabeth. Fanny Rashdall was spending time on the Continent with friends.

Following their tour of Italy, the Marsdens made another, much longer, visit to Paris. The decision to do so was Mary's and it was she who advised Rashdall of their plans: 'Feb 14 1853 Letter from Mrs J Marsden, Paris, announcing thr. arrival from Italy & intent to stay some weeks.'[13] Dr Marsden, whose impatience to return to his clients was no doubt matched by his reluctance to spend time with his morally corrupt daughters, was forced to suppress his irritation and humour his wife. Mary was hoping to develop a better relationship with the girls.

By now the novelty of all things foreign had palled and the doctor booked a suite of rooms at the prestigious Hotel Windsor, decorated in the English style and considered a home from home for wealthy British travellers. The food and wine were said to be of the highest quality, which begs the question as to whether the doctor maintained the bland diet he recommended for his children and patients. Located in Rue de Rivoli, the Windsor was close to the Tuileries and the Champs Elysées, and in convenient proximity to Cité Odiot.

The Marsdens remained in Paris until the end of March. Mademoiselle Doudet took the opportunity to show off her school, her musical accomplishments and her social standing by inviting the couple to several soirées. Madame Espert was among the guests and, as Doudet played the piano, her upstairs neighbour obliged by singing romantic songs the governess thought would appeal to the newlyweds. We might suppose that the young Marsdens were also called upon to entertain the company, although their father still felt his daughters' social graces left a lot to be desired.

When the girls were taken to cafés and restaurants their parents were horrified at the unladylike way they devoured their food. Dr and Mrs Marsden would later say that Lucy and Emily appeared rather thin, but their father refused to consider the possibility that the children may have been hungry; to do so would have cast doubt on the homeopathic diet he had prescribed. According to Mary Marsden, her husband instructed the governess to take the girls to the pastry-cooks every day until they sickened themselves and were cured of their gluttony. She said he was in despair over his daughters, who remained strangely subdued and diffident in their parents' company. They stood with their hands clasped, and whatever one of them said the others solemnly repeated, like trained parrots. When the couple mentioned this to Mademoiselle Doudet she told them the girls were simply shy and awkward, prompting Dr Marsden to give her an extra 300 francs to pay for a dancing instructor.

The girls' lack of warmth towards their stepmother contrasted painfully with the frequent hugs and kisses they bestowed on their governess. Mary suspected she was being cast in the role of 'wicked stepmother' and that the children were being deliberately turned against her. In an attempt to win them over she ordered silk dresses to be made for them as a gift. By now, only three months of the second six-month agreement between Dr Marsden and Doudet remained. Mary told the governess her services would not be required beyond that period. However, it is unlikely her husband would have agreed to the girls returning home, as Doudet insisted they were still indulging in their immoral habits. It was a matter she discussed openly and almost constantly, even in front of her pupils. Eventually Mary asked the governess to stop talking about the subject because it made her husband so wretched. Surprisingly, the girls did not defend themselves against the charges and Mary accompanied Dr Marsden when he consulted a hypnotist, Madame Gavelle, for advice. The consultation may have been arranged at Mary's suggestion as her sister Sarah's husband, William Gordon, happened to be staying at Gavelle's health establishment.

The hypnotist suggested the use of special *caleçons*, undergarments, specifically designed to prevent self-abuse. Perhaps Mary considered the garments a less barbaric solution than Doudet's habit of restraining her pupils with cords. Subsequently, the children were taken to a seamstress to be measured up, another indignity they endured without protest. Given the changes already noted in their demeanour, this unusual passivity should have rung alarm bells, but when their parents returned to Great Malvern they responded to the enquiries of friends and neighbours with assurances that the girls were in good health and spirits. No doubt Mary in particular was anxious to avoid the impression that her stepdaughters had been left in Paris against their will.

Someone who *was* worried about the children's welfare was Zéphyrine Doudet, who felt her sister was far too harsh on them. The only reason she had held her tongue during the Marsdens' stay was because Célestine insisted she was following the doctor's instructions. However, during the first week of April Zéphyrine packed her bags and left Cité Odiot, expressing her concerns to Madame Espert, who had formed a close attachment to the youngsters. The widow sought the opinion of several other ladies before deciding to have a quiet word with her neighbour. Unfortunately, her efforts to help backfired. Incensed at the criticism of her methods, the proud Doudet cut herself off from her mother's old friends and banned the children from visiting them.

Zéphyrine took up a position as a governess in Switzerland, but before leaving Paris she made even more startling allegations against Célestine. She told neighbours and shopkeepers that the Marsden girls were being starved, beaten and kept in solitary confinement. However, she did not inform Dr Marsden or, more importantly, the police. That she failed to do so would turn out to be a terrible mistake.

9. A Strange Letter from Paris

~~~~

U naware of developments in Paris, James and Mary Marsden settled down at their impressive new home, Abbotsfield, in Malvern's Abbey Road. As the new Mrs Marsden, Mary was required to make dozens of courtesy calls to friends and neighbours. She wrote to her stepdaughters telling them she was worn out with making and receiving visits. Dr Marsden threw himself back into his medical work. Hardwicke House and its separate bathing pavilion were now complete and fully operational, with water-cure patients also being offered gymnastic exercises by German 'professors', supervised by Marsden's chief assistant, Dr Blundell. The architect Teulon was re-engaged to build an adjacent property, Elmsdale House, as additional client accommodation. Drs Wilson, Gully and Marsden were now earning upwards of £10,000 a year, a fortune for those times. Dr Marsden's residential fees were between two and two and a half guineas per week,

© ROB CONOLLY, 2010

Elmsdale House today; a reminder of the splendour of Dr Marsden's water-cure complex exclusive of all medical treatment. Patients' servants were boarded at about a guinea a week.

A few weeks after the doctor and his wife returned to Malvern, word came from Mademoiselle Doudet that Emily, Marian, Rosa and Alice had contracted whooping cough, a difficult-to-cure respiratory infection sometimes dubbed 'the hundred day cough'. The condition is characterized by violent spasms of coughing which often end in vomiting. Dr Marsden arranged for a fellow homeopath, Dr Paul Tessier, to treat his daughters. Dr Tessier was immediately struck by the girls' poor general condition. They were emaciated, with pinched noses, sunken cheeks and dark-rimmed eyes. However, he accepted the governess's explanation that this was due to their intractable 'bad habits'. For Célestine Doudet, the outbreak of whooping cough led to a significant financial loss. The infection is highly contagious and her day pupils were withdrawn by their anxious parents.

Meanwhile, the girls' sense of isolation from their family was growing. When they complained that their brother Jimmy did not answer their letters, their stepmother brushed aside their disappointment, telling them that little boys were preoccupied with work and play. Her response was completely lacking in sympathy and understanding. At Cité Odiot the girls were now rarely seen by neighbours. According to the kindly Madame Espert, they had become too weak to run along the cobblestones beside their iron hoops. One day Mademoiselle Bonher, Madame Espert's cook, spotted Lucy trudging up and down the shared staircase at No. 1 without ceasing. Marian explained that her sister was being punished. It upset Mademoiselle Bonher, who feared the girl might have a seizure. After Lucy was called inside, Bonher said she never saw her again.

On 24 May young Marian's condition took a dramatic turn for the worse. Mademoiselle Doudet called in Dr Gaston Gaudinot, who lived closer than Dr Marsden's homeopathic colleague Dr Tessier. Dr Gaudinot arrived to find the child completely paralyzed on her right side. He was told it was the result of a fall. During his consultation Gaudinot, like Tessier before him, noticed that the other Marsden girls appeared weak and severely malnourished. Questioning their governess he received (and did not question) the same explanation for their condition: their addiction to immoral habits. Mademoiselle Doudet also told him that the girls were on a strict diet, ordered by their father. Dr Gaudinot advised that the diet be changed immediately to conform with normal French standards. However, about fifteen days later a letter arrived from Dr Marsden insisting that the old regime be restored. Marsden's decision was almost certainly due to his theory that rich food increased sensuality.

From the time he assumed responsibility for Marian's care, Dr Gaudinot kept Dr Marsden informed of her condition. On 13 June he received a letter from the girl's father thanking him for his bulletins. Dr Marsden said he believed Marian may have suffered a brain haemorrhage during a coughing fit and asked for Gaudinot's prognosis. He added that he was very worried and intended visiting his daughter, but that for the time being it was impossible to leave his water-cure clients.

Marsden's reaction to the news of Marian's illness was in stark contrast to that of Charles Darwin, who reacted so quickly and with such loving concern when advised of the deterioration in his daughter Annie's health. Since her near-fatal bout of typhoid fever in 1848, Marian had been more delicate than her siblings, making Dr Marsden's failure to rush to her side even more reprehensible.

Immediately after composing his letter to Gaudinot, Dr Marsden wrote to 13-year-old Emily about the girls' reported weight loss, judging his older daughter Lucy too dim-witted to comprehend. Despite previously urging Mademoiselle Doudet not to speak to Emily as an adult, his letter reveals he did just that himself. Referring to their restricted diet, Dr Marsden said he did not care whether people approved of homeopathy or not, though he would be annoyed if the intervention of Dr Gaudinot caused a breach with Dr Tessier. To mollify Gaudinot, he told Emily that although it would be better if she and her sisters stuck to their usual regime, milk and water could be replaced with soup at lunchtime if they wished. He then referred directly to Marian's condition: 'We send our best love and kisses to poor little Mary-Ann.' He said he would be coming to Paris to see them but would only be able to stay for a day, and that even such a short absence would be extremely difficult.

The girls' father noted that Fanny Rashdall was travelling in France with some friends and that she too intended visiting them. Still piqued over their demeanour during his honeymoon visits, he commented that he hoped their aunt would find them with more cheerful expressions. Considering Marian's paralysis and the fact that Emily, Rosa and Alice were all sick with whooping cough, it was another example of Marsden's lack of feeling. The letter concluded, 'Uncle John and your mother join me in sending our compliments to Mademoiselle Doudet, and our love to you all.'[1]

Meanwhile, at St Mary's vicarage the girls' Uncle John was relieving his boredom by dabbling in spiritualism, an interest he shared with both his brother-in-law and Dr Gully. On 10 June he had written, 'Table moving in my drawing room by four ladies with entire success.' Five days later news arrived in Malvern that would make the minister look back with longing at those days of ennui. His diary records, 'Strange letter from Paris…' He was referring to an anonymous letter forwarded to Dr Marsden from the French police. The letter contained serious charges against Mademoiselle Doudet, alleging cruelty to her pupils. M. Collomp, the Commissioner of Police, had enclosed his own letter, which stated that although he had investigated the matter and found nothing to justify the charges, he felt it his duty to advise Dr Marsden. Rashdall was impressed by the diligence of the French authorities, 'This is one proof that the strictness of the French Police is not altogether out of place, and without useful purposes and results.'[2] The doctor wrote back, thanking Collomp and telling him that his brother-in-law would be travelling to Paris to investigate.

John Rashdall arrived in Paris on the following Wednesday. He booked in at his favourite hotel, the deluxe Hotel Meurice on Rue de Rivoli, opposite the gardens of the Tuileries. He then went directly to Cité Odiot, and was shocked by what he found:

> For the first time saw the children & was perfectly horrified at the little band of skeletons: Lucy had just taken the Hoop[g] cough, had a long talk with Emily & prayed with her. I mean to do the same with them all. Poor Marian however, is too weak. Then, long talk with Mademoiselle…left very sad, impres[t] with awfulness of sin & the truth of original sin & the rapidity of its growth, a fearful chapter in human nature. How God can find the sore points of one's heart & there send his arrows!![3]

The impression is that Rashdall was referring to his nieces' 'sin' rather than that of their governess. As she had done with their father, stepmother and attending doctors, Doudet had given Rashdall a graphic description of her pupils' immoral behaviour. When a mortified Rashdall questioned them, even the normally self-possessed Emily broke down and cried, saying that if she *was* doing anything bad it must be in her sleep. It was a true *cri de coeur* from a physically weak and bewildered young girl. Her words give a clue as to why she and her sisters so rarely defended themselves against the accusations. If Doudet had told them they were misbehaving in their sleep, how could they deny it?

In an autobiography published in 1892, Englishwoman Mary Smith, who became a governess herself, described her own childhood experience of being wrongly accused and made to suffer a humiliating punishment:

Some ill-natured school child fixed upon me the making of a great noise while the governess was out. As a punishment I was set on the stool, with this horrible cap on my head, opposite the window. A sensitive child, I was overwhelmed with grief, especially as I was quite innocent; but in vain I protested. I was not even noticed, which injustice – child as I was – I thought the worst part of it. At last, seeing how dreadfully I cried, a little girl stepped up to the governess and with a deep curtsey, said that I did not make a noise, but was sitting reading on the form (my usual custom). I was taken down; but I never forgot it. It was a hateful ordeal, robbing a child of its self-respect, which should always be kept inviolate, if at all possible.[4]

Governess Doudet loses her temper with the young Marsdens

How much worse was Emily's situation and that of her sisters? Since they were all branded guilty they were unable to intervene on each other's behalf, and their alleged crimes were far more serious than merely making a noise.

Inconceivably (no doubt at the behest of their father), John Rashdall examined his sick nieces on their French, pronouncing himself disappointed with their progress. He also chastised them for ruining the beautiful, silver-embellished bible their father had given them when they left Malvern. The girls told him it had been damaged when their governess threw it at their heads in anger. But they emphatically denied being abused, and when Rashdall gave them the option of moving to a *pension* they insisted on remaining at Cité Odiot. They continued to profess their love for Mademoiselle Doudet, emptying their purses and asking their Uncle John to buy her a watch. When a bemused Rashdall told them they did not have enough money for such a gift, they begged him to buy her the prettiest thing they could afford.

Abused children have a heartbreaking capacity to adapt to their situation. Given the circumstances, the sisters' professed attachment to their governess was understandable. Their father and uncle had threatened to withdraw their love and support and they had become increasingly unwell and anxious. An emotional vacuum was created, which Mademoiselle Doudet filled, albeit destructively. That same day Rashdall went to see Dr Gaston Gaudinot, who had only good things to say of Mademoiselle Doudet and promised to write a letter of reassurance to Dr Marsden.

On the third and fourth days of his stay the Reverend John Rashdall interviewed various neighbours at Cité Odiot about specific charges in the anonymous letter. He concentrated on the English ex-patriot community, with whom it was easier for him to communicate. Opinion about the governess was divided and it became clear that most of the stories of abuse had originated with Doudet's younger sister Zéphyrine. Rashdall returned to Cité Odiot and had a long discussion with Mademoiselle Doudet. He told her the case against her was grave. She wept bitterly and continued to protest her innocence, claiming her sister had acted through jealousy and had often caused trouble within the family.

Reviewing his investigations, Rashdall wrote, '...there is no getting over the evidence of the Sister, except by the latter recalling or modifying it'. Accordingly, he wrote to Zéphyrine Doudet requesting a first-hand account of her allegations. His diary entry continued, 'It is impossible anyhow to sustain present arrangement with Mademoiselle.'[5] Despite this comment, the girls, including Marian, whose condition her uncle described as 'precarious', remained with their governess.

Mademoiselle Doudet had become worried enough about her situation to confide in two of her late mother's close friends: Miss Jane Stirling and her sister, Mrs Katherine Erskine. Jane Stirling was a 50-year-old Scottish spinster, once described uncharitably by Thomas Carlyle as '...a hoarse voiced, restless, invalid Scotch lady of some rank, mostly wandering about on the continent, entertaining lions and Piano Chopin'.[6] She and her widowed elder sister Katherine Erskine, then in her sixties, had been passionate admirers and patrons of Frédéric Chopin. It was said that Jane wanted to marry the composer and Chopin suspected Katherine was out to convert him. In October 1848 he wrote, 'Mrs Erskine, who is a very religious protestant, good soul, would perhaps like to make a protestant of me; she brings me the Bible, talks of the soul, quotes the psalms to me...'.[7]. It was as members of the Protestant community in Paris that the sisters had become acquainted with Madame Doudet. In the void left by Chopin's death in October 1849, the well-intentioned ladies took up the cause of their old friend's daughter, Célestine.

John Rashdall went to see Mrs Erskine, who insisted Mademoiselle Doudet was incapable of mistreating children. Nevertheless, Rashdall wrote to his sister Fanny, then residing in Orleans. Fanny travelled to Paris

AUDREY EVELYN BONE, JANE WILHELMINA STIRLING, 1804–1859

Chopin's patron Jane Stirling (left) and her sister Katherine Erskine. The pair had been friends of Doudet's late mother and testified on the governess's behalf

with her maid on 30 June and was 'much affected' at seeing the children in such poor condition. Arrangements were made for her to rent an apartment in nearby Rue de Chaillot so she could more closely supervise her nieces.

On Monday 4 July Zéphyrine Doudet responded to Rashdall's letter, withdrawing her allegations and accusing the neighbours at Cité Odiot of 'base exaggeration' and a wish to ruin the prospects of a respectable family. The Reverend noted that while this might serve as an adequate response to the world, it did not satisfy him. And yet, confused by the children's demonstrated affection for their governess and the assurances of Mrs Erskine, he allowed them to remain in her care. There was another reason behind Rashdall's reluctance to take action. He told Mademoiselle Doudet's accusers, who were pressing for prosecution, that Mary Marsden was in the early stages of pregnancy and Dr Marsden did not want his wife upset. However, before leaving Paris, Rashdall arranged for his sister to make regular, unannounced visits to Cité Odiot, an arrangement that led to a great deal of ill-feeling between the embattled governess and the children's aunt.

During John Rashdall's stay in Paris he dined with Mrs Carmichael-Smyth, her son Thackeray, and her granddaughters Anny and Minny. No doubt there was discussion about the Marsden girls' ill health, though it is unlikely anything was said about the rumours surrounding their governess. Thackeray's mother was a fiercely evangelical Christian, famous for expressing her disapproval of those she perceived as lacking in religious devotion. To their chagrin, this included Anny and Minny, although they were fortunate in that their father was far more understanding and liberal-minded than Dr Marsden. He encouraged his daughters to think for themselves and when Anny complained about her grandmother pushing her to read religious books, he advised:

I should read all the books that Granny wishes, if I were you: and you must come to your own deductions about them as every honest man and woman must and does. And so God bless my darlings and teach us the Truth. Every-one of us in every fact, book, circumstance of life sees a different meaning & moral and so it must be about religion. But we can all love each other and say Our Father.[8]

Neither Zéphyrine Doudet's withdrawal of allegations, nor Fanny Rashdall's supervising presence, mollified the governess's accusers. They were incensed that the girls had been allowed to remain at Cité Odiot. The women held a meeting to determine their next course of action and on 29 July their spokesperson, Madame Sudre, sent a furious letter across the Channel to Dr Marsden. Sudre was the wife of the artist Jean-Pierre Sudre. Although she lived just two streets away at 124 Rue Faubourge Saint Honoure, she had never met Célestine Doudet. Perhaps she heard about the children's plight from Madame Martin, wife of a pharmacist who lived in the same street. The Martin children had befriended the young Marsdens, and with whooping cough in the house Doudet would have been a regular customer at the pharmacy.

With heavy sarcasm, Madame Sudre said she understood consideration must be given to the 'interesting' Mrs Marsden (a reference to Mary Marsden's pregnancy), but that it was no excuse for inaction. She was also highly critical of John Rashdall: 'I perfectly understand that as a man of the church the Reverend Mr Rashdall did not believe he should throw Mademoiselle Doudet out the window, but I do not understand, and no-one understands, why he did not put her out the door.' Madame Sudre, who identified herself as the author of the original anonymous letter, added that if whooping cough was given as a reason for the children's dreadful state, it was a lie. She also had an opinion about the girls' refusal to complain about their governess, 'Your children are terrified, like puppies they lick the hand that beats them in the hope of being treated more kindly...Beneath their silk dresses your children have suffered what the children of the poor suffer; cold and hunger.'[9] Madame Sudre referred to Célestine Doudet as an 'odious shrew'. She said that if Dr Marsden or any member of his family protected the governess due to fear of scandal (a reference to Doudet's allegations of immoral habits), it would be a badge of cowardice.

To have been addressed in such a way by a woman, especially a foreigner, would have infuriated Dr Marsden to the point of apoplexy. It is likely the letter served only to fuel his anger towards his daughters, who were continuing to cause trouble at a time when he was preoccupied with his flourishing water-cure practice and Mary's pregnancy. The doctor was still seething over Sudre's interference when on Saturday 30 July a letter arrived at Abbotsfield from Fanny Rashdall. It contained the shocking news that Marian had died at a quarter-past nine on the morning of 28 July. Accompanied by John Rashdall, the girls' father left for Paris the same day.

10. Intermeddling

✧

The Reverend John Rashdall recorded his and Dr Marsden's movements after arriving in Paris on Sunday morning. They went first to Fanny's apartment and then, unannounced, to Cité Odiot. It was mid-summer, and oppressively hot: 'James shocked to see the children look so ill. Found Rosa & Alice in bed, ordered them all up, & took them out for drive.'[1] What Rashdall did not mention was that the governess had initially tried to prevent them from entering Rosa's and Alice's bedroom, no doubt because the little girls were tied together with cords. Apparently Alice was considered to be free of moral sin at the time, prompting an infuriated Dr Marsden to berate the governess, shouting, 'You have tied a living body to a corpse.'[2] He told her she was unfit to be in charge of children. It is sobering to think that his outburst was prompted by fear of Rosa contaminating her younger sister rather than by Marian's death or the dangerously poor physical condition of her sisters.

The next day the men went to see Drs Tessier and Gaudinot, with whom John Rashdall commented they were 'much dissatisfied'. Dr Marsden also went to the cemetery to pay his last respects to his dead daughter. Mademoiselle Doudet had ordered a satin-lined oak coffin for Marian, and as a temporary measure she had arranged and paid for the body to be placed in her late mother's vault. That evening Dr Marsden returned to England, having spent only a few hours with his surviving daughters. It was left to John Rashdall and the governess to organize Marian's permanent burial. The little girl was laid to rest in the cemetery of Montmartre on the following Saturday. Dr Marsden did not return to Paris for the funeral. Mademoiselle Doudet would later pay for a marble monument to be erected on the child's grave.

Not long after Marian's death one of John Rashdall's old Exeter friends, the poet Caroline Leakey, returned to England after spending five years in

Tasmania. In 1854 Leakey published *Lyra Australis*. The final section was dedicated to the Reverend John Rashdall, A.M. [sic] Vicar of Malvern, 'In remembrance of the days that are no more'. One poem, 'To Little Mary', could well have been a tribute to Rashdall's much loved niece. It contained the lines:

> *So bright thou countenance with life*
> *And tender artlessness,*
> *That every laugh of thine doth ring*
> *An echo in my heart.*
>
> *And yet each laugh doth draw a pain,*
> *That all away has past my day*
> *Of lawful gaiety:*
> *Woe worth the heart that thinks it may*
> *Keep mad festivity*
> *When all around a doleful strain*
> *Of strife and sin is heard.*[3]

Following the funeral, Marian's sisters were removed to their Aunt Fanny's apartment in Rue de Chaillot. Before long Rashdall noted:

> Emily & Rosa getting better each day by change of air and good diet. Lucy & Alice still hanging fire. Some disagreeable intermeddling from the Ladies who had taken so strongly agt. Mdlle which I was obliged to put down & insist on being let alone to manage everything in my own way.[4]

The 'intermeddling' from Doudet's accusers referred to the women's insistence that the governess should be charged over Marian's death, as well as for her alleged abuse of the other girls. However, far from following this line of action, Rashdall arranged for his nieces to visit Doudet on a daily basis. He and Dr Marsden would later claim the decision was made for the sake of 'external peace' and to prevent the girls realizing there was anything unpleasant in the air. To be fair, Rashdall's nieces had continued to express their love for Doudet and their desire to remain with her. Of course, this was hardly surprising. Despite everything, she represented stability and security in their lives. As their social isolation increased, so too had their dread of being sent to a *pension*, as their father had threatened or, worse, to an English boarding school. In popular novels such as *Jane Eyre* (published in 1847) boarding schools were depicted as places of unimaginable horror. The orphaned Jane had been branded as 'wicked' on her first day at the infamous Lowood Institution and the young Marsdens had good reason for fearing the same thing could happen to them.

Lady Louisa Antrim, one of Queen Victoria's ladies-in-waiting, had also experienced abuse in the schoolroom. In adult life she wrote a touching description of her childhood, revealing how fear of authority prevented far less isolated and oppressed children than the Marsdens from speaking out against the cruelty of their governess:

> It seems strange that we who were idolized by our parents, and indeed much spoilt by them, should never have told them how unhappy we were with our Fraulein. I suppose we took it for granted that governesses were immovable institutions and fancied that if we complained we should suffer for it afterwards. At any rate we said nothing though once an elder sister Victoria was made to walk for miles with a broken chilblain on her heel, and Mary, learning to read, was often battered and pinched until her poor little arms were pulp. I remember feeling like murder, and clenching my hands with suppressed rage until the nails ran into the palms at this ill-treatment of my sisters. It must have been bad for us to hate as we did then. So miserable were we that Victoria used to pray to die in the night; I used to pray that Fraulein might die![5]

It was decided that the surviving girls should return to England, although it was not until 11 August that John Rashdall arrived back at Great Malvern with Emily, Rosa and Lucy – unhappy and awkward additions to their father's new household at Abbotsfield. Perhaps to relieve pressure on the children's stepmother, little Alice remained in Paris with her Aunt Fanny. A new governess, Miss Bennet, was employed at Abbotsfield, although only Emily and Rosa were well enough to take their place in the schoolroom. Unlike her sisters, Lucy Marsden had not rallied after her removal from Mademoiselle Doudet. She was still suffering from whooping cough and the long journey home took its toll.

As the weeks went by, Lucy's condition deteriorated. On Wednesday 14 September her uncle's diary records that she was gravely ill. He sat with her throughout the night at Abbotsfield, fearing she would die. On Thursday, Dr Black from Clifton was called in. He was one of Dr Marsden's homeopathic colleagues and a personal friend. Both men had attended medical school in Edinburgh and had subsequently studied in Paris. Dr Black felt there was a faint chance of recovery, but Rashdall noted that his brother-in-law had given up all hope. It raises the question as to why Dr Black was called in at such a late stage. Had Dr Marsden's professional pride prevented him seeking help earlier? There is another, even more troubling, possibility. The doctor still believed that the underlying cause of Lucy's decline was self-abuse. A comment he made later suggests that for this reason he may have considered his daughter's death inevitable: '… so terrible is the misfortune of this vice that once it has taken possession of a child, and especially a girl child, it too often only lets go of its prey at the brink of the tomb'.[6]

On Friday morning at 2 a.m. the minister was again called to Lucy's bedside. She died two hours later and he recorded her final moments. For the evangelical Rashdall it was important that the spirit of God should enter the soul of his dying niece…a final triumph over the devil: 'She smiled 2 or 3 times very sweetly & looked up as if in reverend delight during the last ½ hour. She had been peculiarly tender to everyone: taking leave most lovingly of her sisters & emphatically thanking everyone for the slightest attention.' Dr Marsden and his now heavily pregnant wife were also present, but it was the Reverend John Rashdall who had the difficult task of breaking the news to Emily and Rosa: 'I told the children before breakfast & let them have the 1st gush of grief out.'[7] One of the most distressing aspects of Lucy's death was that she had endured two months of separation from her sisters in an effort to prevent her catching whooping cough.

Without the intervention of Célestine Doudet's 'meddling' neighbours, all five Marsden girls might have slipped away at Cité Odiot, victims of whatever virus happened to overwhelm their malnourished bodies. One suspects Dr Marsden, convinced his daughters were infected by an incurable moral malignancy, would have accepted such an outcome as the will of God and perhaps even felt a sense of relief.

That Sunday, services at the Priory Church were conducted by John

Rashdall's young curates, John Garland and Samuel Harris. No doubt there were touching references to the death of the vicar's niece. Rashdall subsequently wrote, 'I trust I feel the sad time sanctifying to my own soul & stirring me to live pure as "dying always".'[8] His words leave the horrible impression that, much as he loved his nieces, he too considered Lucy's life to have been *impure*.

The funeral took place on Tuesday 20 September. Rashdall did not comment on the service, but words from the Anglican Book of Common Prayer were sadly appropriate: 'Man that is born of woman hath but a short time to live and is full of misery.' It is fitting that Lucy, after her strife-torn life, should have been laid to rest beside her mother. Unlike the exacting Dr Marsden, Lucy Marsden would undoubtedly have provided her firstborn namesake with unconditional love, assuring her she was special and that smudged ink and spelling mistakes were not the end of the world. The coffin was followed to the grave by the Reverend John Rashdall and Dr Marsden, each leading a surviving child. The only other mourners were two of the family maids. Rashdall described the burial as '…very quiet but also very solemn'.[9] The public expression of grief associated with Annie Darwin's death was entirely absent. Perhaps this reflected Dr Marsden's belief that Lucy's death was associated with moral vice.

Lucy Marsden's grave in the churchyard at Great Malvern. She lies beside her mother, not far from her old playmate Annie Darwin

Two days later Dr Marsden and his wife left for London, where arrangements had been made for Mary to give birth. Emily and Rosa remained at Malvern, coping with their loss and confusion as best they could. Rashdall's mention of his nieces' 'first gush of grief' reveals their devastation at the death of their older sister. From the time of the prolonged separation from their parents during infancy, the only constant for the Marsden siblings had been each other. Together they had coped with the death of their mother, life with an obsessive and controlling father, the harsh regime at Cité Odiot, and the lingering death of Marian. Now, with Alice still in Paris and James away at school, Emily and Rosa had only each other for comfort.

On 24 September Rashdall received a note from his brother-in-law. The happily expectant father pronounced Mary's confinement as imminent, because he was experiencing sympathetic pain in his loins.

During Dr Marsden's absence there was a serious accident at the construction site of Elmsdale House when scaffolding collapsed and four workmen were injured. Typically, Rashdall did all he could to help, using his Sunday sermon of 9 October to call for a subscription to be raised for the victims' relief.

The doctor's 'labour pains' turned out to be premature as it was not until 17 October that Mary gave birth to a daughter. She was named Isabella, for her maternal grandmother and her aunt, Isabella Macquarie. On Sunday 11 December John Rashdall christened the baby in a public ceremony at St Mary's Priory Church.

In Paris, Célestine Doudet's accusers were still doing their best to convince Fanny Rashdall that the governess should be charged. They now claimed Marian's fall was caused by a blow from Doudet. Quite naturally, Fanny's own feelings against Mademoiselle Doudet hardened after she received word that Lucy too had passed away. Coincidentally, while caring for Alice, she began to find signs of old injuries: a lump on the child's head, scars on her nose, hand, back and ear. Questioned, the little girl confirmed they had been caused by her governess, and as a result the brigade against Doudet gained a new and enthusiastic recruit.

One of Doudet's English neighbours, Mrs Hooper, accompanied Fanny when she took Alice to Dr John Campbell, an English physician living in Paris. Dr Campbell was asked to inspect and certify the injuries. He would later testify that the women tried to pressure him into making the report as damaging to Mademoiselle Doudet as possible, suggesting, for example, that the wounds on Alice's nose had been caused by the governess's fingernails. Campbell refused to be coerced into making any statements about how the injuries might have occurred, simply issuing a certificate describing the marks he found on the child. But it was enough for Fanny and Mrs Hooper, and armed with the document the pair initiated a police enquiry.

As part of the investigation Dr Marsden was invited to provide evidence of physical abuse on the other girls. By now he was forced to accept that his children may well have been mistreated by Doudet, but he said most of their bruises had disappeared, with only a few small marks remaining on Rosa. He commented that he was reluctant to have Doudet charged because he did not want to see his daughters' names attached to a shameful vice invented by the governess to hide her atrocities.

During the police enquiry a number of the accusing neighbours at Cité Odiot were interviewed, but it was decided that much of their evidence was rumour and hearsay. After the governess herself was 'severely interrogated' it was found she had no case to answer. Nevertheless, Fanny Rashdall and Mrs Hooper refused to let the matter drop. On 23 October John Rashdall described the situation in Paris as remaining in an anxious and undecided state. With a view to pursuing Mademoiselle Doudet through the courts, the women took it upon themselves to engage a solicitor, Monsieur Gabriel.

On 3 November Dr Marsden, who had become increasingly irritated by their 'meddling', wrote to Gabriel stating, tellingly, that he did not wish to make a formal complaint because Mademoiselle Doudet's response would be that he had beaten his daughters in her presence. He also admitted that, '...the matter of [masturbation] could up to a certain point be admitted for some of my daughters'.[10] In a subsequent letter to Monsieur Gabriel, Dr Marsden elaborated, confessing he had been so upset and disgusted at hearing of Emily's immoral habits that he had whipped her for several days running with a riding crop. Undaunted, Mrs Hooper and Fanny filed a suit against Célestine Doudet in Dr Marsden's name, without his consent. The doctor was furious and, when presented with an account by Monsieur Gabriel, he told the lawyer to apply to Mrs Hooper for payment. There, for the time being, action against the governess rested.

The question of whether or not Mademoiselle Doudet should be prosecuted placed John Rashdall in an invidious position: caught between loyalty to his brother-in-law and the feeling that he should support his sister. His diary records nothing of this conflict, but an entry on 20 December suggests Dr Marsden may have been persuaded to charge the governess at one point, only to change his mind, or to put the matter on hold. With characteristic restraint, Rashdall wrote, 'In much trouble at the determ^n of James that it is necessary at once to take his wife to Malta, altering all plans.'[11] Was the doctor so self-indulgent that he had decided to postpone any action until after he had enjoyed an extended holiday in the sun? Another interpretation of 'altering all plans' is that the original intention had been for the grieving Emily and Rosa to accompany their parents abroad. Coincidentally, it was Marsden's determination to leave his children and spend the winter on Malta in 1844 that had provoked Rashdall's one and only previous criticism of his brother-in-law.

Dr Marsden, Mary and the infant Isabella left Malvern on 28 December. Emily and Rosa, who were recovering from the measles and would have benefited so much from a change of climate, remained at home to endure an English winter. One wonders what they thought of a father who could not spare a day away from his clients to visit their dying sister in Paris, but was now happy to absent himself for several months.

On New Year's Eve, John Rashdall reflected on the terrible events of 1853, agonizing over his own involvement, 'And so has passed the saddest year of my life & the gloomiest in my domestic circle & Alas, alas. – what has been my spiritual progress! Rather let me say from all my backslidings – Lord Good Lord deliver me! Lord have mercy on me, a miserable sinner!'[12] At the end of January he left for a four-month tour of Italy. Emily and Rosa, who had been staying at the vicarage, were removed to Abbotsfield in the care of servants until their parents returned in the spring.

11. A Complaint is Laid

Thanks to the favourable outcome of the initial police investigation and the continued support of friends such as Miss Stirling and her sister Mrs Erskine, Célestine Doudet had been offered good positions as a governess in England. However, although she was perfectly free to leave France she had chosen to remain – not just in the country itself, but at Cité Odiot. This was despite the antagonism of her neighbours, plus the knowledge that Dr Marsden was still being pushed to press his own charges. For the beleagured Doudet the decision to stay was both an assertion of her innocence and a demonstration of her proud and obstinate nature. The failure of her school meant she had virtually no income, but she refused to allow her accusers the satisfaction of driving her out. As the months went by without word of legal action, she must have felt she could relax and begin to rebuild her life. But suddenly everything changed.

Returning from Italy via Paris on 8 May 1854, John Rashdall was surprised to find James and Mary Marsden staying at the Hotel Meurice. Dr Marsden had just lodged a formal complaint against Mademoiselle Doudet, accusing her of causing the death of Marian and of physically abusing all five of his daughters. The minister's reaction to his brother-in-law's belated charges was one of weary relief: 'So the last of this distressing matter has some prospect of coming to a crisis.'[1] He spent 10 May giving evidence at the Palais de Justice, commenting how strange it was that he should have arrived in Paris just in time to testify, though Dr Marsden had no doubt engineered the 'coincidence'. Two days later Doudet's older sister Louise was examined. That evening Rashdall and the Marsdens visited Mrs Hooper, who was probably congratulating herself over the development. Rashdall wrote:

… now nothing remains but to return home and get the children over as soon as possible: it is a tedious and expensive business to

95

bring them over, first for the preliminary evidence and then again some two months subsequently for the trial. Perhaps arrangements will be made to keep them in France, perhaps in Paris, during the interval.[2]

At Cité Odiot the news hit the governess and her supporters with all the force of Widow Espert's 'globular thunderbolt', especially when Mademoiselle Doudet was arrested. However, it appears Dr Marsden's action was prompted by attacks on his own honour rather than by a desire to seek justice for his daughters. Mademoiselle Doudet, provoked by the earlier police enquiry and the unrelenting campaign by Mrs Hooper and her cohorts, had retaliated by making a series of slanderous comments about Dr and Mrs Marsden. She claimed James Marsden had lived in sin with his new wife for two years before their marriage, that the wedding had only taken place because Mary had fallen pregnant, that she was '...a light woman, that she was hiding her past under the veil of an honourable union'.[3] Was it possible that Doudet, through her Scottish friends Miss Stirling and Mrs Erskine, heard the old rumour of Mary's affair with her brother-in-law Lachlan Macquarie Jr? Naturally Mrs Hooper and Fanny Rashdall informed the Marsdens of the claims in salacious detail.

To account for the death of her pupils, Mademoiselle Doudet was also continuing to trumpet the Marsden girls' addiction to immoral vice, which the doctor viewed as completely humiliating.

The Marsdens returned to England with Rashdall and on 14 May the three held a strategy meeting at Marylebone's Bryanston Square, the London home of Mary's eldest sister, Christiana Meiklam. Early the following morning the doctor and his wife departed for Malvern, leaving the well-connected Rashdall to perform an important service in London. On 19 May he went to Buckingham Palace to see Colonel Charles Beaumont Phipps. The Colonel was a royal insider, equerry to Queen Victoria and treasurer to Prince Albert. Phipps promised to check the authenticity of Mademoiselle Doudet's reference letter from Her Majesty. From this we might conclude that Victoria was made aware of the Doudet affair at a very early stage.

In filing their legal complaint, Dr Marsden and his wife now swore that several weeks after returning to Great Malvern Lucy, Emily and Rosa revealed that, like Alice, they too had been tortured by their governess.

According to Mary Marsden they began, little by little, to talk about what they had endured, their stories corroborated by the state of their bodies. In a declaration later presented in court she stated:

> Rosa was black and scarred from head to foot, Emily was in the same state. Poor Lucy had not only marks on her back but large bruises on her chest, on her side, and on her bowels which were, she told me, the result of blows given her by Mademoiselle Doudet, who had shut her in a dark room alone.

Lucy in particular was said to have been the target of Doudet's cruelty, labelled a 'red-haired devil' and having had her hair pulled out by the handful. Mrs Marsden would give a melodramatic account of her stepdaughter's final days:

> The child would cling to me and clutch my hand with fears; she fell away without any perceptible disease; in her last wandering delirium of weakness it was still the vision of her torturer that was following her. For hours together this sensitive and delicate girl would speak to me of the indignities and sufferings she had undergone. That woman, by means of starvation long-continued, of blows, of fears, had gained such power over her that one day she said to me, – 'Mama, do you know that if she had ordered me to plunge a knife into your breast, I should not have dared to disobey her'.

Mary Marsden also had an explanation for the girls' previous assertions that they loved their governess and had been well treated by her: 'Not satisfied with beating her [Lucy], Mademoiselle Doudet frightened her with ghosts and told her she had power over her soul, and if she ever told what was done to her, even if she [Doudet] were in her grave, she would rise again and murder her.'[4] It might be remembered that John Rashdall, who had also been at his niece's bedside, made no mention of such horrors. Mary's account was in total contradiction to the beatific deathbed scene he described, in which Lucy smiled sweetly, thanked her carers, and made a loving farewell to her sisters.

In fairness to Célestine Doudet, Rashdall's 'diary of the soul' made no reference to any signs of physical abuse on his nieces. One cannot help wondering whether at least some of the allegations were either fabricated or grossly exaggerated and, if so, how the minister reconciled such dishonesty with his conscience. After returning from his trip to Italy in May, he continued his familiar role as the doctor's lackey, interviewing prospective witnesses and obtaining statements. Clearly his disapproval of the desertion of Emily and Rosa after Lucy's death had melted away under the Italian sun.

Contemplating the prospect of a criminal trial, Mademoiselle Doudet was aware that the tide of public opinion would almost certainly be against her. An example of how negative stereotypes of governesses were constantly reinforced can be found in a passage written at the time by William Thackeray, a more liberal-minded man than most. On 15 May 1854, after being interrupted by a knock at the door while writing a letter, Thackeray told his correspondent:

> – who do you think it was? – It was a Governess & Companion
> – and there came in such a simpering ogling sighing sentimental
> spinster that at the end of ½ hour's silly conversation I was glad to
> get rid of her – To console her I told her I was afraid she was too
> handsome: that didn't seem to strike her so I tried her in French
> in wh. she made such an awful igsposure of herself, that the poor
> thing saw it was all over and curtsied out of the room.[5]

For women like Célestine Doudet, such patronizing attitudes added to a core of bitterness that was all too often revenged by cruelty in the schoolroom. However, although Doudet had been employed as a governess by many families, the Marsden camp was unable to find anyone willing to testify that she had physically abused her pupils. The only person with a complaint against her of any kind was Admiral Elliott, who John Rashdall interviewed in London on 22 May. The Admiral provided Rashdall with a written statement concerning Doudet's extreme views on morality. He said that on one occasion, after his young nephew had embraced his sister while they were reading together, Doudet reproved the boy, saying that such behaviour between a brother and sister was unnatural. Admiral Elliott said he considered the governess to be mad.

John Rashdall was able to pass Admiral Elliott's statement on to his brother-in-law when Dr Marsden and his family passed through London that day en route to Paris for the continuation of the committal hearing. A few days earlier Marsden had also obtained a signed statement from the Clifton homeopathist Dr Black, who had attended Lucy the day before her death. Dr Black stated that the girl's terrible condition could not be accounted for by whooping cough alone. He went on to say, '...after the explanation that has been given to me, I have not the least doubt that the treatment the patient was subjected to in Paris strongly contributed to her death'.[6] Of course, the 'explanation' had been provided by Dr Marsden.

The Marsden family returned to Malvern on 29 May, and Rashdall's diary records that the children had given their testimony in 'a most satisfactory manner'. Due to evidence presented regarding Marian's fall, Célestine Doudet was charged with involuntary manslaughter. A trial by jury was set down for Monday 11 December 1854, in the criminal court of the Seine. A separate charge of cruelty against Marian's sisters was to be heard in the Paris Court of Correction at the conclusion of the first trial. The family's confidence in receiving a fair hearing was boosted by the fact that England and France, after their historical enmity, were now allies. The two countries were fighting against Russia in the Crimean War, which had begun at the end of the previous year.

Dr Marsden was well aware of how important his brother-in-law's support would be as he and his lawyers continued to build their case against the governess. Perhaps he also sensed Rashdall's discomfort over some of the allegations being made and that a little flattery would not go astray. On 7 July Rashdall's diary records that Marsden had asked him to mesmerize a lady, '...dreadfully ill with Tick in the eyes; likely to lose her sight'. Like his friend Alfred Tennyson, Rashdall achieved an immediate cure, perhaps with the help of divine intervention. On the following day Fanny Rashdall returned to Malvern with Alice. The child had completely regained her health and Rashdall commented on the deep debt of gratitude she owed her aunt. Nevertheless, Alice had much to come to terms with: the move from Cotswold House to Abbotsfield, the presence of a stepmother, losing her position as the baby of the family and, above all, confronting the deaths of two of her adoring 'little mothers'.

In Paris, the realization that the governess would face trial on two serious charges had created a sense of panic. On 7 June Frederick Baker had called on John Rashdall at the vicarage on behalf of his cousin, '...professing to wish to learn only [the] real state of the case'. The minister simply referred him to Dr Marsden. Then on 15 July one of the governess's titled English supporters visited Dr Marsden suggesting a compromise. Presumably Doudet was willing to admit to a certain level of corporal punishment in return for having the more serious charge of manslaughter dropped. The offer was refused point blank, no doubt interpreted as a chink in the governess's armour. However, the Marsden family had underestimated their adversary. When the offer of compromise was rebuffed, Mademoiselle Doudet employed London solicitor Charles Burrows to search for anyone willing to speak against the character of the Marsden girls and their father. His resulting report would become known as the English Enquiry.

The Marsden camp was also busy. On 22 July John Rashdall interviewed Eliza Burnell at Worcester, noting that her evidence seemed very important: '…altogether against the defense which Mademoiselle wishes to set up'. He was referring to Doudet's claim that his nieces were addicted to immoral habits before she became their governess, and that she had merely restrained them and disciplined them in accordance with her employer's wishes. The final words in Rashdall's diary entry that day reveal the depths of his anguish, particularly regarding the terrible things he knew would be said about the girls in court: '…oh, this sad matter – how heavily it weighs against the heart!!'

Eliza Burnell's sister, Adelaide, had also been recruited as a prosecution witness. Two years had passed since she had been summarily dismissed by Dr Marsden and her resentment had long since faded, helped by the fact that she was now happily married. On 29 June 1853 she had wed John Binnie at the Priory Church in Malvern. The couple would have been disappointed that the Reverend John Rashdall was not there to officiate, but at the time the minister was in Paris, investigating the abuse of Adelaide's former pupils. The deaths of Marian and Lucy were deeply upsetting for the Burnell sisters, who had moved from Exeter with the Marsden family in 1846. Both women would testify that the children had been healthy and likeable, with no bad faults.[7]

Meanwhile, Dr Marsden had begun to employ some dubious methods in an effort to prevent Doudet's lawyers talking to another young woman who had been intimately involved in the care of his daughters. Caroline Matthews had served as the girls' personal maid for about sixteen months prior to June 1852, when her charges left for Paris.

12. The English Enquiry

❦

D r Marsden guessed, quite correctly, that Charles Burrows had been told Caroline Matthews could prove a valuable defence witness. Burrows discovered that the 24-year-old had only recently begun working as a maid in the home of Henry Cox Goodlake, at Painswick in Gloucestershire. Since Goodlake was a member of the medical profession it is likely he was acquainted with Dr Marsden and had employed Matthews as a favour to a colleague. In fairness, the surgeon may not have been aware of Marsden's motives.

Mr Burrows engaged Cheltenham solicitor Henry Thick to interview Miss Matthews and obtain a written statement. In answer to what were probably highly leading, carefully framed questions, the young woman agreed the Marsden children were arrogant, badly behaved liars, that Rosa had been beaten by Dr Marsden and locked in her room as a punishment, and that Emily had also been cruelly whipped for some 'secret immorality'. She said all the children had weak chests, especially Alice, and that Marian had been so delicate, 'I always thought she looked as though she wouldn't live very long.'[1] The statement, dated 20 July 1854, was signed at the neighbouring town of Stroud in the presence of Mr Little, a solicitor with the authority to take sworn statements at England's court of chancery.

The defence team were greatly encouraged by Miss Matthews's declaration. They intended using the information to discredit the Marsden girls' character and to confirm the girls were suffering from delicate health before Mademoiselle Doudet became their governess. While admitting the revelations were unpleasant, the lawyers insisted Dr Marsden's unjust pursuit of Mademoiselle Doudet was equally unfortunate and had forced their hand. Three weeks later Mr Thick was directed by Mademoiselle Doudet to return to Painswick to put some additional questions to Miss

Matthews. However, when the solicitor arrived at Mr Goodlake's house on 11 August he was informed by the servant, and then by Goodlake, that the young woman had left her position without notice about fifteen days earlier. They swore she had not left a forwarding address and said they had no idea where she had gone.

The coincidence of the maid leaving so soon after his initial visit made Mr Thick suspicious and he took on the role of detective. He tracked down the driver who had collected Miss Matthews and her luggage and was told she had been driven to Cheltenham. Further enquiries confirmed that Matthews was being deliberately hidden in a house at Cheltenham by the Marsden family, who were directing her movements. He was informed that prior to her placement with Mr Goodlake the maid had been working in the home of one of Mrs Harriet Marsden's nieces. However, when one of Charles Burrows's agents applied to Mrs Marsden for Caroline Matthews's address in July, the old lady claimed to have no knowledge of her whereabouts, instructing her servant to say that they had not seen Miss Matthews for two years and that she was believed to have travelled to the Continent.

On the following morning, 12 August, Mr Thick staked out the house where he had been told the girl was staying. Sure enough, he spotted her nearby. When he engaged her in conversation the naïve and completely guileless Miss Matthews told the solicitor she was about to leave for the hamlet of Alderton, located about 10 miles from Cheltenham. She said Dr Marsden had arranged for her to stay there at his expense until legal proceedings against Mademoiselle Doudet were over. She also confirmed she had been in recent contact with Mrs Harriet Marsden.

One reason why the Marsden family were anxious to have Caroline Matthews 'on their side' involved the matter of the alleged stolen brooch. Harriet Marsden's sworn account of the incident (admittedly after speaking to the maid at Cheltenham) was as follows: 'I knew that my dear little Rosa had perhaps taken a cake, but I could not believe this accusation…When she was alone with me I said, "Tell me, little one, did you take Mademoiselle Doudet's brooch?"…"No, no, Grandma, I didn't take it."' She added that Caroline Matthews came to her saying, 'Miss Rosa didn't take that brooch. I'm convinced it's in the trunk that Mademoiselle Doudet is in the middle of packing.'[2]

When Miss Matthews left for Alderton later in the day, the solicitor followed her. As an impartial witness he took along Arthur Edward Durham, a medical student at Cheltenham Hospital. Mr Thick knocked at the cottage that the young woman entered and asked to speak to her. Initially the householder refused him entry, but the solicitor insisted: 'I said it was a very grave matter to hinder the course of justice and to hide Caroline Matthews. When I made this announcement I was allowed in.'[3] Mr Thick first asked Miss Matthews to read a copy of the declaration she had made on 20 July. She agreed it was a true and accurate record of her statement, made after careful thought.

In response to the additional questions framed by Mademoiselle Doudet, the maid confirmed Rosa had been accused of stealing a brooch. She also said it was true that Emily had been made to sleep separately from her sisters and that Marian had fallen from the first floor landing on the night of the Cotswold House dinner party. Doudet was obviously hoping the little girl's death could be linked to this accident.

Mr Thick then asked Miss Matthews to make a second written statement, but much to his frustration she refused. The solicitor was shocked when she explained her reluctance:

> She told me she believed that if she did so, Dr Marsden would say she had spoken against him, and that he would refuse to pay her the money he had promised if she acted according to his wishes. She said she did not see how she could take Dr Marsden's money if she did as I asked.[4]

Mr Thick told her she must not be influenced by personal considerations; she should do the right thing and not worry about anything else. When she still demurred, he found himself in a dilemma. Although the maid had openly admitted being bribed by Dr Marsden, he knew this would be denied in court. And since Matthews was in the pay of her old employer, she would almost certainly say she had been pressurized into making her original statement, which had been entire fabrication. It seemed all Mr Thick's investigative efforts would be wasted.

To some extent the damage was mitigated when Charles Burrows obtained written declarations from two other ex-Cotswold House domestic servants: Fanny Burford and Caroline Fox. Both swore the Marsden girls told lies and were generally badly behaved. Like Caroline

Matthews, Fanny Burford spoke of Dr Marsden's severe punishment of Rosa and Emily shortly before they went to Paris. Burford described Rosa's beating over the missing brooch as so serious she was twice placed in a warm bath to reduce the welts and bruises. It is worth noting that the only incidents of corporal punishment mentioned occurred after Mademoiselle Doudet joined the household. A worrying aspect of the statements was that Miss Burford's evidence regarding the children's health, especially that of Marian, was almost identical to that of Caroline Matthews. Had some prompting taken place before Burford conveniently produced the words, 'I always believed that it was unlikely she would grow up'?[5]

Next on Mr Burrows's list of prospective witnesses were Dr Marsden's landlords and closest neighbours during the period he and his family were at Cotswold House: the Candler family. Initially, Hester and her siblings refused to speak against the family they had lived alongside for nearly seven years. Their reticence was understandable. They had watched the motherless children grow up and had grieved the loss of Marian and Lucy. Only when they were told (incorrectly) that Mademoiselle Doudet could face the capital offence of murder did they agree to co-operate. In their hearts the Candlers also found it difficult to believe a woman with a previously unblemished character, initially so highly regarded by Dr Marsden, could be guilty of such dreadful crimes.

At the beginning of August Mr Burrows sent a list of questions to Hester, Annabella, Mary and William Candler relating to the health and character of the children:

1. Were Emily and Rosa frequently punished by their father while they were at Cotswold House, and for what faults in particular as far as you know or believe?

2. Had anyone ever been obliged to put Rosa in a warm bath by the orders of her father and rubbed with arnica or other ointment to remove the marks of his severe punishment?

3. Were the children in the habit of lying or committing thefts, or did they have some other bad habit?[6]

And so the list went on.

Over the following two weeks the Candlers responded by sending Mr Burrows a series of signed statements, witnessed by magistrates and justices of the peace. Their declarations confirmed virtually all the negative reports on the girls he and Mr Thick had obtained from the ex-servants. Yes, Hester and her siblings believed the children were all badly behaved and untruthful. Yes, they knew Rosa had been accused of theft. Yes, Marian in particular had been in extremely delicate health. Annabella went on to claim that, like themselves, Adelaide Binnie (née Burnell) sympathized with the predicament of her successor, Célestine Doudet. She said that when she met Mrs Binnie in Malvern the previous month, Adelaide told her she had never recovered from the stress of the children's illness at Dunkerque in the summer of 1850. Referring to the charges against Doudet, Mrs Binnie had added, 'How lucky it was for me that Alice did not die at Dunkerque, because otherwise what would have been my position!'[7] In reality the situation had been quite different. At Dunkerque, Adelaide had shared responsibility for the children with their Uncle John Rashdall and their maternal grandmother.

Annabella and Hester Candler also provided a story about the dismissal by Dr Marsden of a young Hungarian refugee employed to teach the older girls German. (God help poor Lucy, already struggling with French!) One evening early in 1852 the language master had apparently stayed too late with his pupils while the doctor was absent. The implication was that this had compromised the girls' reputation, although their father's reaction may have been linked to secret guilt over his love affair with Mary, then his in-house patient. William Candler made one more very interesting comment. He said that when the family left Cotswold House the children's mattresses were in a deplorable state. It suggests they were bed-wetters, and probably chronic sufferers of anxiety and emotional stress. Punishment over bed-wetting would also be mentioned by a maid at Cité Odiot. The Candler sisters reported that they were often upset at hearing the children's cries while they were being punished.

Importantly, the Candlers refused to comment on allegations that the Marsden girls were masturbators. This was a disappointment to the defence team, as the report of the English Enquiry explained:

This matter of vice in the children is the principal question in the legal process as, on one hand, it helps explain the character and health of the children, the punishments inflicted by their father and later, the advice given by him to the governess, and on the other hand this vice was the cause of a great slander by Mr Marsden in regard to Mademoiselle Doudet.

But finally, in a clear indication that pressure had been placed on the Candlers, the desired information was forthcoming: 'When the Misses Candler understood the urgency of the situation and when they were sure that Mademoiselle Doudet was definitely going to appear in front of the Court of Assizes, they could no longer allow their scruples to hold them back.'[8]

It was actually Hester Candler alone who contacted Mr Burrows again on 28 November 1854, just days before the charge of manslaughter against the governess was due to be heard in Paris. She now agreed to provide a declaration about the girls' immoral habits. The defence were aware the material had not been sworn in the usual manner, but hoped it might carry some weight in the minds of the magistrates, adding, 'We sincerely regret the necessity to put these documents before the court, but the defence of Mademoiselle Doudet is contained in these pages, as Mr Marsden has accused her of inventing the vice.'[9]

In her initial letter Hester Candler wrote:

Dear Sir

I very much regret not having told you all I know, when you were at Cheltenham this summer, regarding the painful affair of Mademoiselle Doudet...

She said she had been aware of the Marsden girls' 'deplorable habits' and was now willing to put aside any feeling of modesty: 'I feel I am only fulfilling a duty, and I leave the rest in the hands of the All Powerful.'[10] Her promised declaration was sent two days later. In it she claimed the children had voluntarily confessed their habits to her while playing in the garden at Cotswold House, and that this occurred prior to the arrival of Mademoiselle Doudet. It is difficult to believe the girls would have confessed *any* misdeed to a middle-aged neighbour likely to inform their martinet father, let alone behaviour for which Emily had already been thrashed.

Reviewing the information Mr Burrows had gathered, Doudet's lawyers drew up a list of the Marsden girls' alleged faults:

> The children were not truthful; they were cunning.
> One of them had the habit of committing small thefts.
> They were violent, bad tempered, and ill-mannered.
> They were dirty.
> They were perverted.
> Their father used severe punishments on them.
> Their health was bad.
> They had suffered serious illnesses.
> Their hygiene was bad.[11]

It was a true character assassination. However, due to concern that Caroline Matthews would revoke her original statement and that Hester Candler's eleventh-hour statement alleging immoral vice was not legally admissible, the lawyers reluctantly put the English Enquiry documents aside to concentrate on other aspects of the case.

13. The Court of Assizes

On 18 November 1854, sixteen months after Marian Marsden's lingering death, her body was exhumed from Montmartre Cemetery for an autopsy. The religious rituals surrounding death and burial were of enormous importance to the Victorians, and for the Reverend John Rashdall in particular the desecration of Marian's body was unbearable. Significantly, he avoided all mention of it in his diary. Despite questions surrounding Lucy's death, her body remained undisturbed beside her mother. It was a small act of grace for a young girl who had been subjected to so many indignities in life.

Three weeks later, on Thursday 7 December, the Marsden family and their servants set off for Paris to attend the manslaughter trial. They were accompanied by Fanny Rashdall and several ex-servants willing to testify in person against the governess, including Caroline Matthews, Eliza Burnell and the temporary governess Miss Dowmann. The elderly Harriet Marsden provided a written deposition, but insisted that if her health had permitted she would have travelled not just to Paris to defend her beloved grandchildren but around the world.

There were fifteen to twenty people in the Marsden party – a logistical nightmare and costly exercise for Dr Marsden, who had no idea how long they would be required to stay. John Rashdall had travelled to Paris a day earlier as a one-man advance guard, booking in at the familiar Hotel Meurice and taking apartments for the Marsdens and their retinue at No. 5 Rue Lord Byron. The following days were spent in gloomy anticipation of the trial. Fortunately, Saturday's London papers provided some distraction as Rashdall's friend Alfred Tennyson's poem on the disastrous Charge of the Light Brigade appeared in print for the first time:

Half a league, half a league.
Half a league onward,
All in the valley of Death
Rode the six hundred.
'Forward, the Light Brigade!
Charge for the guns' he said:
Into the valley of Death,
Rode the six hundred.

On the same day a brief paragraph in *The Law Times* made an oblique reference to the trial:

The Independent of Brussels mentions a case which is shortly to come before the Paris court, and will greatly interest a portion of the English female aristocracy. A governess, who has had the confidence of some very high families in England, and could even produce gracious testimonies from our Queen, is to answer for having by cruel treatment caused the death of two children under her care.

The family arrived at the Court of Assizes on Monday morning surrounded by a throng of spectators and newspaper reporters. However, the correspondent for one London newspaper directed his attention to the accused's brigade of well-born English supporters:

This case, which for many weeks past has excited extraordinary interest in all classes of society in Paris, both French and English, stood for trial today. The demand for tickets of admission was about unparalleled. The President of the court was under the necessity of refusing many English ladies who made great interest to be present. Additional seats were placed in every part of the court where space could be found for them without obstructing the entrance, and several of the ushers usually present were ordered out, so as to leave as much room for the public as possible. It is understood that many persons of rank and station have come from England on purpose to give evidence in favour of the prisoner. It will be seen that the indictment (acte d'accusation) alludes to the number and highly-flattering nature of her testimonials.[1]

For those who gained admittance, anticipation was followed almost immediately by a corresponding sense of anti-climax. After the indictment was read the court was informed that the case was to be postponed until Friday 15 December, Célestine Doudet having pleaded serious illness.

That evening Dr Marsden and Mary attended an 'at home' with Lord and Lady Cowley at the British Embassy. Lord Cowley, the nephew of the 1st Duke of Wellington, had been appointed Ambassador to France in 1852. The occasion was an opportunity for the doctor to exert some influence in diplomatic circles, countering the effect of Doudet's coterie of English friends.

Frustration increased for both the public and the prosecution when the trial was delayed a second time. On Friday morning Doudet's advocate stood up and explained that three doctors had certified his client as unable to withstand a court case expected to last for a minimum of several days. Having just left Mademoiselle Doudet, who was in a court-approved health clinic, he was able to give a graphic account of her condition. She was bedridden and at one point her teeth were clenched so tightly she had to be fed soup via a nasal tube. He doubted she would ever recover. When examined, the trio of doctors confirmed the defendant's ill health. According to a report in *Lloyd's Weekly* on 24 December, they had found her in a catatonic state. Her eyes were closed, and although enough pressure was applied to her lids to produce a scream in a healthy person she gave no indication of pain.

The Reverend John Rashdall noted in his diary that the governess had also arranged to be bled, inferring she had done so in a deliberate attempt to appear pale and anaemic. One can imagine him feeling the family's action against her was as doomed to failure as Lord Cardigan's misguided Crimean charge when he wrote bitterly, 'She will never stand trial!!'[2]

Two days later, on 17 December, Mary Marsden was forced to return to England, most likely due to the grave illness of her younger sister, Barbara. With little prospect of the trial commencing in the foreseeable future, Dr Marsden and John Rashdall also left, accompanied by their servants and witnesses. Only Fanny Rashdall and the children remained in Paris, where they celebrated Christmas. It appears young Jimmy Marsden spent the festive season at school, but Dr Marsden, Mary and John Rashdall assembled at St Mary's vicarage on Christmas Day for a roast turkey dinner. On 18 January 1855 everyone was back in Paris, only to be faced with yet another lengthy postponement due to the defendant's continuing ill health.

Meanwhile, life in England went on and while waiting for the commencement of proceedings, John Rashdall attended an evening party at his mother's elegant town-house in Cheltenham. He was shocked at the manner in which young people danced together:

> How strange to an unused eye it seems that modest English girls shd. be allowed or willing to join in the polka or the waltz. In Germany & on the stage it is a very different thing. The persons never come into contact with each other, but are kept at greatest possible distance: here in England at the private parties − whether by clumsy dancing or design − I observe the gent & lady actually hug one another; I shd. say such amusement is positively dangerous, & sensually provocative.[3]

In the weeks ahead Rashdall would be so mortified over charges against his nieces, his sister, and even himself, that the 'sin' of close dancing would pale into insignificance.

It was not until Wednesday 21 February that the governess was finally deemed well enough for the trial of involuntary manslaughter to begin. Rashdall, Dr Marsden and the prosecution witnesses returned to Paris for the third time, though without Mary Marsden, whose evidence would be presented in writing. Only the most uncharitable would have found anything to criticize in her absence. Her 31-year-old sister Barbara died at Leamington Spa in Warwickshire on 26 February, from tuberculosis.

The press reported that many people stayed away, having given up all hope of seeing the monstrous Doudet in the dock:

> In consequence of the repeated postponements there was nothing like the crowd as on former occasions. The general belief was that her state of health continued to be such that she would not be able to appear. There was, however, a great many fashionable ladies present, most of whom came to give evidence in favour of the prisoner. She appeared at the bar dressed in black, with a large bonnet, which almost entirely concealed her features.[4]

Unlike the Marsden girls, the accused was spared the humiliation of arriving and leaving the court in public view. For the duration of the trial she would be held within the Conciergerie prison, part of a huge complex making up the Palace of Justice, located near Notre Dame cathedral. Each morning Mademoiselle Doudet was transferred from her prison cell to the adjacent Court of Assizes via an internal staircase.

In the bloody aftermath of the French Revolution Marie Antoinette had been imprisoned in one of the Conciergerie's medieval dungeons before being led to the guillotine in 1793. It was said the condemned queen was ill and in pain, the dampness of the cell having caused rheumatism in her knees. She was also haemorrhaging, forced to stem the blood and perform other bodily functions in the presence of uncaring, card-playing guards. Conditions for Célestine Doudet were far less barbaric and she could rely on the loving support of her sister Louise, who spent every moment possible at the prison. Nevertheless, the governess would have shared Marie Antoinette's sense of injustice. The dead queen's cell had recently been converted into a chapel known as the Chapel Expiatoire, where it might be supposed Mademoiselle Doudet prayed for a miraculous deliverance from her enemies rather than as an act of expiation. Transference to prison had brought a chilling realization of her situation. Dear God, how had a squabble with Zéphyrine and the mutterings of a few meddling neighbours come to this?

At twenty-past ten on the morning of 21 February the prisoner entered the courtroom. She was escorted to the dock, though allowed the luxury of an armchair as a concession to her delicate health. A nurse stood by, smelling salts at the ready in case her charge had an attack of the vapours. London's *Morning Chronicle* described the governess as expressionless, extremely pale and plainly in a state of feebleness and depression. She acknowledged her advocate, Monsieur Nogent-Saint-Laurens, with a brief gesture. Questioned by the President, Monsieur Hatton, Doudet gave her full name and confirmed she had been born in Rouen on 15 June 1817. She gave her address as No. 76 Rue de Bac, in the Saint Germain neighbourhood of Paris. This was Dr Pinel's Maison de Sante, the clinic Doudet had been staying in before her transference to the Conciergerie. It had been named in honour of a famous French psychiatrist.

The President of the Court of Assizes had unusually wide-ranging powers. He formed the jury (elected by lot), personally directed the twelve members in their duty, and explained the case they were to deliberate on. In exercising these functions the law allowed him *pouvoir discrétionnaire*, or unlimited discretion, meaning he was able to do anything he judged useful in an effort to discover the truth. Some writers on French law criticized such power, arguing that if a president was not a man of honour and conscience, *pouvoir discrétionnaire* could be a dangerous weapon against an innocent person.

A hung jury was a highly unlikely outcome in the trial as under French law only a simple majority rather than a unanimous verdict was required. Nor, if found guilty, was Doudet in danger of sharing Marie Antoinette's awful fate, although involuntary manslaughter did carry a heavy prison sentence.

The *Greffier*, or clerk of the court, then read out a detailed 'act of accusation', which was effectively an outline of the prosecution's case. It was a painful and humiliating experience for Doudet. For the first time the jury and members of the public heard the exact nature of her alleged mistreatment of her pupils. Next, she was interrogated by Monsieur President. The very first question addressed to her was whether, *before* she left for Paris with the children, she was aware their father intended remarrying. She replied that she had heard it spoken of, presumably among the servants. He did not pursue the matter, but it raises the possibility that Doudet used that information to her advantage. She may already have been thinking of establishing a school, particularly if she knew her mother did not have long to live. Were her allegations against the girls aimed at exploiting both Dr Marsden's horror of masturbation and his preoccupation with Mary Campbell? If so, the ploy was successful. As soon as she broached the idea of a school, the lovelorn doctor breathed a sigh of relief and delivered his five 'corrupted' daughters into her hands.

Monsieur Henri Nogent-Saint-Laurens opened the case for the defence by speaking about the honourable reputation of the Doudet family. In an ill-disguised play for the sympathy of the jury, he said his client and her sisters were entirely on their own. They had recently lost their mother and their naval officer father had died many years earlier in the service of his country. He delivered a glowing tribute to the loyalty and affection of Louise Doudet, declaring that from the moment her sister had been accused, Louise had supported her with the care of a mother. She had been in constant attendance at the prison, happy to sacrifice her health

© ANTONIO ABRIGNANI/SHUTTERSTOCK

Defence advocate Henri Nogent-
Saint-Laurens, who made much of
Doudet's past connection with
British royalty

and livelihood if she could lighten the 'clouds of calamity' engulfing her sibling. Warming to his cause he went on, 'When I think of this generous and devoted woman my heart swells with emotion and involuntary tears come to my eyes.' Then, in a deliberate juxtaposition, he made a curt reference to his client's younger sister, whose widely reported accusations, despite her subsequent retraction, had been the primary source of Célestine's troubles: 'Zéphyrine, you have heard from.'[5]

Naturally, a great deal was made by Nogent-Saint-Laurens of his client's time at Buckingham Palace. According to a newspaper report in England, Doudet's patron Mademoiselle de Chabaud-Latour testified that the Queen ordered her secretary to provide French judicial authorities with a letter verifying Doudet's service. However, the royal testimonial may not have been all that it appeared. It is difficult to believe anyone would have left such a prestigious position voluntarily, particularly to become a governess. The wording of the reference confirms that the decision for Doudet to leave was Queen Victoria's: '...her education has been too good for her situation of wardrobe woman with me, and I think that of governess would suit her better'. But this explanation is illogical; if anyone could have been expected to be surrounded by people of good education it was the Queen of England. Nor was it an opportune time for Victoria to part with one of her wardrobe ladies.

Célestine Doudet was at Buckingham Palace during the spring of 1842, as preparations were underway for the royal couple's first costume ball, inspired by the medieval Plantagenet kings. On 19 April Victoria wrote to her Uncle Leopold, describing a scene of feverish activity:

THE ROYAL COLLECTION © 2012, HER MAJESTY QUEEN ELIZABETH II

Queen Victoria in her robes of state by Franz Xaver Winterhalter, *c.*1870. In her role of wardrobe woman, Célestine Doudet handled the monarch's priceless jewels

I am quite bewildered with all the arrangements for our bal costume, which I wish you could see; we are to be Edward III and Queen Philippa, and a great number of the court to be dressed like the people in those times...but there is such asking, and so many silks and drawings and crowns, and God knows what, to look at, that I, who hate being troubled about dress, am quite confused.[6]

Had the haughty Doudet argued the point over some historical detail until she was viewed as an unpleasant French cuckoo in the nest? Whatever the case, it must have been galling for her to read reports of the ball (held on 12 May) at second hand, especially if she had helped create the fabulous, diamond-studded bodice worn by Victoria and valued at over £60,000.

Ironically, the prosecution may have been able to turn the tables on the defence by arguing that Queen Victoria had been an astute judge of character and that her 'recommendation' was in reality a diplomatic letter of dismissal.

The prosecution, headed by Monsieur Gustave Chaix-d'Est-Ange, set out to portray the defendant as a sexually obsessed spinster. In her written statement that must have caused a stir in the courtroom, Harriet Marsden claimed Doudet had told her that while she was employed by Queen Victoria, Prince Albert had made sexual advances towards her. Given the repressive nature of Victorian society it is difficult to believe Doudet would have spoken openly about such a matter, and virtually impossible to view the royal consort in the role of seducer! Albert was a devoted husband and father, praised by Victoria as a paragon of virtue, and scorned by Her Majesty's more loose-living subjects as a boring prude. Nevertheless, Mrs Marsden said she had feared Doudet would make similar charges against her son, and that she warned the doctor to be on his guard: 'The way she [Doudet] spoke to me about Prince Albert, her insinuations about him and herself, convinced me of her vile machinations.'

The old lady's deposition also addressed the issue of her granddaughters' 'immoral habits':

> If the insinuations against the children were true, I alone should have heard them. It was indecent to speak about them to a young widower. But that was part of her plan, she knew he would keep it secret. My son was fooled by the recommendations of people in high places, and by modest manners and affectations of piety.[7]

A number of servants who had been employed at Cotswold House either testified in person or provided statements swearing they had been unaware of any 'immoral habits' in the girls. So too did the governess Miss Dowmann, employed during Doudet's absence in Paris at the time of her mother's death in May 1852. The defendant interjected as Miss Dowmann spoke from the witness box, insisting they had often spoken about the problem. The witness became very agitated, crying out, 'That's wrong, that's wrong, very wrong. Never! Never!'[8]

Dr Marsden's barrister Monsieur Chaix-d'Est-Ange strenuously defended the girls' purity. At one point he addressed the governess directly, telling her she had not only killed the body of Marian but that she had also tried to destroy the child's soul with her horrible insinuations. Finally, he reminded the court of the surviving sisters' complete recovery: 'They breathe health and innocence, the sight of them is worth more than any certificate.'[9] For those present who believed that masturbation led to physical decline this should have dealt the final blow to Mademoiselle

Dr Marsden's principal advocate Gustave Chaix-d'Est-Ange. Portrait by Etienne Bocourt, engraved by L. Chapon. Chaix-d'Est-Ange passionately defended the Marsden girls' moral purity

© RMN-GP (MUSÉE NATIONAL DU CHÂTEAU DE COMPIÈGNE)

Doudet's accusations. If the girls were unable to curb their behaviour despite severe corporal punishment and the threat of rejection by their family, then how were they suddenly able to do so after leaving Cité Odiot?

The confusion and contradictions regarding the children's immoral habits is illustrated in an exchange between the President and the accused:

'Were all these girls afflicted with this shameful vice?'

'Yes, monsieur le President.'

'But you have said that only two were?'

'Dr Marsden told me that they all were, and he begged me to take severe measures to correct them.'

'But he only spoke to you of two of his children, and you understand that the cause of the decline of the three others must be found in your bad treatment.'

'All five had these habits but they weren't noticeable until they had whooping cough, and that complicated matters and made them worse.'

'But the whooping cough didn't come till 1853, and in the autumn of 1852 we had these words "They are spectres – shocking to see." '

No answer.

'You actually forced these little girls to write to their father a terrifying description of their habits. It is against nature.'

'The father wrote to the children about the habits and they had to reply.'

'But Dr Marsden says it was you who revealed to him the existence of these habits. That is why he wrote to you to be severe in the matter.'[10]

By the time the trial began, Dr Marsden had conveniently 'forgotten' he had known of the alleged bad habits before his daughters left Malvern, insisting he had heard about them only after the girls were in Paris. The defence successfully challenged this by producing his letter of chastisement to Emily in which he had said, 'I beg you in your own interest to make every effort to follow the advice and instructions I gave you before you left...' The governess had kept all the letters to the children from their parents and uncle. It seems a terrible invasion of their privacy that she was able to present them as evidence.

Mademoiselle Doudet was also questioned by the President as to why she had constantly discussed the children's immoral habits with outsiders. He told her that even if such behaviour had taken place it should have remained a private matter within the family. Revealingly, Doudet replied, 'I realize that I lacked discretion. But as it was the occupation of my entire life to break these habits, my mind was constantly occupied by them and so I talked about them to comfort myself.' The President surely voiced the opinion of the entire assembly when he commented, 'That is a very strange explanation.'[11] It also said much about the governess's obsessive nature and her own difficulties with sexuality, which she may have projected on to innocent young girls.

The court heard that the first person to act upon rumours of mistreatment at Cité Odiot was Doudet's upstairs neighbour, Madame Espert. On 31 May 1853, the 52-year-old widow wrote to the governess, having assumed the role of spokesperson for a number of her friends. The damning letter was found among Mademoiselle Doudet's effects when she was arrested:

Dear Mademoiselle

You have always seemed to wish to be on intimate terms with us, and we have every reason to be pleased with your behaviour towards us but it is absolutely necessary that there should be a candid explanation between us before going further. Very painful rumours are abroad concerning the way in which you treat the poor children confided to your care, and this makes us anxious and uncomfortable.

The sequestration of Lucy for the last month is a fact so serious that I must have the matter cleared up before treating you again as a friend. It was not to prevent her catching hooping-cough (as you have said) that you thus shut her up alone – it is by way of punishment; and people even say that Poppy [Marian] owes the cruel state in which she now is to your severe treatment. There are persons who have heard you beat those unhappy children and their aspect shows clearly that they live under the dominion of terror. And when all this agrees with what your sister has said when she left you on this account, not being able to remain a witness to your severities; when it agrees also with what the servants who have left you, have said, my heart revolts and sickens at an exterior of goodness and exceeding kindness joined to a severity of conduct so long continued and so cruel. I wish to believe, dear Mademoiselle, that all this is only due to mistaken ideas on the best mode of education: but believe me, if persevered it will prove as fatal to you as it will be to your victims.

If you are a Christian woman restore peace and joy to those around you, otherwise you will compromise the health, the minds, and the well-being of your pupils, and you yourself will cease to be worthy of esteem and respect. It is such a great and wonderful task to bring up the young, especially when you replace a mother in the care of orphan girls. You, who speak so well of this mission, you must be able to appreciate it, and I leave your conscience to guide you. Did your mother treat you so, let me ask? Will you who seem to regret her, in her name I beg of you to return your system of education to some gentler plans – more like those your parents used towards you.

Formerly the children came to see us sometimes. Why is it not so now? Mademoiselle Doudet, believe me I speak to you still as a friend, moderate your severities towards those children or I shall be obliged to drop all communication with you, for I will not appear to countenance such conduct by holding any intercourse whatever with you. Reflect on what I say and decide. Lucy must be restored to favour, and I must see her at your side, or I go no more to your house; and I warn you openly, I will write to the father; for it is impossible he can authorize such severities; and, if he did, you cannot without dishonour undertake to carry them out.

I regret dear Mademoiselle to write you such a letter, as painful to me as it is to you, but it is my duty to speak the truth to you, and I hope you will take it as it is meant.

Believe in the regard I have for you,

WIDOW ESPERT[12]

The letter was read to the court by the President, greatly affecting those present. Madame Espert appears to have spoken purely out of concern for the children's welfare, prompted by her own observations plus the allegations by Doudet's servants, neighbours and, most importantly, by her sister Zéphyrine. Even Mademoiselle Doudet, when questioned by the President, could not bring herself to question Madame Espert's motives:

'Do you suspect the sincerity of this woman?'
'No.'
'Has it all been an error on her part?'
'Yes.'[13]

It is true that Zéphyrine Doudet subsequently retracted her allegations. She did so again in court, saying they had arisen from a private quarrel between herself and Célestine that had nothing to do with the children. The nature of this quarrel was never revealed, but the domestic arrangements at Cité Odiot were bound to have created friction. When the autocratic Célestine established her school, Zéphyrine found herself in the subservient role of unpaid assistant in her late mother's home. She later testified that although she had disapproved of the harsh regime at Cité Odiot, it was Dr Marsden she blamed, not her sister: 'My sister punished the children sometimes, but much less than if she had followed the orders of their father.'[14] Zéphyrine said that the neighbours had exaggerated her reports of ill-treatment. She added that at the time she left Cité Odiot she was unwell, which may have contributed to her speaking unfairly about Célestine.

The court heard that Mademoiselle Doudet did not respond to Madame Espert's letter for two days. This was interpreted by her accusers as an admission of guilt, as an innocent person would have refuted the allegations immediately. Questioned about the delay, Doudet explained it was because she had been so busy caring for her sick pupils, particularly Marian, who by that stage required round-the-clock care. She had eventually invited Madame Espert to her apartment to explain the situation and to defend herself against her sister's accusations. She told her neighbour that Lucy was being kept in a room on the ground floor to prevent her catching whooping cough and that it had to be locked for the sake of the girl's security. As we know, Espert and her friends remained unconvinced. They continued their campaign against the governess, leading to the anonymous letter being sent to the French police on 3 June.

Called to the witness stand, the police commissioner Monsieur Collomp said he acted on the letter without delay, making an unannounced visit to Cité Odiot early the following morning. He said he found two of the children taking lessons from a professor of French and two others ill in bed, apparently suffering from whooping cough. Collomp described one child (presumably Marian) as 'evidently dying'. Lucy, who he thought looked very ill, was in bed alone in a room on the ground floor. However, he said it was not a cellar, as had been alleged. The room opened on to the courtyard and had a window, although the shutters were closed. The French master had also noted Lucy's long absence from the schoolroom. Perhaps because Doudet had already been criticized for keeping the girl downstairs alone, he was told she had been sent to the countryside to avoid catching whooping cough. Disturbingly, others alleged that Mademoiselle Doudet's explanation for Lucy's seclusion was that she had been caught flirting with young men in the street.

The poet Désirée Pacault from the third floor at Cité Odiot went to see Lucy (possibly with Madame Espert) when rumours circulated that she had been locked away. She said the girl took her hand with an air of despair: 'That made an impression on me!' Pacault said it had been difficult to gain admittance to the room because Mademoiselle Doudet said she could not find the key: 'But we would not give way. We wanted to see the little girl, and we saw her.'[15] Those present at the trial were about to have the opportunity of seeing Lucy's surviving sisters.

14. All This is False

There was intense interest among spectators when the Marsden girls entered the courtroom. They were reported as wearing tartan plaid outfits and Scotch caps, a fashion popularized by Victoria and Albert's love affair with Scotland, and possibly a deliberate riposte to the governess's much vaunted association with the British monarch. The girls sat quietly with their maid and did not appear to be intimidated by their surroundings, or by the presence of the governess. One reporter suggested they could have been attending a prize-giving ceremony rather than a court case. Their rosy cheeks and clear eyes were in stark contrast to the pallor of the accused. Fanciful Marsden supporters might have felt justice had already been served in that the tormentor had taken on the once deathly aspect of her victims. Mademoiselle Doudet moved towards the girls and was heard to mutter, 'At last!' as though she fully expected their testimony to exonerate her. She was held back by a police officer. Her performance was clearly aimed at the jury – an attempt to demonstrate her confidence that the girls would not condemn her, even though they had already done so at the committal hearing.

Emily was the first of the sisters to give evidence. She said the governess had locked them in the cellar for hours on end, withheld food, and hit them with anything that came to hand. Questioned about the length of time she had been deprived of food, Emily replied that on one occasion it had been 'From Wednesday morning until Friday evening', adding that such punishment was for making '...little mistakes in our lessons'. Asked if she had been made to get out of bed during the night she said yes, 'At the least movement in our beds [a veiled reference to the alleged self-abuse] Mademoiselle made us get up. We had to stand in our nightdress at the foot of the bed with our arms held out.'[1] The testimony echoed Rashdall's report of a tearful Emily telling him that if she was doing anything wrong it must be in her sleep. It is important to remember that the girl was now fifteen, when being forced to speak about such a delicate matter in public would have been utterly humiliating.

One reason for the children's restlessness at night would have been the misery of chilblains, from which they all suffered. Chilblains are painful, itchy lumps, usually on the feet and hands, caused by sudden changes in temperature. According to one of Mademoiselle Doudet's day pupils there was a fire in the schoolroom, but not in the rest of the apartment. The girls were also more susceptible to chilblains due to their bad nutrition.

Questioned by the President as to why she did not complain to her father during his first visit to Paris, Emily said she had been afraid of the governess:

'Did she say she was punishing you on the orders of your father?'
'Yes.'

Mademoiselle Doudet's response to Emily's testimony was, 'If this young girl was afraid of me she was more afraid of her father…All this is false.'[2]

But Rosa and Alice gave similar accounts of ill-treatment. Alice was asked by Monsieur Chaix-d'Est-Ange whether she had been left with a torn ear, to which the little girl replied 'Yes', removing her cap to show the injury. The court was then told that Alice had other scars, caused by falling on to a chamber-pot. This related to an incident when Alice was made to relieve herself while her legs were tied. As she was trying to do so, the governess allegedly pushed her and the china pot shattered, causing lacerations to the child's buttocks. When Fanny Rashdall was questioned about the scars she highlighted the prudishness of Victorian society, causing amusement in court by blushing and telling Monsieur President that in England no one would ask such questions. At the conclusion of the children's evidence, Doudet looked shocked and discouraged.

The girls' claims were substantiated by the maid, Léocadie Bailleux, said to have been sacked for following Zéphyrine's example in telling neighbours about her mistress's cruelty. The governess's response was that if she had feared what the maid might say it would have been foolish to dismiss her. Revealing a certain insecurity about her own attractiveness, Doudet suggested that people believed Bailleux because she was young and pretty, and that her youth made her susceptible to Dr Marsden influencing her testimony. The defendant added that another servant who claimed to have witnessed acts of mistreatment was not credible because she had been sacked for stealing an umbrella. When her evidence came into direct conflict with prosecution witnesses, Doudet accused them of lying. For example, in addressing the matter of the girls being tied to their beds the President asked:

'Did you ever tie up the children?'
'I tied them sometimes by the arms, never otherwise.'
'But there are witnesses who saw them tied by the feet, and one-to-another.'
'There are people who saw things that never existed.'[3]

Other witnesses were called to give evidence about the girls' continued weight loss after their parents returned from Italy in April 1853. The dressmaker employed to produce the silk outfits ordered by Mary Marsden testified that by the time they were ready to be fitted, the sisters were skeletons. She said she was forced to make radical alterations. In a written deposition the elderly porter at Cité Odiot, Louis Tassin, whose lodge was adjacent to No. 1, admitted he had not noticed any signs of physical abuse by the governess but said her young charges looked malnourished and unhappy. He and his wife deposed that if the girls were in the garden when they were having a meal they would '…devour the food with their eyes'.[4]

Louis Tassin made another particularly astute observation. Questioned as to whether the girls appeared frightened of their governess he said no, but that he had been struck by the feeling that she could '…make the children walk through fire with a single look from her eyes'.[5] Tassin said he never once saw all the girls playing together. This was probably a reflection of Doudet's unpleasant regime of always casting at least one child as 'transgressor', while granting privileges to the others. More damaging was his statement that at one point Doudet had approached him for support, saying Dr Marsden was coming to Paris to see his daughters and she feared being blamed for their ill health.

Several residents of Cité Odiot were then produced by the defence team. Monsieur Rapelli, a doctor of theology, shared the ground floor space at No. 1 with Mademoiselle Doudet. Rapelli said he had heard no sounds of violence from the first floor apartment, but *could* hear the sick girls coughing. This enabled the defence to point out that although the building was clearly not soundproof, neither the occupant on the third floor nor, despite her letter of accusation, Madame Espert on the second, reported hearing any suspicious sounds. Monsieur Rapelli kept to himself and said he had rarely spoken to Mademoiselle Doudet, but had never seen the children crying or appear upset when they played in the vestibule or under his window. He said he was astonished to hear of the allegations. The defence also presented evidence from the residents at Nos 2, 4 and 6 Cité Odiot, who all claimed to have seen the children acting affectionately towards their governess.

Frederick Baker, who had farewelled his cousin Célestine when she left England with the children, provided a declaration stating that the young Marsdens had already appeared delicate. Baker said that he and his wife travelled to Paris a few months later, visiting Cité Odiot on consecutive Mondays: 4 and 11 October 1852. He described everything as appearing perfectly normal. The children's diet was simple but healthy, consisting of bread, soup, boiled mutton, etc. Mademoiselle Doudet explained that she gave the children more than Dr Marsden had authorized and that he did not like them to eat meat. The governess told her cousin she had sent several letters to Dr Marsden asking about unpaid fees and whether her first term of engagement would be extended. As she had received no reply, Mr Baker subsequently wrote to Dr Marsden on Mademoiselle Doudet's behalf. According to the Bakers, the children showed great fondness for their governess and seemed 'extremely happy and content'.

Dr Marsden's lawyer, Monsieur Chaix-d'Est-Ange, argued that Doudet's psychological domination of the girls accounted for their apparent attachment to her, as did their failure to complain of abuse. He referred to the case of a woman who had occupied the same seat as Mademoiselle Doudet three years earlier. She had been executed for killing her own daughter, despite the fact that the child had steadfastly refused to make any accusations against her mother. Even at the point of death, when asked who inflicted her terrible injuries, the little girl murmured, 'I injured myself'.[6] The court was visibly moved by the lawyer's speech.

The most outspoken of Doudet's supporters was not a resident of Cité Odiot, but a woman from the Midlands in England. She was Mrs Julie

Schwabe, who also maintained a house in Paris, where she moved in the same circle as Jane Stirling and Katherine Erskine. Although the recently widowed Mrs Schwabe had been married to a wealthy Manchester manufacturer, she was no lady of leisure. She took an active interest in social issues, particularly the education and welfare of young women. Her various causes had led to a friendship with Florence Nightingale. But the Doudet case also had a personal connection for Mrs Schwabe. Through her friendship with Jane Stirling and Katherine Erskine, she had known the late Madame Doudet and had employed Célestine as governess to her own large family from the autumn of 1846 until early in 1848. Mrs Schwabe travelled to Paris to give evidence in person and published a pamphlet championing the governess in an effort to influence public opinion. Together, Mesdames Schwabe and Erskine and Miss Stirling formed a formidable trio in their crusade to have Célestine Doudet acquitted.

Mrs Schwabe told the court, 'I have come because we were told in England that Dr Marsden made the charge [against Doudet] in France because the country has a great love of children, and that she would have no one from England to defend her. So I thought, well!, I'll go myself, and

© ROEHAMPTON UNIVERSITY

The wealthy widow Julie Schwabe, Doudet's strongest supporter and previous employer. Mrs Schwabe's advocacy of women's education had led to a friendship with Florence Nightingale

here I am.' During her evidence she explained, 'I am the mother of seven children, and if I believed that Mademoiselle Doudet was capable of one-tenth of what she has been accused of, I would not have travelled from England to testify.' She insisted that although Doudet *did* affect grand airs, she had treated the children very well and certainly never hit them. When Mrs Schwabe asked one of her daughters how the governess reacted if they misbehaved, the girl laughed and said Mademoiselle Doudet would simply draw herself up and say 'Leave!' Schwabe added that her own maid, who adored the children, had said, 'I am so pleased you are going to defend Mademoiselle Doudet. She is too good, too kind, and too Christian to have done what people say.'[7]

But Julie Schwabe was unique among employers of governesses. As an advocate for women's education, she respected their profession and valued their accomplishments. Such was her wealth that she felt no temptation to extract the last ha'penny of value from her children's teachers by setting them endless hours of hem stitching. The 1851 census reveals Mrs Schwabe's home in Manchester, Crumpsall House, had a staff of sixteen, including a full-time needlewoman. In the Schwabe nursery there was no cause for a governess to express her resentment with undue severity. In the lead-up to the court case Julie Schwabe had written to Dr Marsden telling him that if Mademoiselle Doudet was guilty, which she simply did not believe, then the governess had already suffered enough. If she was innocent, the trial would be a travesty of justice. The doctor responded that she did not know the facts and that he would send her a memorandum, which he duly did. Needless to say, it did not alter Mrs Schwabe's opinion one iota.

Two of Mademoiselle Doudet's day pupils at Cité Odiot also testified on behalf of their governess. They were Marguerite and Céleste Lebey, daughters of the proprietor of the Hotel Odiot. The girls had taken lessons with the young Marsdens from October 1852 until January 1853, for two hours in the morning and two in the afternoon. Marguerite Lebey said, 'She [Doudet] was always very good with us. She sometimes rebuked the young girls when it was merited but I never saw her hit them.' Her sister Céleste agreed. When the girls' father was examined, he said they lived close by and that '...the little girls came to play in our garden the day after their arrival, and my wife remarked to me that the children looked delicate and suffering'.[8]

Other witnesses who made the journey across the English Channel were Hester and William Candler. They had been encouraged to appear in person in order to repeat the allegations they made against the Marsden family in the so-called English Enquiry. By now, relations between the two families had degenerated into bitter animosity. Following the committal hearing, William Candler and Mrs Schwabe presented themselves before the Procureur Général, offering to lodge bail of 50,000 francs to secure Doudet's release. They were thwarted due to the French policy of refusing bail in criminal matters.

Mr Candler testified that after the Marsdens returned from Paris in the spring of 1853, both James Marsden and John Rashdall expressed their full confidence in the governess, and that the doctor had said he was considering engaging her for a further six months. Candler also told the court that when he met Emily and Rosa after they returned home following Marian's death, the girls said they had been well cared for in Paris and wanted to return.

Hester Candler repeated her claim of having heard the children speaking about their 'immoral habits' while they played in the garden at Cotswold House. Asked why she did not report this to Dr Marsden, she said it was not her business. This conflicts with statements Miss Candler made to Charles Burrows about her intimate relations with her neighbours. By her own admission she had been so closely involved with the children's day-to-day lives that she was almost a member of the family, supervising when their father was absent on medical visits and helping to serve their meals.

She accused the girls of being liars, and so unmanageable that their father regularly beat them. Miss Candler also claimed the children's grandmother, Harriet Marsden, told her the youngsters had been delicate from as early as 1847. She told the court she had agreed to testify in order to establish the untruthfulness of the children's declarations against the accused. It is worth noting that although the Candlers spoke of misdemeanours and severe punishments, they themselves had apparently never experienced a single incidence of discourtesy or misconduct on the part of their lively young neighbours. This was despite living at exceptionally close quarters for many years.

Nor does Miss Candler's negative view of the Marsden sisters equate with a letter Mary Marsden wrote to her stepdaughters on 6 May 1853:

'The Misses Candler were very pleased with your presents and think that you were very kind to remember them. They send their best love to you all.'[9] There is no hint here of any animosity towards the girls. That the children bought gifts for their neighbours (and also for the governess) surely indicates generous spirits. Ironically, it was the defence lawyers who produced Mary Marsden's letter in court, their object being to refute Dr Marsden's claim that the two families had fallen out and that the Candlers' allegations were prompted by spiteful revenge.

While travelling in France another neighbour, the elderly Mary Hind from Malvern Lodge, had made at least two visits to the girls at Cité Odiot. It was further proof that they were regarded with warm affection by those who knew them.

Countering the Candler family's testimony were written declarations from two of their own ex-servants, Hannah Smith and Thomas Trehearn. Both had been long-term employees at Abberley House. Yardsman Trehearn, aged fifty-eight, stated that he knew the Marsden children very well, had watched them playing every day on the garden terrace, and had often helped them build their play-houses. He said the girls were good and pleasant in every way and that the Misses Candlers had always been full of praise for them. On each of the children's birthdays his employers would send a cake next door to Cotswold House. Hannah Smith's declaration was similar. She said she had seen the young Marsdens every day, that they were very healthy, good children and she had never heard a word against them.

In response to such witnesses, and more particularly to the prosecution's Parisian army of accusing neighbours and servants, the defence produced an equal number of local residents willing to speak of Mademoiselle Doudet's kindness and exemplary care of the girls. These included shopkeepers, tradespeople, dance, language and music teachers, and, of course, Dr Gaudinot. But had the governess simply put on a good front for visitors? Not surprisingly, the President appeared to attach more weight to the evidence of those who had lived in the apartment: Doudet's sister, the maids, and, of course, the surviving Marsden sisters.

There was a sensation on the fourth day of the trial when a row of 'barristers' occupying some of the best seats in the house were discovered to be impostors, dressed formally in legal gowns and wigs. A petition objecting to their presence was presented to the President, who abruptly ordered them to leave. To the amusement of the crowded courtroom, twelve young men rose and shuffled out. They were considered lucky to escape with a warning as they could have been charged with contempt and gaoled for up to two years.

A depressed John Rashdall updated his diary that evening. He made no mention of the bewigged interlopers, although he would have considered their behaviour despicable and an affront to his nieces, particularly given the delicate nature of the evidence, which he *did* refer to: 'The trial has proceeded as far as conclusion of Exam. of witnesses on both sides. The details very painful & the defamation of the defence very gross: leveled at the children & very disgustingly agt. their Aunt Fanny.'[10] Rashdall's last comment referred to Doudet's bizarre claim that the children had been introduced to their immoral habits at Great Malvern by Fanny Rashdall. He could not bring himself to mention that he too had been defamed. According to the governess, his nieces reported that he had once entered their Aunt Fanny's bedroom at Rue de Chaillot and behaved 'very jovially' with her.

The defence attempted to substantiate this allegation by calling Félicité Desitter, a maid who entered the service of Mademoiselle Doudet on 13 June 1853, remaining at Cité Odiot after the children were removed to Rue de Chaillot. She said the girls told her that their aunt had behaved immodestly. However, her credibility was somewhat damaged when the President, perhaps suspecting that Mademoiselle Desitter might have been coached, interjected:

'From whom did you learn these details?'
'From all the children, from Emily, Lucy and Mary Ann [sic].'

The agent général leapt upon her error:

'Mary Ann, poor child, was dead at that time!'
'Ah! I forgot!'[11]

Nevertheless, Emily, Rosa and Alice were called in and asked if they really had seen their Aunt Fanny behaving immodestly and whether they had said so to Mademoiselle Desitter. All three denied this, prompting the President to address a specific question to Rosa:

'But, in a letter dated from Chaillot written by you, Miss Rose, there is the following sentence: – "My aunt was very indecent this morning at her toilet." Why did you write that?'
'Because it would please Mademoiselle Doudet, who was always speaking ill of our aunt.'[12]

Desitter also claimed that when the girls visited Cité Odiot from Rue de Chaillot they were so excited over who would be the first to embrace the governess that Rosa once tripped on the stairs in the race to the front door. She said the girls complained of being half-starved at their Aunt Fanny's flat, while in her opinion the food at Mademoiselle Doudet's was perfect: '...we had eight pounds daily of the best bread and meat, in proportion with vegetables and fruits, it was all excellent. The little girls ate pretty well, but they were not very fat; they were gay and lively without excess, as is suitable in a house of education.'[13]

Who to believe? The jury had been given an almost impossible task. Having listened to a vast amount of conflicting evidence relating to Doudet's general abuse of her pupils, they now had to consider the circumstances of Marian's fall and the specific charge of manslaughter.

15. A Fête of the Heart

Emily Marsden was the only eyewitness to what took place between 12-year-old Marian and the accused on the evening of 24 May 1853. Mademoiselle Doudet's royal connection had influenced the ambitious Dr Marsden to employ her, so it was ironic that Marian's ultimately fatal fall should have occurred on Queen Victoria's birthday. The President questioned Emily about the circumstances leading to the incident:

> 'May 24…what did you do?'
> 'Mademoiselle took me to the Jardin des Plantes with Alice and Léocadie [the maid]'.
> 'Where were your sisters?'
> 'In the house. Lucy on the ground floor, Mary-Ann in the cellar and Rosa on the first floor tied to the bed.'
> 'What happened when you came back?'
> 'Mademoiselle untied Rosa then went to find Mary-Ann in the cellar.'

Marian, Lucy and Rosa had been left at home due to misbehaviour and given extra schoolwork as punishment. Emily said that when they returned Rosa, who had completed her task, was given a piece of bread. However, Marian was scolded for disobedience then struck a blow that knocked her over. She got up, but was hit again and fell to the floor, unconscious. Asked what happened next, Emily replied that the governess picked Marian up and cried, 'Speak, speak, and I will forgive you.' She told Emily, 'The doctor will say that I have killed your sister,'[1] though she was already claiming that Marian had thrown *herself* to the floor in a fit of temper. In the midst of the drama, a terrified Emily ran down Rue Washington into Rue du Faubourg Saint-Honoré to Monsieur Martin, the pharmacist, where she said her little sister had broken her neck. It was the pharmacist's wife who returned with Emily and saw Marian lying motionless, unable to speak.

The maid, Léocadie Bailleux, confirmed Emily's account of the outing to the Jardin des Plantes and the whereabouts of the children who had remained at home. Mademoiselle Bailleux claimed to have heard Marian fall, although she was in an adjoining room at the time. She said Mademoiselle Doudet shouted for her to run and fetch Dr Gaudinot and to tell him Marian had tried to throw herself out of the window. It would be alleged that the governess's intention was to convince the doctor that the little girl's addiction to vice was so extreme that she was suicidal.

The governess's courtroom account of what happened was published in the *Worcester Journal*:

> 'The 24th May', she [Doudet] said, 'is the anniversary of the birth of the Queen of England. She is my benefactress, and I have made a vow to celebrate that fête wherever I may be; I would give holiday to my pupils; everything about me should breathe enjoyment; it was a fête of the heart. We all went for a walk; at our return Alice was seized with a fit of coughing, and I was holding her in my arms. Unfortunately, at the same moment, Mary Ann was taken with a similar fit; I could not assist her, and she had a fall.'

What an unfortunate coincidence! The paper, admittedly always rather colourful and prejudicial in its accounts of proceedings, concluded:

> This story would lead us to suppose that all the children were out walking but Léocadie Bailleux tells us that Mary Ann was shut up in the cellar, Lucy in her bedroom and Rosa strapped across the body to a bed. Thus did Mdle. Doudet celebrate the natal day of her benefactress, the Queen of England. All about her was to breathe enjoyment, and out of five pupils three were in confinement and torture! This was her 'fête of the heart!'[2]

Léocadie Bailleux returned to the apartment with Dr Gaston Gaudinot, who said *he* was told Marian had fallen from a chair during an attack of whooping cough. Someone else who examined Marian in the days that followed was Dr Shrimpton, the late Madame Doudet's English physician. Dr Shrimpton had maintained his connection with Cité Odiot and had been treating the Marsden girls for whooping cough. He testified that Doudet had told him Marian had thrown herself to the floor in anger after being chastised over her 'appalling habits'. This hypothesis was as strange and shocking as the 'attempted suicide' story mentioned by the maid Bailleux, but there was no reason to doubt the doctor's testimony. In all other aspects Dr Shrimpton was warmly supportive of Mademoiselle Doudet, stating that she was kind to the children and that they were well cared for. He did think they were unusually pale and thin, but the governess attributed this to their homeopathic diet and he accepted her explanation.

The President reminded Doudet that she had given a number of different versions of Marian's fall, adding:

> 'Your sister attributed the death to blows inflicted by you.'
> 'She is too principled to have said that.'
> 'When you carried the child in your arms, didn't you say, "Speak, only speak and I will forgive you?" '
> 'I did not say that.'
> 'Standing by the bed of [Marian] and noticing her expression, didn't you say, "Look at her smile! She is saying that she pardons me"?' (A comment reported by Madame Tassin, the porter's wife.)
> 'I did not say that.'[3]

Brigitte How, a local dressmaker, gave evidence for the prosecution relating to the governess's behaviour prior to Marian's death:

> One day Mademoiselle Doudet asked me to come and look after young Mary-Ann, who was very sick. She told me that the Commissioner of Police had been to interview her and added that she didn't want to stay alone with the patient in case the girl died and she was compromised. I stayed the night next to the girl, who was unconscious and when I left the next morning the concierge told me that Mary-Ann's illness had been caused by violent blows from Mademoiselle Doudet. I spoke about this to the governess, who told me there was nothing to justify it.[4]

The defence countered by again calling the servant Félicité Desitter. Mademoiselle Desitter stated that the governess had often stayed the entire night beside the failing child. She said she had never seen her mistress hit the children except for a few smacks on Alice's bottom when the little girl was being silly. Mademoiselle Doudet's Scottish supporter Mrs Erskine testified that in light of the charges being made she had questioned the maid herself, asking whether Desitter had noticed any bruises on the children when undressing them, to which the answer was no. It was also Mrs Erskine who told the court that having cared for Marian like a mother, Mademoiselle Doudet had paid to have the dead child's coffin placed within her own mother's vault until a permanent burial could be arranged.

As well-known figures in French society, the testimony of Mrs Erskine and her sister Jane Stirling carried great weight. The accused's advocate, Monsieur Nogent-Saint-Laurens, highlighted their credibility by producing a letter from the diplomat Duc de Broglie (one-time French Ambassador to London). While admitting he was not conversant with the details of the case, de Broglie said he had known Mrs Erskine and her sister for more than thirty years and that in the whole of Great Britain there was no one more worthy of respect, or whose word could be more totally relied upon. However, de Broglie's claim that he knew nothing of the case was disingenuous. His wife moved in the same circles as Mesdames Erskine, Schwabe and co., and she too was a strong believer in the governess's innocence.

An opportunity for Monsieur Nogent-Saint-Laurens to score valuable points over the prosecution came when Dr Marsden swore he had been kept completely in the dark about the seriousness of Marian's condition. He testified that in the weeks following the incident on 24 May: '…we received no more news of Mary Ann. My other daughters continued to send me letters in which they repeated their eulogiums of the kindness with which Mdlle. Doudet treated them, but never said a word of the state of the little sufferer.'[5] This was shown to be untrue when the defence produced the letter in which he had thanked Dr Gaudinot for his regular bulletins and discussed the details of his daughter's paralysis. There was also the note to Emily in which he had written, 'We send our best love and kisses to poor little Mary-Ann'. This letter also revealed Marsden's reluctance to follow Dr Gaudinot's advice by improving his daughters' diet, even though he had been told they were all alarmingly thin. Similar correspondence was produced in which Dr Marsden had written to Lucy and Emily commenting on Marian and Alice's bad state and declaring the only 'ray of sunshine' for him was hearing that the girls were finally trying to correct their faults.

Due to Dr Marsden's delay in laying charges against the governess it was more than a year after Marian's death that an autopsy was performed. A team of three surgeons operated, led by Dr Auguste Ambroise Tardieu, the nineteenth century's foremost forensic scientist.* A detailed account of the findings was published in England after the trials by Dr Marsden, who felt the evidence had not been fully or accurately reported:

> ...three of the most eminent surgeons in Paris, made a post-mortem examination on the body of the child. They each and all verified and gave evidence that there was a gash **outside** the skull, that the plates of bone forming the cranium were separated, that there were the remains of a clot and effusion within the skull opposite the point of this outside blow, that the sutures of the bones forming the skull were burst open close by the blow, an event which frequently occurs in early age, instead of the fracture which takes place from blows in those of older years, when the bones are firmly knit together. These gentlemen all agreed that this state could neither be accounted for by any effusion consequent on a fit of whooping cough; nor by that of slipping from a chair on a carpeted floor of a slightly made child, especially in the reduced state in which she, in common with her sisters, was at that time.[6]

Put simply, the surgeons concluded that the injury was the equivalent of a fractured skull in an adult, caused by a powerful blow or fall rather than a coughing fit. However, Mademoiselle Doudet's advocate preferred to attribute Marian's death to other factors, putting the following scenario to the jury, 'The young girls had been consistently weak and ill. Couldn't the

---

* In one sense, Marian's death contributed to the protection of other vulnerable children. In 1860 Dr Tardieu published a groundbreaking report on child abuse based on the many court cases and autopsies he had been involved in. It anticipated by almost a century what is now known as the battered child syndrome.

Dr Auguste Ambroise Tardieu, the pioneering forensic surgeon. Tardieu headed up the delayed autopsy on the body of Marian Marsden

© ACADÉMIE NATIONALE DE MÉDECINE, PARIS

* 1818   TARDIEU   † 1879

death of Mary-Ann be attributed to the same sickness? It was two months and four days after May 24 that she succumbed. Does anyone dare to claim that the blow she received that day caused her death?'[7]

One point the prosecution failed to capitalize on was that Marian's injury occurred on Queen Victoria's birthday. This was surely no coincidence. The occasion would have given Doudet cause to reflect on how significantly her life had changed since her glory days in the personal service of Her Majesty. By the spring of 1853 she no doubt regretted ever meeting Dr Marsden, whose eccentric regime she at least partly blamed for her sister Zéphyrine's defection. The stress of her situation increased when she found herself caring for several sick children, with very little help. Her day students had been withdrawn due to the fear of infection, and if Mary Marsden succeeded in having the girls return home at the end of June, she would lose the very nucleus of her school. It is likely that in her frustration she lost control after returning from the park, delivering the blows that led to Marian's death.

On the seventh day of the trial the opposing lawyers delivered their final arguments. That the surviving girls risked being sacrificed to the fear and ignorance surrounding sexual morality became clear when Monsieur Nogent-Saint-Laurens stated, '…the only possible mode of explaining the whole of the present case was to believe, as he firmly did, that the little Marsdens were stained with the vicious habits spoken of. Then, everything became clear, and his client's conduct consistent and justifiable.'[8] In other words, he believed the children's decline was caused by masturbation, therefore his client's efforts to control the habit could not be considered physical abuse. He then spoke to the jury about their heavy burden of responsibility: 'I conclude gentlemen, with a last word. I have fulfilled a great duty, you will fulfil a still greater one: you are going to judge.'[9] Referring to the frenzy of public interest he said they must be calm and cool; that the woman who had been thrown into court due to slander and passion must leave due to justice and reason.

If Doudet *had* caused the death of Marian, what had been her motive? Possibly jealousy over Dr Marsden's marriage, the prosecution argued. Monsieur President appeared to support this theory. He compared the accused's case to that of a young woman called Marie Menier. In September 1854 Menier had been sentenced to six years' in jail for the attempted murder of a 12-year-old girl, first by suffocation, then by strangulation. She confessed that the man she loved had abandoned her and she had revenged herself by hurting the niece he adored. In a grave tone Monsieur President asked the governess if this story was not similar to her own? His words created visible emotion in the courtroom. Mademoiselle Doudet rejected the hypothesis in a feeble voice. Monsieur Chaix-d'Est-Ange then suggested that evil did not necessarily require a motive to exist. He spoke of a Marchioness who removed orphans from a hospital in Rouen supposedly as an act of Christian kindness, then tortured them: 'Elle leur fait manger leurs excrements!'[10] He had defended the woman because he could not believe the accusations against her, yet evidence proved his aristocratic client was guilty.

On the final day, 28 February, proceedings opened at midday. In his summing-up, which lasted for an hour and a half, it was felt the President leaned strongly towards the prosecution's case. When he demanded of Mademoiselle Doudet if she had anything to say in her defence she replied, 'I rely on what has been said by my advocate. Only, I protest with all my strength against the accusation. Be assured Mr President, that no ill-treatment was ever exercised, that no blow was ever struck at Mary Ann, and that the scene never occurred of which so much has been said.'[11]

By now, Doudet's supporters had virtually abandoned all hope of an acquittal. In their minds even the governess's most charitable acts had been twisted to portray her as a monster. One example was that Mademoiselle Doudet's motives in paying for Marian's monument and tending her grave in Montmartre Cemetery were questioned. The prosecution contended that her actions were self-serving and driven by guilt. In an impassioned speech, Monsieur Chaix-d'Est-Ange said that to have cared for the grave of a child after torturing her in life was sacrilege…and an insult.

The jury retired to consider its verdict. At the end of their deliberations each member was given a slip of paper reading, 'On my honour, and on my conscience, my declaration is YES/NO [guilty/not guilty]'. The papers were marked in a secret ballot and placed in a box for the foreman to open and tally. Waiting to hear her fate, the accused was reduced to a state of nervous collapse. While being attended by medical staff, including the court-appointed physician, Dr Bonnet, she made a comment about her situation that would come back to haunt her.

At 2 p.m., after deliberating for just twenty minutes, the jury returned to announce that six of their twelve members had found in the prisoner's favour, and accordingly Flore Marguerite Célestine Doudet was pronounced not guilty. Monsieur President ordered she be set free unless there was any further reason to detain her. The Advocate-Général immediately stepped forward and announced, 'Mademoiselle Doudet is to be detained for another case.'[12] As she was led away the court rose in an atmosphere of agitation and excitement. Those present, not least the governess, found it difficult to absorb the shock of the acquittal.

What had persuaded half the jury that Doudet was not guilty of manslaughter? Certainly the time-lag between Marian's fall and her death on 28 July was a factor, plus the long delay before a postmortem was conducted. Was masturbation considered some sort of justification for violence? Did Dr Marsden's own harsh treatment of his daughters weigh against the prosecution? His advocate, Monsieur Chaix-d'Est-Ange, would have much to reflect upon before Doudet faced trial for cruelty.

In retrospect, it seems strange that Chaix-d'Est-Ange did not raise the potentially damaging issue of Doudet's supporters seeking a compromise in July 1854. This, in conjunction with Marian's fall occurring on Queen Victoria's birthday, could have tipped the balance in favour of a guilty verdict.

That evening the Reverend John Rashdall opened his diary and wrote, 'Acquitted!!! To the surprise and indignation of all.' In an unchristian rush to judgement he added, 'I have no doubt they [the jury] were bribed.'[13] The comment was ironic given Dr Marsden's documented corruption of the witness Caroline Matthews.

William Thackeray's mother, Mrs Carmichael-Smyth, had followed the trial very closely and she too expressed outrage at the verdict. In a letter to her granddaughter Anny dated 6 March she wrote:

...the wretched Doudet is acquitted; by 6 to 6 whc. is considered a verdict for the accused – there is a general indignation against her & the jury, & no scruples as to how the verdict was obtained – the death of Nicolus [Tsar Nicholas of Russia, who died on 2 March] has not caused half as great a sensation – Everybody one met, Every shop keeper – had the same burst of indignation – What the 2ᵈ trial may produce who shall say – a French Gentᵃⁿ in the court said to Mr Chase [sic] 'I blush for my country' – & well he might...in all my experience of human nature I have never seen such an instance of malignancy & practiced duplicity. I yielded half credence to her horrid reports of those dear children, deceived by the power she seemed to have over them wh. made them speak as if she was kind to them.

Carmichael-Smyth said she had spoken to Mr Rashdale (John Rashdall) at length about Dr Marsden. The minister had assured her a more generous, kindhearted and affectionate father did not live, but that he had erred by 'weakly suffering himself to be alarmed by this horrid woman upon a matter which he could not arrive at but through her'.

Further on in the letter she returned to the Doudet case. She had been out walking when an acquaintance called to her from a carriage saying the governess was acquitted. Mrs Carmichael-Smyth told Anny she had retorted, '...is she I'm glad of it wretched woman for her punishment is her own conscience & may God forgive her'. When the acquaintance suggested she was judging the governess unfairly, her response was, 'I can do no other, knowing what I do.' She claimed to have inside knowledge of the case: 'Some circumstance proving her guilt & the terror in wʰ she kept the poor children, from one of their own people who was not a witness.'

Unfortunately she did not name the person, or explain why they did not present their evidence. The old lady was even more upset when her walking companion entered the fray: 'There's a dilemma; if she's innocent the others [the Marsden sisters] are guilty [i.e. of masturbation].'[14] Mrs

Carmichael-Smyth was speechless with fury, but the woman was merely voicing what many people felt.

Thackeray's daughters passed news of the verdict to their father. In a letter dated 22 April 1855 he could not resist a dig at the 'fire and brimstone' brand of religion his mother shared with the Calvinistic Mrs Erskine and Jane Stirling, 'The girls told me about Mrs Erskine & the Doudet flare up. So here's another instance in w^h. religion isn't peace but a sword. I suppose they are so interested in the woman because she is a convert – and they wont see the truth about her, and hate those who do.' His last words referred to the fact that his mother, a friend of Mrs Erskine and her sister Jane Stirling, had fallen out with them over the case. Pronouncing his own judgement on the governess, Thackeray added, 'What a fiend! I wish she could be locked up in that closet where she kept the poor girls.'[15]

At the very time Mrs Carmichael-Smyth was railing against Doudet and the French jury, an American correspondent was filing a report on the trial for the New York publication *Harper's New Monthly Magazine*. It appeared in May, amid pictures of the season's promenade gowns, silk bonnets and fashionable black lace mantillas. After explaining the background to the Doudet case, the correspondent highlighted the widespread shock at the governess's acquittal:

There was what the French called a 'grande sensation' in the courtroom. Everyone was taken by surprise; and the next day nothing was talked about in the salons or in omnibuses but the strange verdict of the Doudet trial. Some attributed it to bribes; others to the influence of the royal recommendation of Victoria; still others to an anti-British influence, which refused justice to an English complainant against a woman of French birth.

The journalist alluded to rumours that the governess had been crossed in love by Dr Marsden and that her cruelty may have been motivated by insane jealousy:

There are, however, certain mysterious circumstances belonging to the trial which might lead one to suppose that the accused had, in this particular case, forgone her previous character for amiability, crazed with the intent of wreaking a private vengeance for secret wrongs inflicted by the plaintiff.[16]

Hinting that more would be revealed during the cruelty trial, the article concluded with the remark that the case was creating as much gossip in Paris as the 1847 murder of the Duchess of Praslin. Americans were well aware of this case and understood the subtext of the comment. The Duke of Praslin had repeatedly stabbed his wife in a frenzied attack following her accusations that he had been having an affair with Henriette Deluzy, their children's 'very clever' governess. Mademoiselle Deluzy was initially suspected of being an accomplice and imprisoned, but was found to have no connection with the crime. She escaped the wrath of the French public by moving to New York. In 1848 she married wealthy clergyman and author Henry Field of Stockbridge, Massachusetts.

Oddly enough, the same issue of the magazine contained a serialized extract from William Thackeray's new novel *The Newcomes: memoirs of a most respectable family*. The book, considered one of Thackeray's finest, was based on the snobberies and absurdities of Victorian middle-class society.

The manslaughter trial had been widely reported in England. Criticism of homeopathy and testimony that the girls' father had been complicit in the mistreatment of his daughters prompted a letter to a leading medical journal from Dr William Marsden. In 1851 Dr Marsden had founded the world's first specialist cancer centre in London (now known as The Royal Marsden Hospital). He wished to make it clear that he had no connection to Dr James Loftus Marsden:

> Sir, – At the request of many friends I am induced to ask the favour of the insertion of this note, in reference to the unfortunate case of a Dr Marsden and his daughters, now under investigation in the Court of Assizes, Paris, and a report of which has appeared in many of the English newspapers.
>
> The said Dr Marsden is no relative or connection of mine, neither have I any knowledge either of him or any of his family. I am not a widower, neither have I any daughters, and I believe I am the only one of the name in the medical profession in London.[17]

With the most serious charge against her dismissed, Doudet's legal team prepared for the second trial. Their client was feeling more relaxed, justifiably optimistic of another positive outcome.

16. Hymns of Praise

❦

On 9 March 1855 the charge of cruelty against Marian's sisters began in the Court of Correction under the direction of President Martel. The Deputy Imperial Prosecutor was 33-year-old Pierre Ernest Pinard. Once again Dr Marsden was represented by Monsieur Chaix-d'Est-Ange, and Célestine Doudet by Monsieur Nogent-Saint-Laurens. Unlike the Court of Assizes trial, judgement on the accused would be passed by a tribunal of magistrates instead of a jury.

Much of the evidence presented had been aired previously. However, the prosecution now raised even more startling allegations of cruelty. Some of the claims must have been difficult for the magistrates to believe. Dr Marsden testified that Alice had been so deprived of fluids she was

Pierre Ernest Pinard, Deputy Imperial Prosecutor, as photographed by Pierre Louis Pierson. Pinard went on to become chief prosecutor in the famous *Madame Bovary* obscenity trial

forced to drink her own urine and that all five girls had been reduced to drinking soapy water. He said Alice had been made to eat soap, and that on one occasion the governess had tried to pull her tongue out. This was said to have been because the child responded to Monsieur Tassin, the porter, when he requested the doctor's address (presumably to pass on his concerns regarding the children). Alice told the court that when her nails were being trimmed the governess deliberately cut her fingers with the scissors. At this point President Martel was impelled to interject:

'My child, is what you are saying really true?'
'Oh, yes Monsieur!'[1]

John Rashdall swore under oath that the family had agreed not to influence the children's testimony, to allow them an entire 'freedom of action'. However, one suspects it was the minister who instigated the pact and that he was the only person to honour it. Perhaps the greatest contrast in character between Dr Marsden and his brother-in-law was that while Rashdall was tortured by his conscience to the point of being an emotional cripple, Dr Marsden gave no appearance of possessing one. During the trial Rashdall's diary records that he had 'a rather severe talk' with Marsden. Was this a reaction to the more extreme allegations now being made? One such example was the accusation that Doudet knocked the girls' heads against their bedroom wall with such force that the imprint of their hairnets remained on the paper. If this *was* invention, it was certainly creative.

More credibly, Rosa testified that when her feet were painful from chilblains Mademoiselle Doudet punished her by stamping on them until they bled, a claim substantiated by the maid, Léocadie Bailleux. The accused retaliated by stating that at Cotswold House she witnessed Dr Marsden's own brutality towards his children. She said that after one of the girls committed a minor misdemeanour he strode out of the house, picked up a fallen branch, and thrashed the child until the branch broke in two. According to Doudet, he asked her to fetch a riding whip so he could continue the beating. This was *her* version of the incident Dr Marsden referred to in his letter to Fanny Rashdall's solicitor, Monsieur Gabriel, in October 1853, when explaining his reluctance to press charges. Of course, Dr Marsden claimed he whipped the child in response to the governess's report that she was a masturbator.

When the prosecution suggested that Doudet continued her employer's regime of corporal punishment in Paris she protested strongly. She insisted her motive in mentioning the doctor's violence was simply to show that the girls were frightened of him. She said that this explained why they were accusing her of such terrible things: that they had been forced to repeat learned lines to avoid Dr Marsden's fury. Interestingly, in a lecture delivered to Malvern's Mechanics' Institute some years later, Dr Marsden noted that fear was one of the strongest passions of the human mind:

> From the hair of the head to the sole of the foot there is not the breadth of a pin's point, that is not instantly affected, and affected injuriously, by this passion, which, you know, of course, is one of the depressing ones. And there is scarcely a disease, that it has not on some occasion or other brought out, or brought on, from the passing effect of shivering and trembling to insanity and catalepsy.[2]

It is likely that between their father and their governess, the young Marsdens had become so emotionally damaged that their understanding of the truth was severely compromised. If they *had* been coached to lie or exaggerate they were blameless – with their behaviour merely reflecting the influence of their parents. For a man of John Rashdall's integrity, false allegations must have been difficult to deal with. No doubt he eased his conscience by telling himself that the end justified the means. Both he and the Marsdens were justifiably incensed that Doudet had been acquitted of causing Marian's death. They were determined that the outcome of the second trial would be different. But significantly, Rashdall himself did not testify to seeing bruises or scars on his nieces. It might also be remembered that his account of Lucy's beatific death was the antithesis of the appalling scene described by Mary Marsden. During his visit to the girls at Cité Odiot after the initial rumours of abuse, Rashdall mentioned only their skeletal appearance. Thanks to the governess, he attributed this to their unfortunate 'addiction to vice'.

Once again, charges of immoral vice meant the girls were as much on trial as Mademoiselle Doudet. The prosecution repeatedly countered the defamation with statements attesting to the children's good character. The most touching was by one of their former governesses, Miss Maria Hayne, who said she had known the girls since 1846, when their mother was

alive. Miss Hayne had accompanied the family from Exeter to Great
Malvern and remained in touch after leaving her position in 1848. Such
was her affection for her ex-pupils that she had even visited them at Cité
Odiot. She said she had been shocked to find the girls so subdued and
altered in spirit.

The stark change in the demeanour of the girls was addressed during
an exchange between Monsieur President and the accused after Doudet
again refuted the many reports of ill-treatment. It also reveals her brief,
antagonistic responses, which did her no favours:

> 'But some ocular witnesses saw them ill-used. The woman
> Bohner [Widow Espert's cook] saw you make Lucy run up and
> down stairs fifty times running; and insisted upon [you] desisting
> from such a punishment. The woman Patin declares that you left
> them in winter without any fire; and that she remarked to you
> how deplorably sad they were, and you replied, oh stuff! It's the
> English character.'
> 'The children were gay enough with me.'
> 'And what do you say to the needle woman Chardonnel, who
> would not work for you, she was so indignant with your conduct.
> And to Lecodie Bailleux?'
> 'She is under bad influence. I don't know whose service she is in
> now.'
> 'But there are twenty four other witnesses, all people of the
> highest respectability, are they too under bad influence?'
> 'It is a mere persecution and pride on their part.'[3]

Throughout both trials Célestine Doudet contended that the best proof of
her innocence was that, until the girls returned to Malvern and the
influence of their parents, they had openly expressed their fondness for
her. This was undeniably true, having been noted by the newlywed
Marsdens in December 1852, and when they returned from their
honeymoon in Italy the following spring. Even when John Rashdall
visited them in June 1853 the 'little band of skeletons' insisted on
remaining with their governess.

During the trial Rashdall admitted the children had no reason to
pretend an attachment they did not genuinely feel. He said he had known

them since infancy and had their complete confidence. There was nothing to prevent them speaking frankly to him, and Emily in particular was not the sort of girl to suffer abuse in silence. Rashdall had conveniently forgotten that he had threatened to abandon his nieces if they did not follow their father's wishes. To the girls, this meant submitting to the will of their governess without complaint.

The prosecution insisted the girls' declarations of affection for Doudet were manifestations of abject fear. As Madame Sudre had put it, they were like terrified puppies licking the hand of their tormentor. The accused rejected this theory, saying the children had begged to return to her care even after they were removed to their Aunt Fanny's apartment. As proof, letters written by the girls during their time at Rue de Chaillot were presented. It is not known whether Doudet's lawyers advised her against this move, but they certainly should have done. The letters were extraordinary. Their style, content and, above all, the question of their veracity presented a conundrum that confounded the best legal minds of the day. From her Aunt Fanny's apartment Emily wrote:

My dear 'demoiselle

I think of you very often and I hope very much to come back and live with you. It is shameful to have been separated from you like this. I dreamt last night of little Mary-Ann; what a shame that she could not have been buried near the grave of Madam Doudet [Mademoiselle Doudet's mother]. You must be very lonely in your apartment on your own and I can assure you I regret it very much and think that Lucy and Rosa feel the same as me. Uncle John says we can spend an hour or two with you every day. I am very happy to learn that we won't be leaving until Tuesday…I will try to write every day that we are here. I know that you love to receive little notes from us. I have told my aunt that Papa promised you a lock of Alice's hair, which she is going to cut soon. Don't forget that you promised us some of your hair. You cannot believe how upset I am to have been so bad when I was with you.[4]

Even the most ardent of Doudet's supporters must have found it difficult to accept that this letter was written by a 13-year-old, particularly the reference to Madame Doudet's grave. By so clumsily over-egging the pudding Doudet betrayed her own hand in its composition. That she was fighting to save her livelihood and reputation against an orchestrated campaign of rumour and accusation is no excuse, but perhaps explains why she was driven to such extremes.

The letters from the other girls were in exactly the same vein, hymns of praise to Doudet's goodness interspersed with litanies of remorse over their bad behaviour and immoral habits. The 9-year-old Rosa, who sent her governess six letters within a two-week period (while visiting her almost every day), wrote, 'You don't know how many times I have cried all night thinking of all your kindnesses to me and how ungrateful I was to you. Alice is sicker here than she was at your house.' Rosa added that she had called her doll 'Tinny' (a diminutive of Célestine) and she would write to Mademoiselle Doudet often when they returned to England, signing off, 'I think of you always my dear Zelly. I am your affectionate little ex-pupil.'[5]

Most poignant of all were letters from Lucy, by then very sick: 'Would you accept this little notebook to carry in your pocket? The little locket I want to buy is for your hair. I hope you will accept this small remembrance. I have done my best.'[6] She too thanked the governess for her loving care of them all, especially Marian, apologizing for the anxiety she had caused through her bad schoolwork and misbehaviour. As mentioned previously, the girls also denigrated Fanny Rashdall and their Uncle John, suggesting the pair had behaved inappropriately together.

The children would testify that the letters had been dictated by the governess on their daily visits to Cité Odiot. They described taking the drafts back to Chaillot and dutifully copying them out. They also insisted that none of the accusations against their Aunt Fanny were true; they had only made them to please Mademoiselle Doudet, who they knew disliked Miss Rashdall. Rosa in particular was very upset about the imputations she had made against her aunt.

Naturally, the defence leapt upon inconsistencies in the girls' stories. At one point they said they copied their governess's dictation onto slates – admittedly implausible considering one of Emily's letters comprised sixteen closely written pages. On another occasion Emily said that rough sheets of paper had been used. However, given the time lapse between the girls' removal from Doudet and the trial, it is hardly surprising that their memory of events was imperfect.

Undoubtedly the letters were the governess's 'insurance policy'. Accusations of cruelty had already led to visits from Police Commissioner Collomp and John Rashdall. Marian's death was certain to raise more questions. One of the letters from Emily was to Louise Doudet, which makes perfect sense. It was essential for Célestine to gain the support of her older sister in the face of Zéphyrine's damaging accusations. The letter informed Louise that Marian had died in her beloved teacher's arms: 'It is a great consolation to us to know that she is buried here, and dear Mademoiselle has promised to visit her grave very often.' Zéphyrine had already been advised of the tragedy by the frail Lucy in a letter written on the very day of her sister's death. Emily's letter to Louise contained more saccharine praise of Mademoiselle Doudet: 'Apart from her untiring care of our dear little sister she has been the best of friends to us. Neither a mother, nor a governess, nor a professor, could have taken more pain and effort to help us in our studies…always helping and encouraging us.'

The letter then turned to criticism of the governess's enemies, particularly the disloyalty and injustice shown by those closest to her. Although 'Emily' wrote coyly, 'I had better not mention any names',[7] the target was clearly Zéphyrine. Even disregarding the content of the letter, Louise must have thought it odd that a child had written in place of her sister at such a distressing time.

Accepting Mademoiselle Doudet as the real author raises another puzzle. How could someone previously so highly regarded as a governess have imagined the letters expressed the true sentiments of children? Zéphyrine, consumed with guilt and regret over her sister's downfall, clutched at straws by suggesting they were written by the girls' family as a ploy to discredit Célestine. But if so, why did the governess present them in court as part of her defence instead of dismissing them as absurd?

Ironically, it was letters between the Marsden girls and Zéphyrine that most clearly showed that they had been dictated, or at least written at Cité Odiot rather than at Rue de Chaillot. As Dr Marsden would explain after the trial, the correspondence came into his possession by chance. In his letter to *Berrow's Worcester Journal* published on 24 March 1855, the doctor wrote:

The children's declaration that they [the letters] were chiefly written on loose sheets of paper at the Cité Odiot, and transcribed at their Aunt's in the Rue de Chaillot, is curiously and wonderfully corroborated by a letter that fell into my hands, having been forwarded to England as they had left Paris before it arrived [at Chaillot]. It is from Zépherine [sic] Doudet to the children. In it she sends them back their own letters written from the Rue de Chaillot at the same time as their letters to the governess. The letter runs thus, and is a clue to many things.

The letter Dr Marsden was referring to was addressed to Lucy. In a restrained and dignified response, Zéphyrine Doudet reveals *she* certainly believed her sister's hand was directing the girls' pens. The letter also confirms that she had attempted to soften her sister's regime at Cité Odiot. However, it makes no mention of the horrors they were alleged to have undergone, saying only that she had tried to make them 'more comfortable':

> My Dear Lucy, – as we staid some days at Pau, I only received your letter yesterday. I must say I was much surprised to receive such a letter from you, and, as I am perfectly sure that *every word has been dictated to you* by another person, I send it back to you, for I am persuaded that you are not ungrateful enough to have forgotten that all the time I was with Mademoiselle, I did all I could to make you comfortable, and if it had depended upon me, you would have been so. Be kind enough, if you please, to tell Emily from me, that when she writes to any one she should think a little of what she says.
>
> I never persuaded your papa to send you to school: I never wrote to anyone against Mademoiselle; all she says is perfectly false.
>
> I hope your hooping cough is better.
>
> Goodbye dear Lucy, I make the best wishes for your happiness and am your affectionate friend.

(Signed) ZEPHERINE [sic] DOUDET

The letter from Emily that had so upset Zéphyrine was also published. It read as follows:

Dear Miss Zépherine,

As my sister Lucy received your letter after she had finished hers to you, she has not answered it. I am very sorry we cannot grant your wish to have anything that belonged to dear little Marian; dear Mademoiselle has her hair, and we have not the liberty to do as we like with the little things that belonged to her; moreover, I am sure she would disapprove of our giving you anything.

You used to tell us when you were here ['here' is proof this was being penned at Cité Odiot rather than at Chaillot] that we should be very unhappy when you left us; allow me to tell you that we could not be more happy than we have been, if the illness of Marian had not taken place.

My dear Mademoiselle has always been more than a mother to us; her only desire is to have us around her, and to do all she can for our instruction, our amusement, our pleasure.

I love Mademoiselle very much, but she has not bought our affection, as I am sorry to say, you tried to do; but let me tell you, that you succeeded with none of us. Papa has taken us away from Mademoiselle's; we are very sorry to leave her, and we are sure it is your fault by persuading papa that it would be better for us to go to school.

We have passed many happy days with Mademoiselle, and we hoped to have passed many more. I beg you to reflect on your conduct; I am sure your conscience cannot be at rest: think of all the harm you have tried to do to Mademoiselle, and ask yourself if she deserved it at your hands! She would go through fire and water to serve you, and ever since I have known her she has ever shown herself the best of sisters in every respect. We are on the point of leaving her; she is losing all that could be a comfort and a consolation to her. You aught to be her best friend, and are you so? Oh dear Mademoiselle, I beg of you to think seriously about it; humble yourself first and ask pardon of God, and then of Mademoiselle; I assure you she is ready to forgive you. Become once more a good and tender sister to her, and pray never write or say anything harsh or unkind to her.

She has already suffered so much; and instead of telling all sorts of falsehoods against her, you aught to try and show that you are wholly changed and are really a good sister. This is the last request I have to ask from you; pray grant me this favour.

I cannot bear to see my dear Mademoiselle surrounded as she is by enemies, and left without a single friend. I beseech you to make friends with her; you will then both be happier. *Perhaps you will think that Mademoiselle has dictated this letter, but she does not even know that I am writing*, or if I intend writing at all.

I am, yours faithfully.
(Signed) EMILY MARSDEN

P.S. – I have not written this letter at Mademoiselle's but at my aunt's. *Mademoiselle begs me to say that she will* write to you soon, when she is more tranquil.

Dr Marsden's italics highlight the fact that Emily first insists Mademoiselle Doudet is unaware she is writing or even intending to, then promptly passes on a message from her!

There were a few more lines to the postscript, containing another barb for Zéphyrine. Emily wrote that her father's decision not to extend his agreement with the governess was due to Zéphyrine's defection. This was because Dr Marsden claimed that the original contract had been on the understanding that both sisters would be involved in the girls' education.

Unquestionably the letters were written under the direct influence of Célestine Doudet. The most obvious reason that the children allowed this to happen can be found in the well-documented Stockholm syndrome, in which kidnap victims bond with their captors and become detached from reality. During their time at Cité Odiot the Marsden sisters certainly felt they had no means of escape. Kidnappers often tell their victims that their loved ones have abandoned them, but perhaps the saddest part of this story is that Doudet had no need to do so. The girls had already been rejected by the two people closest to them: their father and their uncle. It is also true that their spirit and sense of self had been damaged years before Mademoiselle Doudet entered their lives.

17. The Chill Wind of Defeat

࿇

On the third and final day of the trial, Monsieur Pinard, the Deputy Imperial Prosecutor, delivered a memorable closing speech. He told the magistrates that Mademoiselle Doudet's accusers included neighbours, servants, shopkeepers and, above all, her own sister. While acknowledging Zéphyrine's retraction of her allegations, he maintained that witnesses had clear memories of what she originally said.

Monsieur Pinard suggested that the governess had acted from vengeance or simply cold-blooded cruelty. He rejected the possibility that she was insane, though many saw this as the only explanation as to why a woman of previously impeccable character would suddenly become a monster. The hypothesis of madness was canvassed in a piece published a few weeks later in the *New York Times*:

> On the recent extraordinary trial of a French governess in Paris for unheard-of cruelties towards her pupils, two young English ladies, a case was cited of a young man who committed suicide last November, and who left in writing the following explanation of the act. 'Ever since I came to years of discretion, I have been possessed by a mania for assassination. I strove against it, but some day or other I may be overcome, and I would rather die than dishonour my family.'[1]

The Prosecutor dismissed the Chaillot letters as being dictated. He stressed that even if the girls *had* been guilty of bad habits, the accused's cruelty could in no way be justified. Allowing, as he put it, his heart to speak under his legal robes, he also referred to Doudet's disrespectful behaviour in asking the dying Marian for pardon. There was a sensation in the courtroom when he said: 'Célestine Doudet may receive the pardon of the dead, and the pardon of God, but human justice must not pardon her.'[2] Finally, he contrasted Doudet's cruel treatment of her sick pupils with the consideration she had been shown by the judiciary during her own illness prior to the manslaughter trial. It was said that the Prosecutor's address flowed like clear water, and that as they listened the accused's supporters felt the chill wind of defeat.

Summing up for the defence, Monsieur Nogent-Saint-Laurens returned to Doudet's passionate and highly reputable supporters, including her connections with English royalty and the nobility. He reminded the court that not one claim of mistreatment had been made prior to the governess joining the Marsden household. While admitting there was reason for *suspicion* that his client had been too severe, he contended there was no proof: 'Doubt exists everywhere. I search in vain for proof of a crime, or even a misdemeanour.' He completely rejected the charge of deliberate physical abuse: 'That she corrected these children, I will allow; but it is impossible to believe in the cruelties imputed to her. It is so difficult to prove them that recourse is had to some idea of vengeance or jealousy [yet] Dr Marsden has with all loyalty declared that Célestine Doudet never made advances to him.' But the advocate then made an ill-judged comment that betrayed a crack in his confidence: 'Gentlemen, I believe in the innocence of Célestine Doudet; you will smile perhaps at my credulity – at my weakness; I persist nevertheless in my belief, and I never will believe her guilty.'[3]

In expectation of a verdict, spectators had filled the stairs leading to the courtroom and crammed into surrounding corridors. After retiring for about an hour, President Martel returned and read the tribunal's judgement. It was found that in 1852 and 1853 Célestine Doudet had been guilty of cruelty towards Lucy, Emily, Rosa and Alice Marsden. She was sentenced to two years in prison and ordered to pay a fine of 200 francs plus costs. Informed that she was to be conveyed to St Lazare prison, she reportedly said in a matter-of-fact tone, 'I expected it.'[4]

The trial launched Pierre Pinard's career. Two years later he was appointed chief prosecutor in the famous obscenity trial against Gustave Flaubert's novel, *Madame Bovary*. He would also enter politics, serving as France's Minister for the Interior.

The verdict against the governess was an important and long-awaited victory for Dr Marsden, who felt his honour had been restored. Mademoiselle Doudet had been condemned as a defamer and a liar, perpetrator of extreme acts of cruelty against his daughters. In the eyes of the world (if not his own), the children had been judged morally pure. However, the sentence of two years was viewed as totally inadequate. There was also the prospect of the judgement being overturned on appeal.

In Great Malvern's Priory Church one of the most arresting carvings on the ancient misericords is of three mice hanging a cat, symbolizing the victims of oppression rising up against their tormentor. Two owls flank the gallows, representing the wisdom of the judicial system. But for the surviving Marsden sisters, the conviction against Célestine Doudet would never erase their psychological scars. More to the point, when they looked at the carving in years to come, who would they most clearly identify as the cruel cat: their governess or their father?

Such had been the publicity surrounding the two trials in Paris that Emily and her sisters became minor celebrities. Before leaving the city they were presented (at her express wish) to Princess Mathilde, niece of Napoleon Bonaparte. At her chateau outside Paris the princess conducted a lavish literary and artistic salon. The occasion would have been an unforgettable experience for the girls. Princess Mathilde had a passion for roses and her rooms were decorated with Ming vases full of perfect blooms, cultivated within the grounds of the chateau. The princess also owned a fabulous collection of jewellery. Since Célestine Doudet had enjoyed the privilege of handling the Queen of England's jewels it would be lovely to think her young victims were shown Princess Mathilde's spectacular, newly commissioned corsage ornament. It was a life-size, 200 carat Tudor rose made of over two and half thousand diamonds.

There was another affirming moment for the girls when they returned to Great Malvern a few days later. The townspeople expressed their support by ringing the bells of St Mary's Priory Church in welcome. But lurid newspaper accounts of the trials aroused primitive instincts and there was intense anger towards those perceived as having turned against their own. John Rashdall reported that on the night of his nieces' homecoming, effigies of Miss Hester Candler and her sister Annabella were paraded through the streets and then ceremoniously burned on the Common. Wild celebrations continued long into the night. On 24 March an editorial in *Berrow's Worcester Journal* confirmed the effigy burning, though it stopped short of naming the Candlers. In the same issue, the *Journal* published a lengthy letter to the editor from Dr Marsden. By now, the girls' father was aware that if Mademoiselle Doudet had been labelled a monster, he too was being judged harshly in the court of public opinion, and his lucrative medical practice could suffer.

The doctor defended himself against accusations that he displayed a lack of care and affection for his daughters, particularly after Marian's death:

> It has been asked how I could leave the children under the woman's care after witnessing the scene I described in my charge against her. The question is simply owing to a misstatement. After the receipt of the anonymous letters against the governess (which we did not at all credit) I was myself in Paris only for a few hours on one occasion, in which I instantly removed them from under her roof and placed them with their Aunt, Miss Rashdall, under the kind supervision of the Rev. T [sic] Rashdall, in the Rue de Chaillot, where they remained whilst their mourning dresses etc were making.

The newspaper's readers might well have asked whose fault it was that Dr Marsden had spent so little time in Paris?

Fortunately, the Marsdens and the Candlers were no longer living side by side, but Great Malvern was still a relatively small town and reports of the vengeful 'witch-burning' episode increased tension between the families. John Rashdall and the Misses Candler served together on the local school committee, but at the next meeting the Candlers were conspicuous by their absence. Nevertheless, the ladies were unwilling to lose face completely and as the Priory Church was the centre of the community, Rashdall found himself in an almost impossible position: 'Sunday 23rd March 1855 – The children & their papa app^d at church, and Miss Candler [presumably Hester] in her pew!' As vicar, Rashdall could not avoid acknowledging one of his parishioners, galling though it must have been. It would be interesting to know the subject of that day's sermon. Somehow the minister managed the situation without alienating his prickly brother-in-law, but several weeks later the relationship between the two men would fall apart under different circumstances.

The Doudet case was the cause of painful self-examination in England, shaking the nation's smug confidence in its moral superiority. Following the governess's conviction for cruelty, the illustrated Sunday newspaper *Lloyd's Weekly* published 'THE ROD IN ENGLAND: AS SEEN IN PARIS (From our own correspondent)'. It was a long and passionate essay on the damaging contrast between French and English domestic life. The support of Célestine Doudet by so many upper-class English women, including the well-intentioned Mrs Schwabe and her friends, was of special concern to the author:

> In addition to the long list of bad qualities for which we enjoy a reputation in this country [France], another may now be added. We are conspicuous among the nations for cruelty to our children. We are barbarians with faith only in the birch. To us kindness is unknown as a governing power. If we spoil our children it is not by sparing the rod...They [the French] find that Mademoiselle Doudet has for supporters − English ladies: and that Dr Marsden's children have for support French people of rank. The French think Mademoiselle Doudet should be torn to pieces: the English protect her, and spend money to shield her from the legitimate consequences of her crimes...We all know how fond the French people are of drawing general conclusions from isolated facts. From this trial they will be quite ready to write us down cruel. Their impressions will help them to this verdict. The coldness which we exhibit, in contrast with the effervescence which they call life, will appear to them as the results of hearts steeled against all the tender emotions of human nature. For this trial has created a deep impression here. It has long been the talk of the Salons:− already it is being carried about the country for the enlightenment of the provincial intellect. A description of Mademoiselle Doudet is given, in which black is the only colour used; and then this hideous figure is presented as the protégé of the Queen, and a select circle of English ladies. In contrast to these patrons, the Princess Mathilde, and the French ladies are shown as lavishing kindness upon the little English victims! The contrast is, at the very least, unfortunate for us. It is capable of the widest extension − and the French will push it as far as it possibly can be pushed...[5]

Attempts were made by the British press to dismiss Queen Victoria's testimonial to Mademoiselle Doudet as fraudulent:

> Up to the present time, it is by no means clear that the letter from the Queen, produced at the trial, is a genuine document: and it is remarkable, as an illustration of the slovenly manner in which criminal trials are conducted in France, that the authenticity of such a document as a royal testimonial should be taken for granted.[6]

Of course, we know that John Rashdall investigated the character reference at Buckingham Palace at the earliest opportunity. His subsequent silence on the subject suggests it was indeed genuine.

That the French courts paid Dr Marsden's costs in the first trial despite Doudet having been acquitted was cause for further discomfort. The *London Daily News* described the payment as an act of chivalry, 'which we would do well to recognize and emulate'.[7] Adding salt to English wounds, Paris's *Exposition Universelle* was due to open on the Champs-Elysées on 15 May, an attempt by the French to surpass London's Great Exhibition of 1851. Ambassador Lord Cowley was accused by the press of paying more attention to the exhibition than to defending his country's reputation by addressing the issues raised by the Doudet case.

The *Daily News* also attacked the British system of education for young girls: 'It is hard for an English girl, educated in the orthodox way, to be an original thinker. Expensive, mindless, unpractical, and useless, our schools turn out accomplished machines whose minds are, like Chinese feet, cramped out of all symmetry, power and normal use.'[8] The article criticized the practice of sending young children to school in foreign countries in the care of strangers, stating that it had been this 'fatal facility' that had allowed Célestine Doudet to perpetrate her cruelties.

Not surprisingly, the experience of the Marsden sisters had an enduring, adverse effect on French boarding schools catering to the English middle classes. A piece written by the proprietor of one such establishment appeared in Charles Dickens's *Household Words* two years later, assuring readers its pupils were happy and healthy and that a monster such as Mademoiselle Doudet would never be tolerated:

It would be impossible for any of our schoolmistresses to become a Célestine Doudet; I beg their pardon for putting such a hypothesis, even as a suppositious case...The French law forbids flogging children, except in extreme cases of rebellion. Not that monsters do not now and then appear at intervals...such as the afore-mentioned wretch, Doudet.[9]

Unhappily, evidence that children continued to suffer in the schoolroom was provided years later by Lord Curzon, who grew up to become Viceroy of India. He and his siblings endured a reign of terror in the 1860s that had striking similarities to the Marsden case. Of their terrifying governess Miss Paraman, Curzon wrote:

I have often thought since that she must have been insane. She persecuted us and beat us in the most cruel way and established over us such a reign of terrorism that not one of us ever mustered up the courage to walk upstairs and tell our father or mother. The governess tied the children to chairs, locked them up in darkness and, forced us to confess to lies which we had never told, to sins we had never committed, and then punished us severely as being self-condemned.[10]

18. Everyone Here is Ruined

In Paris, Célestine Doudet began her sentence at Saint-Lazare, an infamous women's prison built in the twelfth century as a lepers' hospital. The sober but well-cut costume she had worn as a governess was replaced by shameful prison garb: a black cotton cap and rough blue serge dress. For a woman of Doudet's sensibilities, conditions at Saint-Lazare were appalling. There was no segregation by social class and the vast majority of inmates were prostitutes. After what she described as 'a distressing visit' in 1847, the English prison reformer Elizabeth Fry wrote that she had seldom witnessed such as scene of disorder and deep evil: 'gambling, romping, screaming'. It was with great difficulty that she gathered a few Protestant women together for a Bible reading.

Life within the prison inspired the plaintive song 'A Saint-Lazare', by the mid-nineteenth-century writer and performer Aristide Bruant. It contained the line, 'C'est la misère. Ici tout l'monde est decare.' ('It's pitiable. Everyone here is ruined.') Little had changed half a century later when the convicted anarchist Madam Maitrejean spoke of her own experience:

> I cannot think of the common régime without a shudder…try to imagine a large, sordid room, with fifteen or sixteen bunks side by side, in daytime used as a workshop, and alive with insects. In one of these rooms I was quartered, and they gave me as companions vulgar street-walkers and a few thieves and habitual criminals. Women occupying the other cells were no better. The scandalous scenes that took place by night in one of the rooms were imitated in the next one to us, and the Sisters of Mercy who were in charge shut their eyes, for they could not stop it![1]

But women of the street have their own strict moral code. Often forced into the profession due to a background of violence and sexual abuse,

Saint-Lazare prison, long synonymous with human misery

CHARLES-LOUIS MULLER

they are especially protective towards the young and vulnerable. The inmates of Saint-Lazare would not have taken kindly to the arrival of a haughty governess convicted of cruelty to her pupils. Doudet was almost certainly subjected to verbal if not physical abuse and ostracized by her fellow prisoners.

Louise Doudet loyally continued her prison visits, trying to buoy Célestine's spirits and urging her not to give up. The sisters were obliged to converse through metal grating, with a prison officer in attendance. An appeal was being prepared, although Célestine was fretting over how she could continue to pay for her defence. The two trials had exhausted her funds. According to her lawyers, she was still owed 1,500 francs by Dr Marsden who, judging others by his own standards, had refused to pay up, claiming the money would be used to corrupt witnesses. Surrounded as she was by so many wealthy supporters, the governess had no real concerns about legal fees. In fact, the defence team would be strengthened at the appeal hearings by the addition of the brilliant advocate Antoine Berryer. Monsieur Nogent-Saint-Laurens approached Berryer for assistance following the adverse Court of Correction verdict. Monsieur Berryer was at first reluctant, but after studying all the documentation he not only took on the case but pronounced himself so convinced of Mademoiselle Doudet's innocence that he waived his normally hefty fee.

The appeal was heard before a panel of magistrates at two sittings, the first on 13 April. Having reviewed all available evidence, the President,

© ROB CONOLLY

Antoine Berryer, Doudet's celebrated appeal advocate, who had distinguished himself as a statesman and parliamentary orator

Monsieur Zanglacombe, addressed the prisoner. He went straight to the heart of the case. How could it be that so many witnesses had spoken against her? And if she had been so good to her pupils, why had they too testified to her cruelty? Mademoiselle Doudet told the President that if he took the trouble to examine the witnesses, he would see that few had been in a position to judge conditions at Cité Odiot. In the case of Madame Sudre, Doudet insisted the woman had never set foot in her home. She said the first time she saw Sudre was at the Court of Assizes.

Responding to the inference that the young Marsdens would not complain without reason, the prisoner said:

> It is still more inexplicable I think that the children, if there had been mistreatment, should have always asked to remain with me. While their father was in Paris [February–March 1853] I frequently took them to him, where I left them. They could have complained then if mistreatment had occurred. No-one can say they were under my influence when they were living at la rue de Rivoli [the location of the Hotel Windsor] and I was at la barrière de l'Etoile [near Cité Odiot].

Monsieur Zanglacombe replied:

> 'They were under your influence because they had to return to
> you in the evening – they were terrified.'
>
> 'But Monsieur, that's not so. On the contrary, they were only
> meant to stay until the month of June, and one evening when I
> went to find them at their father's they told me it had been decided
> that they would stay another six months. They clapped their
> hands. They were delighted.'[2]

The President was forced to admit that this was a mystery, adding that
sometimes even judicial proceedings failed to throw light on certain
aspects of a case.

The details of the Marsdens' visit to Paris after their return from Italy
had been the subject of dispute during the trials. In his original complaint,
Dr Marsden said he and his wife had stayed 'about a month'. However,
Doudet's lawyers checked the register at the Hotel Windsor, proving the
couple had stayed almost *two* months, from 7 February until 30 March. It
allowed them to query how a father who was also a doctor could have
spent so much time with his children without noticing any signs of ill-
treatment. In response, the prosecution also referred to the original
complaint. Dr Marsden had said that although he and Mary called at Cité
Odiot almost daily, they were rarely allowed to take the girls out, the excuse
being that the children had misbehaved or that outings would disrupt
their studies. It has to be said that the doctor's evidence lacked credibility.
He was hardly the sort of person to be dictated to by a governess.

By 24 April, when the second appeal sitting began, the defence had
decided to strengthen their position by presenting the report of the
English Enquiry compiled by Charles Burrows. It was contained within a
117-page dossier titled *Memoire pour Mademoiselle Célestine Doudet
contre Le Ministére Public et M. Marsden, partie civile.* The dossier
promised to cause quite a stir, containing as it did a detailed account of Dr
Marsden's bribery of Caroline Matthews and his elderly mother's
complicity in concealing the maid's whereabouts. Doudet's lawyers were

---

* During my research for this book I managed to locate a copy of the suppressed
Memoire in, of all places, the rare book department of Glasgow University Library.

taking a calculated risk. They knew they might alienate the magistrates due to the unpleasant nature of the evidence against the children.

The reason the defence needed all the ammunition they could muster was because, between the first and second sittings, the public prosecutor counter-appealed against the leniency of Doudet's original sentence. As grounds for this *appel de minima*, as it was known, it would be argued that the governess's cruelty was premeditated and thus should have been heard under a different law carrying a harsher penalty. The prosecution claimed there was direct proof of premeditation in a remark by Mademoiselle Doudet at the completion of the manslaughter trial. It was overheard by the Conciergerie physician, Dr Bonnet. While waiting for the jury to deliver their verdict, Doudet allegedly said, 'I am innocent, but if I am condemned I am consoled in thinking that M. Marsden will also suffer in the honour of his daughters.'[3]

The prosecution's interpretation was that at the moment of judgement, even though she fully expected to be found guilty, the accused's satisfaction in harming Dr Marsden outweighed the misery of her own situation. In a written report, Dr Bonnet stated that the deputy-matron also heard the remark and would testify if required. Questioned about the incident the governess, visibly shaken, explained she had been in a swoon and could not remember *what* she had said. Her advocate Monsieur Berryer argued that Dr Bonnet only conveyed what he judged to be the 'sense' of Doudet's comment, not a verbatim account. He said his client might just as easily have been making a sad comment on the whole affair: 'I am innocent, but if I am condemned, I will suffer less than Monsieur Marsden because the process will leave a grave stain on the honour of his family.'[4] He said two words in Dr Bonnet's version, 'in thinking', changed the context of the comment, giving the impression Mademoiselle Doudet had sought revenge on her ex-employer.

As premeditation inferred a motive, the public prosecutor set out to prove Doudet had acted from the motive of jealousy. He suggested she deliberately targeted Dr Marsden as a wealthy widower, investigating his background before insinuating herself into his household. To support this argument he quoted a remark made to the doctor by Adelaide Burnell when Mademoiselle Doudet first arrived at Cotswold House: 'It's very odd: Mademoiselle Doudet knows all your business, and all your friends, as well as you do.'[5]

Much was also made of evidence previously given by Madame Espert. The widow had claimed that when the governess first arrived in Paris with the children she sang the praises of Dr Marsden and placed his photograph in pride of place on the mantelpiece. However, on hearing news of his remarriage she allegedly burst into tears, saying, 'With so many children it is shameful for a man to remarry.'[6] The photograph came down and, according to Madame Espert, Doudet defamed the doctor as a womanizer. She said the girls had sworn they would never call their stepmother 'Mother'. When Espert mentioned this last point to Zéphyrine, the governess's sister allegedly replied, 'These are not the feelings of the children. It was my sister who said that.'[7] Mademoiselle Doudet denied making any of the statements, insisting she had given her pupils a holiday to celebrate their father's marriage.

The homeopath Dr Tessier had testified that when he began treating the girls for whooping cough, he was startled to hear the governess describe Dr Marsden, in front of the children, as a pleasure-loving man who enjoyed success with the ladies. She said he was more interested in his romantic life than the welfare of his daughters. On this occasion Doudet said she could not remember having said such a thing, but if she had, she would not retract the remark because it was true!

On their part, the defence quoted Chopin's patron Miss Jane Stirling, who had insisted that far from plotting to marry Dr Marsden the governess expressed early misgivings about her placement at Malvern: 'When she came to Paris on the occasion of her mother's death she appeared to regret being at M. Marsden's house. I urged her to leave the position: she appeared to consider my advice, but more as someone resigned than someone convinced.'[8]

There are several reasons why the theory that Célestine Doudet viewed Dr Marsden as a potential husband does not hold up. First, when she accepted the position of governess in March 1852 the doctor was already romantically involved with Mary Campbell. And as her lawyers pointed out, why would Doudet suggest setting up a school as far away as Paris if her object was to become mistress of Cotswold House? The prosecution's response, that the Paris venture was never intended to be permanent, seems a little weak. Finally, there is the issue of the rigid English class system. Célestine Doudet may have been well born and highly accomplished, but she was still a governess. As Kathryn Hughes points out in her book, *The Victorian Governess*, 'In real life governesses did not marry Mr Rochester and not just because there was something nasty in the attic. On the whole they chose their male equivalents, marginal men whose occupations as curate or teacher could offer them no fairy-tale ending.'[9]

But if Doudet had no aspirations to marry her employer, it *is* reasonable to assume she was envious of the newlywed Marsdens' happiness, especially when the couple left to spend the winter in Italy while she shivered in Paris, caring for five increasingly unwell children. She was poorly paid and obliged to institute Dr Marsden's strict regime, which contributed to her sister's defection. By all accounts, Doudet's abuse of the girls became more serious after Zéphyrine left in April 1853.

The prosecution would have been closer to the mark if they had argued that the governess was motivated by self-interest rather than jealousy. When she arrived at Cotswold House she was in her mid-thirties and worried about her future. Within weeks her sense of security had been shaken by the doctor's arbitrary dismissal of Adelaide Burnell. She also knew her authority within the household would be reduced when her employer remarried. Was it mere coincidence that after being told of Rosa's small acts of larceny, Doudet should accuse the girl of stealing her brooch? And that after being warned to keep an eye on Emily, she should discover that all five girls were masturbators? There is a distinct possibility that she callously fabricated the charges. The doctor's revulsion over his daughters' alleged behaviour ensured that her suggestion of establishing a school in Paris was welcomed. For as long as the girls continued to confess to being liars, thieves and moral degenerates, she could be confident he would not want them to return home.

Meanwhile, Dr Marsden's lawyers were studying the published report of Charles Burrows's English Enquiry. They were appalled by the damaging nature of its contents. Monsieur Chaix-d'Est-Ange did his best to discredit it: 'The solicitors, he said, had searched the country looking for witnesses, quoting the names of eminent people, and the name of a woman in danger of her life, poised on the edge of her grave; sparing neither effort, nor money, nor influence.' He declared that testimonies obtained in such a way had little value: 'In what form are they given? The safeguard of [being sworn under] oath does not exist…These testimonies are simply certificates, given without contradiction. These, they say, will be received in evidence in the Court of Justice. Yes, but with the sole authority of a certificate.'[10]

Monsieur Chaix-d'Est-Ange reminded the court that Fanny Marie Burford and Caroline Fox, two of the ex-servants interviewed during the enquiry, later swore under oath that Dr Marsden's daughters were morally pure. He then moved on to the children's maid, Caroline Matthews:

> This witness you accuse M. Marsden of having sent away, of having hidden; this witness M. Marsden feared so little that he brought her twice before the Court of Assizes. If Caroline Matthews did not testify it was because Mademoiselle Doudet was not in a state to appear. Being unable to return a third time, this girl left a certificate with the [prosecution] attesting to the fact that Mr Burrows had found her, had told her that M. Marsden and his daughters had slandered her, and that she would never find another place. She had been made to sign a declaration that she had not even read.[11]

He dismissed the argument that the report would not be circulated outside the courtroom, commenting that Mademoiselle Doudet's supporters were so powerful that the information it contained would receive wide publicity.

There was immense relief for the prosecution when the report, in particular pages 7, 9, 10, 11 and 21 (which included Miss Matthews's admission that she had been bribed), was judged defamatory to Dr Marsden and his daughters, and suppressed. For the defence lawyers it was a major defeat. However, it vindicated their decision to have Hester Candler travel to Paris; otherwise, her testimony regarding the Marsden girls' alleged faults and character flaws would never have been aired.

Julie Schwabe contributed to the appeal with a written statement:

> My interest in Mademoiselle Doudet is not due to sympathy but to my love of the truth, and this conviction is so complete and entire that, when I visited her in Saint-Lazare, the day before my departure, I said that if she were acquitted I would receive her within my family as before...[12]

Her sincerity and good intentions were never in question, but the Advocate-Général, Monsieur de Gaujal, argued that although honourable witnesses testified to the accused's good character, they were referring to an earlier period in her life. He pointed out that Doudet may have been a governess for twelve years without a complaint, but her previous pupils had been under the eye of their parents, which had not been the case with the young Marsdens.

Monsieur de Gaujal also dismissed the defence's suggestion that Dr Marsden's long delay in filing charges implied doubt over the prisoner's guilt. He said it was understandable that the doctor had been reluctant to pursue the matter given that he would be forced to discuss prurient allegations against his daughters in front of strangers and in a foreign court. When it came to the infamous Chaillot letters, de Gaujal said he could take them one by one and show they were all written under the inspiration and thought of the governess. Monsieur Chaix-d'Est-Ange went further, stating that the correspondence provided the final proof of the governess's cruel regime.

The appeal was not only denied, but the prosecution's *appel de minima* granted. As a result, Mademoiselle Doudet's sentence was increased from two to five years. Upon hearing the verdict she asked to speak, but the President summarily dismissed her: 'Il y a arrêt. Emmenez la prévenue.' ('That's the judgement. Remove the prisoner.')[13] As she stood to leave, an official offered his arm, but Doudet brushed him aside with a hurt expression and walked from the courtroom alone.

For Célestine Doudet, the prospect of five years in gaol was overwhelming. By the time she had served her sentence she would be in her forties, an age when it was difficult for any governess to find a place, let alone a woman convicted of premeditated cruelty against children. Her last hope was an appeal in the Court of Cessation against the *appel de minima*. It was held on 6 July 1855, but after deliberating for two hours the court again found against the prisoner.

In mid-August, Queen Victoria and Prince Albert arrived in Paris on a state visit. Given the constant references to Her Majesty throughout the trials, Buckingham Palace must have been relieved the case was over and no longer the talk of the salons. The Queen was accommodated at Chateau Saint-Cloud, where she and her wardrobe ladies occupied the gorgeous apartments once belonging to Marie Antoinette. No expense had been spared in preparing for the royal visit: 'The boudoir was upholstered in light blue, festoons of roses running along the walls, and priceless Dresden groups distributed everywhere, the dressing rooms were hung with pale green, with garlands upon garlands of violets.'[14] There is a strange parallel when we remember that during the trials Célestine Doudet had been held in the dank cells of the Conciergerie, where Marie Antoinette languished before her execution. Victoria and Albert were guests of honour at a grand ball held at the Palace of Versailles, where Her Majesty danced with Emperor Napoleon III. The Emperor would eventually play his own role in the Doudet affair.

Julie Schwabe maintained her campaign on Célestine's behalf, pressing for clemency or a re-trial. Unable to enlist the support of her friend Florence Nightingale, who was busy ministering to sick and wounded soldiers in the Crimea, Schwabe turned to the social activist Charles Dickens. She sent the celebrated novelist a letter of appeal and a box of supporting documents. It was a serious error of judgement. In a terse reply written from Folkestone on 22 July 1855, the author cited the complexities of the case and lack of time as reasons for not taking up the cause. It is more likely that his sympathies lay with the children. Doudet had already become the female equivalent of Dickens's fictional character Wackford Squeers, who ran the brutal boarding school Dotheboys Hall in the novel *Nicholas Nickleby*.

Dear Mrs Schwabe

I have this morning received your letter and box of papers. The arrival of such a heap of documents leaves me but one course.

It is incumbent on me to represent to you that I cannot enter on the examination of a case which requires to be pursued through such a labyrinth. I had begun to read the account of Miss Doudet's trial, but I now abandon it in despair. My life is a busy one, my thoughts are intently set upon a new book [the serialized *Little Dorrit*], I am surrounded by occupations which have their plain ends and uses, I have innumerable correspondents who have a right to my punctuality and attention, and I cannot plunge into this sea of distraction. I have no other impression of Miss Doudet's case, than I have of any other case in which a person has been tried and found guilty and has been in no wise benefitted by an appeal. That she does not want friends, your generous devotion and that of the lady whom you mention, sufficiently assures me. To waste my energies in turning from the work and duty that I have clinging to my sleeve, to wander through a maze like this, would be to write my life and purpose into the sea-sand now lying before my window.

I will immediately send the whole of the papers to the Household Words office in London, addressed to you, to the care of Mr. Wills there. That gentleman will send them on to any address you may forward to him for that purpose.

Faithfully yours
Charles Dickens[15]

In November, Dickens left to spend the winter in Paris, where his portrait was painted by the romantic artist Ary Scheffer, another Doudet supporter and a close friend of Mrs Schwabe. One wonders whether the predicament of the governess was raised during the novelist's daily sittings.

Reviewing the verdict of premeditated cruelty against the governess in *Causes Célèbres de Tous Les Peuples*, Armond Fouquier said he considered the judges to have been influenced by the French love of children and their pity for the helpless. Fouquier thought the contrast between the gentle French method of education and the harsher British system gave the regime at Cité Odiot the illusion of criminal cruelty. He suspected that justice had not been served in the case, but that the greatest adversary of Mademoiselle Doudet had been Mademoiselle Doudet herself: 'This attitude before the court of bitter haughtiness, bristling with pride and prudishness; this preoccupation with her dignity that prevailed at all times during the terrible accusation she was faced with, did not dispose the judges in her favour.'[16] Célestine Doudet was both victim and product of the worst aspects of Victorian society: religious zealotry, class division, moral hypocrisy and the subjugation of women.

On 6 December 1856 the prisoner was transferred from Saint-Lazare to France's largest women's prison, located at Clermont in the Alsace region. In her wake followed Mrs Schwabe and several other high-ranking ladies – a show of support that allowed the governess to maintain a little self-respect amid the humiliations of the prison process. Once again the majority of her fellow inmates would be coarse, rough-tongued thieves and prostitutes. The women were required to work a twelve-hour day in the prison laundry or bakery, forbidden to speak during working hours or at mealtimes under threat of solitary confinement. The food at Clermont was curiously similar to Dr Marsden's own homeopathic regime: predominantly bread and vegetables with meat served only twice a week. Each dormitory held between seventy and eighty women. Thirty years later the French anarchist Louise Michel was incarcerated at Clermont. Describing conditions, surely much improved since the 1850s, Michel wrote, 'The beds are low and very close together, consisting of a sacking bottom, a mattress, a pair of sheets and two blankets, with a pipeclay dish which serves as a washbasin. In none of the dormitories is there a lavatory.'[17]

At the end of August 1857 a report appeared in the English press stating that the imprisoned governess was seriously ill. No doubt the story originated with Mrs Schwabe and her loyal band, who were pressing the French authorities for Doudet to be granted preferential treatment at Clermont. Curiously, evidence suggests they were successful. In 1875 Adolphe Bélot published *Une Maison Centrale des Femmes*. Based on Clermont, it included anecdotes from Monsieur Bailie, the prison's long-time director. Bélot wrote:

> Among the criminals of a higher station might be mentioned… Mademoiselle Doudet, the English governess who was sentenced to ten [sic] years confinement for having inflicted atrocious tortures on the children confided to her care. The case of this last was a curious one, on account of the protection and sympathy which were accorded to her…Solicited on all sides, forced at last to obey formal orders from those higher in authority, the director was obliged to separate Mademoiselle Doudet from the other women, to give her a spacious apartment as a bedroom, and to supply her table with delicate food. In the interest of discipline, M. Bailie soon obtained the removal of Mademoiselle Doudet from his establishment.[18]

There is a ring of truth to the story as on 22 April 1858 Doudet was transferred to Haguenau prison. Her influential friends now redoubled their efforts to have her released on medical grounds. Within weeks the institution's doctor, Monsieur Jacobs, completed a report stating that continued detention would constitute a death sentence. He added that the prisoner had been suffering since the day of her arrest on 8 May 1854.

On 27 June 1858, Célestine Doudet was officially pardoned, effectively cancelling the majority of the additional sentence she received in the *appel de minima*. According to a report published in the *Western Daily Press* on 12 July, it was Emperor Napoleon III who exercised his prerogative of mercy in the case, prompted by the intervention of the Bishop of Nancy, his chief almoner. No doubt Mrs Schwabe and her group had been making representations to the bishop on the prisoner's behalf. The author of the report clearly supported Doudet's cause:

> Notwithstanding the prejudice which ran so high against the prisoner, and the decision of the Tribunal, there were not a few who, after close and patient investigation, arrived at the conviction that, in spite of all appearances Miss Doudet was innocent of the charges brought against her…The matter has been for some time before the Emperor − His Majesty very properly took time to consider, and it may be presumed that he shared the opinion of Miss Doudet's venerable advocate and her zealous friends, as he has done the most graceful act a monarch can perform for the suffering and the innocent.[19]

The words 'suffering' and 'innocent' might equally have been applied to the Marsden children, two of whom were beyond the help of any monarch.

On her release, Mademoiselle Doudet spent time recuperating in the spa town of Baden in Germany and then in England, cared for and encouraged by her supporters. Subsequently, she returned to Paris, where it is said she was still able to find families willing to employ her as a governess. In total she had been deprived of her freedom for four years and nineteen days. However, perhaps her greatest punishment was that all the shades of grey in the case were edited out until she became a caricature, a story-book monster like the wicked witch in *Hansel and Gretel*. In 1856 an article in Dickens's *Household Words* described the neglected botanic gardens in Ghent, Belgium, in which the dying plants were likened to the Marsden girls: 'Other unhappy captives, lank and lean, bald and mangy, beg hard for someone to have compassion on them...He (the nurseryman) is the Celestine Doudet of greenhouse evergreens; his pupils do not thrive; his oleanders are in the last stage of suffering.'[20] Doudet's cruelty against defenceless children would remain in the French psyche for generations. Jacob Axelrad introduced her into his 1944 biography of the writer Anatole France, a boy of eleven during the Paris trials:

> Mademoiselle Lafont, the tutor, was a young lady whose blonde hair smelled of heliotrope and whose eyes were of a rich, violet colour. The boy delighted in her person...There was another lady, whose eyes were not dark as violets, whose hair held no odour of heliotrope. She was Mademoiselle Doudet, a strict disciplinarian of unsavoury reputation...[21]

To this day, the case of Mademoiselle Doudet is cited in books and articles on child abuse. Despite the passage of over 150 years, at least one of the governess's distant relations confesses to a feeling of shame and embarrassment over the familial connection. In June 2011 the following posting was left on a website relating to Dr Marsden and his daughters: 'I found out recently doing some family research that I'm related to Celestine Doudet! I knew I'd find a skeleton somewhere and I have...I hope you appreciate why I haven't left my name!'[22]

Célestine Doudet died intestate on 26 December 1893 at 13 Rue Vernier in Paris, aged seventy-six. She left an estate of £947.00. Probate was granted the following year to her English relative, Frederick Parker Baker, who testified on his cousin's behalf in 1855. In her declining years Mademoiselle Doudet shared a home with her sister, Louise, who died eleven months earlier. It is interesting to note that Mademoiselle Doudet died on Boxing Day. Perhaps Christmas without Louise proved too much and she simply lost the will to live. Her lonely state was emphasized by the wording on the probate papers. She was described as 'A spinster without Parent, Brother or Sister, Uncle or Aunt, Nephew or Niece'. The date of Zéphyrine's death is unknown. There is a saying that old crimes cast long shadows and this was certainly true in the Doudet case. Given Zéphyrine's perceived betrayal of Célestine, it is unlikely there was ever a *rapprochement* between the sisters.

The effects on the Marsden siblings would also be permanent, leading inexorably to another tragic death. What would be the precipitating factors and who would prove most vulnerable – Emily, Rosa or Alice?

19. A Family Breach

❧

T he failure of Doudet's appeals and the significant increase in her sentence was greeted with satisfaction at Great Malvern. But for the surviving girls the drawn-out legal process simply lengthened their exposure to public scrutiny. They had returned home as young heroines, but whenever they ventured from Abbotsfield they were the object of whispers and curious stares. Their emotional confusion had deepened during the trials as the moral ground shifted beneath them. There is no doubt that their testimony was corrupted by their parents. Their father, who had berated them all their lives for their perceived misdemeanours and shortcomings, repeatedly lied under oath.

It is unlikely Dr Marsden ever forgave his surviving daughters, particularly Emily and Rosa, for 'dishonouring' the family name. Emily was the first to have been suspected of moral vice. The doctor considered her the brightest of his offspring and therefore responsible for the collective sins of her sisters. Rosa had been labelled a liar and a thief, as well as a self-abuser. In the doctor's eyes their behaviour had sullied his relationship with Mary and threatened his stellar career. Nor could he be sure they had abandoned their unspeakable habits. One can imagine him checking to see if their spines were beginning to curve, or feeling their necks for signs of the goitrous growths he warned Emily about in 1852. Their presence in Malvern was an embarrassment, a constant reminder of everything he wished to forget.

It was in this climate that Emily and Rosa were told they were to be sent to boarding school, a fate the socially withdrawn and insecure girls had always dreaded. John Rashdall's diary suggests the original plan was to separate them. He mentions Mary Marsden taking Emily to Clifton in Bristol, where Mary's youngest sister, Augusta, had attended a young ladies' academy in 1851. Several days later, on 1 May 1855, Rashdall records a dispute over the girls between their Rashdall aunts and their stepmother:

Cheltenham. Found painful convers. had taken place between Mrs James Marsden, E & F [Elizabeth and Fanny Rashdall] conc. the child.: — all over excited: but I feel sure the former was in wrong. I had convers. with her subseq[y]. which I fear only riveted the diffce. & the consequences I fear also will be permanent. What a fatality seems to rest upon these children! God set things right: it is beyond human skill.[1]

Without Mademoiselle Doudet as a target, the women, nerves shredded by grief and stress, had turned on each other. No doubt Elizabeth and Fanny felt it harsh and insensitive to banish the girls a second time. There were other long-buried resentments to fuel the dispute. Mary Marsden had replaced the Rashdalls' beloved sister Lucy and perhaps there was also jealousy over Alice, who remained in Fanny's care for almost a year after her sisters returned from Paris. It is easy to imagine the row degenerating into destructive blame-laying over the fatal delay in removing the children from Célestine Doudet's care. Did Mary suggest that John and Fanny Rashdall had failed in their supervisory role? And did Fanny and her sister hit back with accusations of selfish neglect on the part of Mary and her husband? In general, the British press had refused to criticize the children's family, though there were notable exceptions. In an article dated 14 March 1855, the plain-speaking *Liverpool Journal* strongly censured Dr Marsden, John Rashdall and Fanny, declaring that the only parties who exhibited real kindness and humanity towards the children were the French neighbours and visitors of Mademoiselle Doudet.

John Rashdall made a serious mistake by weighing into the argument, and more particularly by taking the part of his sisters against Mary Marsden. In the patriarchal society of the 1850s, he assumed that no matter what position he took in a 'foolish women's quarrel', he would be viewed by Dr Marsden as acting with reason and good sense. However, as a bachelor he failed to appreciate the power of a young wife over a new and ardent husband. Despite John Rashdall's long friendship and unswerving loyalty, the doctor sided with his aggrieved spouse and cut off all communication with his first wife's family. For Rashdall, who had invested so much emotion in the children, the separation was devastating.

However much they may have protested, Emily and Rosa were soon attending Miss Wilson's academy in Brighton, presumably a compromise to Emily going to Bristol alone. Once again Alice was separated from her older sisters. She remained at home with her stepmother, supplanted as the baby of the family by her half-sister, Isabella. The faithful Miss Dowmann was engaged as her governess. James Jr's education had also taken a new direction. To his father's disappointment the boy lacked the academic ability to warrant sending him to a public school as a preliminary to university. In September 1855 the 13-year-old was enrolled in the Royal Naval academy at Portsmouth, with the hope that a cadetship could be arranged through the patronage of Sidney Marsden's influential family. It might be remembered that Sidney, the daughter of a Welsh peer, was married to Dr Marsden's brother, Frederick.

James too had coped with a great deal during the previous three years. Within the protective environment of school he had been shielded from the trauma of the Paris trials and the distasteful nature of the evidence, but nothing could spare him from the knowledge that his sisters had been abused and ill-treated to the extent that two of them died. During the same period Dr Marsden had not only remarried but become estranged from some of the most familiar and significant figures in his son's life – including the entire Rashdall family and the Candlers. It is little wonder the boy felt an increasing sense of disconnection from his family. Writing about preparatory schools in *The Victorian Family: Structure and Stresses*, historian Anthony Wohl comments, 'That intimacy which the father did not give was found in the close friendship of boys. It was an intimacy that was entirely masculine and one which valued manliness, courage, loyalty, honour, even the daring and mischievous, more than it honoured piety, intellect or sexual fastidiousness.'[2] The flaws that would eventually emerge in James Jr's character were both a reflection of his troubled childhood and a confirmation of his father's theory that impressions and images shape the mind.

Occurring so soon after the Paris trials, the rupture between John Rashdall and the Marsdens could scarcely have gone unnoticed in Malvern. The once constant comings and goings between St Mary's vicarage and Abbotsfield ceased abruptly, setting tongues wagging. The sympathy of locals would definitely have favoured John Rashdall, the town's much loved minister. Dr Marsden, by comparison, was a remote and intimidating figure whose medical practice catered to the visiting gentry.

In early August Mrs Rashdall, Fanny and Elizabeth arrived to stay at the vicarage, providing their son and brother with much needed moral support. The women remained until the end of September, by which time Mary Marsden and her infant daughter had left to spend a few months in the South of France. On this occasion Dr Marsden remained at home, attending to what John Rashdall described as his 'professional necessities'. Soon afterwards Fanny Rashdall made what was to be a permanent move to Brighton, presumably to be closer to Emily and Rosa, but perhaps also to make a point to their parents.

Rashdall himself was also on the move, leaving the Priory Church in the hands of his curates yet again as he set off for a lengthy sojourn in Germany. On 30 September he met Mrs Carmichael-Smyth, while on his way to church in Hamburg. Thackeray's mother was full of gossip on what the Reverend John Rashdall described as 'the old subject of the Doudet'. She gleefully reported a rumour that the governess had made a suggestion to the governor of Saint-Lazare prison that she educate his children. The astounded gentleman had reportedly replied that he did not want his children murdered in either body, mind or reputation. Carmichael-Smyth also had something to say on the matter of Doudet's transfer to Clermont. Rashdall's diary records:

> When she [Doudet] heard that she was to be removed to the South of France she was outrageous, tore her hair etc., etc. Her object in remaining in Paris was to have the benefit of seeing constantly her infatuated friends, or those to whom Mrs Erskine and co. might entrust the commission to care for her. Whereas she will now be forgotten, though these friends still cling to her and profess to believe her innocence.[3]

John Rashdall's prediction that the family rift would be long lasting was correct. It was complicated by the fact that he was young Jimmy Marsden's godfather, a duty taken far more seriously in Victorian times than in today's secular society. He also remained as one of the trustees for Mary Marsden's marriage settlement. Nevertheless, it was approaching Christmas, the season of goodwill, before he swallowed his pride and attempted to patch things up with Mary, then six months pregnant with her second child. His reluctance is evident in a diary entry written immediately after the meeting. Significantly, it had taken place the day after Rashdall's birthday, always an occasion for painful self-reflection on his moral and spiritual progress:

> 20th December 1855 – This morning hav^g written a note to apprize her called on Mrs J. L. M & as far as may be, made up the diff^{ce} in the hope that J. himself will respond.
>
> I felt it a plain Xn [Christian] duty – to be done – however painful & difficult & doubtful.

Unfortunately his humiliating back-down failed. Mary, sensing that the Reverend's heart was not in it, remained unmollified. The implacable Dr Marsden was equally unmoved by his brother-in-law's overture.

The continuing breach prompted Rashdall to review his future as vicar of St Mary's Priory Church. Lack of intellectual stimulation in Malvern had been an issue from the time he moved there. Estranged from the Marsdens and with the older children away at school, he decided it might be best to return to London and resume the incumbency of Eaton Chapel. His diary entry on New Year's Eve 1855 is full of regret and sadness: 'What a year this has been – what sorrow, anxiety, trial & sin! The Paris trial: the family Separ^n. The perplexing questions concerning Malvern & Eaton Chapel yet unsettled.'

A degree of diversion was provided on 10 January 1856, when Great Malvern celebrated the arrival of gas-lighting. For the first time, residents could appreciate the full beauty of the town's elegant new street lamps, with their brass fittings, decorative iron brackets and barley-twist columns. Adding to the excitement, Drs Marsden, Gully and their fellow commissioners had decided to mark the occasion with a giant bonfire on Worcester Beacon. For weeks in advance wagon loads of fuel were hauled up the hills above Malvern: 450 faggots [bundles of sticks], 5 cords of wood, 4 loads of old hop-poles, 2 loads of furze, 12 poplar trees, 2 tons of coal, 1 barrel of naptha, 2 barrels of tar, and 12 empty tar barrels. Eventually the pile stood 30-feet high and 30-feet in diameter at its base. At seven in the evening the bonfire was lit, preceded by the firing of twelve rockets. What a shame that of the Marsden siblings only 10-year-old Alice and little Isabella were on hand to enjoy the spectacle.

Bonfires have been used throughout history to symbolize spiritual cleansing and to ward off evil, but New Year brought yet more heartache for the Marsden family. Mary went into early labour and at the end of January she gave birth to a stillborn baby boy.

For Dr Marsden, the Paris trials had been a public relations disaster and he was anxious to restore his reputation. In 1856 he published a second edition of *Notes on Homeopathy*. It was typical of his arrogance that despite questions raised over his daughters' extreme homeopathic diet, he refused to acknowledge the slightest flaw in the system. In the preface to the new edition he made an extraordinary statement:

> I have altered nothing, because all I have stated are simple facts, as I saw them; and all my opinions have not in any way changed with regard to the value of homeopathy — the greatest step forward in the practice of the art of medicine that has ever been made since the recorded annals of the world began.

There was one part of the book he may later have wished he *had* altered. When the new edition appeared, the *Monthly Homeopathic Review* questioned Dr Marsden's judgement in quoting the example of his son's recovery from typhoid in 1847:

> …we must confess to a strong objection to anything like the expression of his private feelings on the part of a physician. It is, or ought to be, taken for granted, that every physician, to whatever school he may belong, acts towards each and all of his patients to the best of his ability, and with the same degree of conscientious solicitude as he would towards any member of his family.[4]

Some of Dr Marsden's figures regarding 'cures' he witnessed in Vienna were challenged, as was his boast that he had introduced the Swedish Professor Ling's medical gymnastics to Great Britain. How embarrassing to have received such criticism from the country's principal mouthpiece of homeopathy.

In August the same year, the doctor leased a property bordering Malvern Common called Peachfield, with the intention of providing inexpensive accommodation to the genteel poor, including clergymen – and governesses! Many must have viewed this as a cynical move and there was certainly a strong element of self-promotion. A large advertisement appeared in the local paper for weeks prior to the official opening. Dr Marsden made it known that he had assumed personal financial responsibility for the lease of Peachfield and its furniture. Additionally, he and his partner, Dr John Dauglish, intended providing medical attention to the residents free of charge.

Dr Dauglish had recently arrived in Malvern to study hydropathy and was also experimenting with water for a different purpose. He had developed the process of forcing aerated water into bread dough, to produce lightness without the need for yeast. The automated method was not only fast, but more hygienic, with no manual kneading required. Even the doyenne of the Victorian kitchen, Mrs Beeton, welcomed the innovation in her *Household Management*. The new bread proved far more successful than the Peachfield clinic, which quickly folded.

At the end of the year the periodical *British Friend* published an essay by James Grant titled 'A Few Days at Great Malvern'. Like many before him, the author waxed lyrical about the town: 'There is something so joyous, so exhilarating in the atmosphere at Great Malvern that the visitor feels as if he had been transplanted to some healthier and happier planet.' But although Dr Marsden's Hardwicke House was then one of the town's largest and most technically advanced water-cure establishments, only those of Drs Wilson, Gully and Grindrod were mentioned. Grant also tried to scotch what he described as 'the prevailing impression that at all hydropathic establishments the patients are half-starved'.[5] It is tempting to believe that this impression had been accentuated by press accounts of the emaciated Marsden sisters and that the failure to mention Dr Marsden was deliberate.

Although Lady Foley urged John Rashdall to stay at Great Malvern he moved back to London (and Eaton Chapel) in February 1856. Late that year he heard Mary Marsden had become 'dangerously ill' and was being treated in the capital by no less than three physicians. In complete contrast to his conduct prior to Marian's death in 1853, Dr Marsden left his patients without hesitation to be at his wife's side. He had arranged for Mary to be operated on by the Scottish surgeon Mr William Fergusson, Surgeon-Extraordinary to Prince Albert and described as having the most aristocratic practice in London. The attending anaesthetist was the equally celebrated Dr John Snow, who had famously administered chloroform to Queen Victoria in 1853 during the birth of her eighth child. Dr Snow's case notes of Saturday 16 November 1856 reveal Mary's operation was for the scarcely life-threatening condition of...piles! 'Administered chloroform to the wife of Dr Marsden, of Great Malvern, whilst Mr Fergusson operated for haemorrhoids by ligature...'[6] Whether Mary had already tried other forms of treatment is unknown, but in his book *The Water-Cure in Chronic Disease*, Dr Gully summarily dismissed surgery as a cure for piles, insisting that wet-sheet packing and sitz baths were infallible for even the most troublesome of cases.

Rashdall went to visit Mary on 21 November, motivated by Christian kindness but also the hope that it might finally pave the way to reconciliation. Delicacy prevented him from mentioning the nature of her complaint, and he did not comment on the meeting except to say her condition was much improved. However, on 13 December Rashdall had what he described rather formally as 'an interview' with his brother-in-law, followed by another visit to Mary. His diary reveals that his efforts to make peace were as disastrous as before: 'Called on Mrs JLM & had a most painful conversation with her.'[7] 'Painful conversation' was always Rashdall's euphemism for an argument.

Abbotsfield was advertised for lease that year from December until May. It appears that Dr Marsden was intending to spend another winter on the Continent, allowing Mary to recuperate in a warmer climate. Alice and Isabella may have accompanied them, but Emily and Rosa remained at school.

Despite the continuing family rift, John Rashdall had never been banned from seeing his nieces. This may have been because he was still able to perform a useful service for Dr Marsden. When the girls arrived from Brighton by train en route to Malvern for holidays, their uncle would meet them in London and escort them to Euston station for the final stretch of their journey. In June 1856 he reported they were looking well and that there was 'a very good account of them from Miss Wilson's hand'.[8] The report was just as positive the following year.

The year 1857 brought an unexpected but happy change in John Rashdall's private life. On 15 April the 48-year-old married 26-year-old Emily Hankey at St George's Church in London's Hanover Square. The couple moved into a newly built home in St Georges Road, Kensington. Emily was the daughter of wealthy London banker Thomas Hankey. She and Rashdall were well suited as the Hankey family were deeply religious. Thomas was a member of the evangelical and social reforming Clapham sect and in 1866 Emily's sister Kate would write the well-known hymn, 'Tell Me the Old, Old Story'. For Rashdall, who had resigned himself to life as a bachelor, marriage and the birth of his son Hastings the following year provided fulfilment and solace. But regret over his nieces' suffering would torment him for the rest of his life and his loving concern for the girls remained undiminished.

20. Disgrace and Exile

A t the completion of their schooling in Brighton circa 1860, Emily and Rosa returned to Great Malvern. The watering-place was described in a contemporary visitor's guide as a flower-filled town which had retained the quaint atmosphere of a village, thanks to its unique architecture: '...scarcely two houses are built alike, either as regards style or position. They face every possible direction, so that, if a "smart shower" of houses had fallen from the clouds, the effect could scarcely have been more diverse.'[1] Dr Marsden's water-cure clinic and private residence were mentioned among other substantial buildings near the Priory Church.

The girls' days would have been filled with church functions, charity bazaars and visits to the sick; their evenings with ladylike pursuits such as music, embroidery, and the reading of suitable novels. There were also letters to be written to their brother James, now serving as a junior officer in the Royal Navy aboard HMS *Diadem*. His cadetship had commenced in March 1856; it was arranged not through the patronage of his Aunt Sidney Marsden's relatives but after a chance remark to a friend by the estranged John Rashdall. However, the biggest piece of family news that year involved Uncle Frederick Marsden. He and Sidney were now living with their family in Cheltenham. Frederick had retired from army service in India with the rank of Lieutenant Colonel and in May 1860 he was awarded the prestigious Order of the Bath by Queen Victoria.

At the centre of the Marsdens' social circle at Malvern were James Gully, his devoted sisters, and Gully's particular friends Charlotte and Fanny Dyson, the spinster daughters of a retired clergyman. Gardening was a particular passion among the group. The names of Dr Gully, Charlotte Dyson and eventually young Alice Marsden appear in lists of prizewinners at the local horticultural show. Meanwhile, Dr Marsden had instigated a competition of his own, offering a gold medal for the best essay on the usefulness of Mechanics' Institutes. It was probably no coincidence that both he and Dr Gully had recently delivered lectures at the Malvern Institute!

In 1860 the rail line reached Malvern and the quiet routine of life was interrupted by the opening of the railway station on Friday 25 May. As with the arrival of gas-lighting, it was an event long anticipated by the Improvement Commissioners, the biggest boost for the town since Malvern spring water cascaded from the crystal fountain at the Great Exhibition. A song was written and performed for the occasion, titled 'The Beauties of Malvern'. Set to the rollicking tune of 'Yankee Doodle', it was aimed at prospective day-trippers rather than the gentry. Song-sheets illustrated with a steam train were printed, enabling the townspeople to join in, no doubt accompanied by the Rhine band:

> *Improvements are going on so fast,*
> *In Worcester and at Malvern,*
> *Now we all shall have a chance at last,*
> *To go and visit Malvern.*

The chorus was a rousing:

> *So rise the steam and come along,*
> *Old and young come hither.*
> *And taste the water, which, they say,*
> *Will make you live for ever.*

Old and young certainly did 'come hither'; it was estimated that 10,000 passengers arrived over the Whitsunday holiday weekend. Malvern's villagers and gentry alike gazed wide-eyed at what the press described as 'The most curious specimens of the British shopkeeper and artisan on an outing'. Inevitably, the noisy hoards from the Black Country wore out their welcome, prompting the suggestion that since the excursion trains did not arrive until 11 a.m. and generally departed by 6.30 p.m., Malvern's visitors, as opposed to day-trippers, should take their walks before or after the 'invasion'. Alternatively, since the trains arrived only three days per week, visitors could arrange to spend these days on drives or rambles into the countryside.

Emily and Rosa were now young women. A man of Dr Marsden's standing might have been expected to have taken a house in London for the annual social season, providing a base for his daughters' 'coming out' and the opportunity of landing suitable husbands. The highly competitive Victorian marriage market inspired some cynically comic lines in *Punch Magazine*:

> *Daughters to sell! Daughters to sell!;*
> *They cost more money than I can tell;*
> *Their education has been first rate;*
> *What wealthy young nobleman wants a mate?*
> *They sing like nightingales, play as well,*
> *Daughters to sell! Daughters to Sell!*

But there would be no expensive parties or presentations at court for the tarnished and unmarriageable Misses Marsden of Abbotsfield. Although Dr Marsden had defended his daughters' purity in 1855, he had been motivated by the desire to protect his *own* reputation. In his heart he had always perceived the girls as sexual deviants. No doubt he sympathized with Queen Victoria who, blaming her degenerate son Bertie for the death of Prince Albert in December 1860, said she would never be able to look at her son again without a shudder.

It was John Rashdall who provided his nieces with a brief 'London experience'. In the summer of 1862 his sister Elizabeth arrived with Emily, Rosa and Alice to spend a few days at Kensington. James Marsden was on leave from the navy and Rashdall took the whole party to the city's second great International Exhibition. As Poet Laureate, the minister's friend, Alfred Tennyson, had written a choral ode for the occasion, which included a tribute to the recently dead Prince Albert:

> *O silent father of our Kings to be,*
> *Mourn'd in this golden hour of jubilee*
> *For this, for all, we weep our thanks to thee.*

The Exhibition was a let-down for those who had experienced the excitement of 1851. Joseph Paxton's fabulous Crystal Palace was a hard act to follow and the 1862 building was described as 'a wretched shed' by the prestigious *Art Journal*. Its twin domes were laughingly dubbed 'soup bowls'. The young Marsdens were among the underwhelmed; according to their uncle, they were far more impressed by a visit to the Houses of Parliament. The family visit culminated with the baptism of John Rashdall's third and last child, Agnes Emily, who had been born in June.

Three months later James Marsden, who was serving on HMS *Resistance*, blotted his copybook by being charged with misconduct. Dr Marsden was mortified when his son was court-martialled. The incident had occurred at Portsmouth on 18 October 1862, as *Resistance* was about to weigh anchor. Young Marsden was not at his station and Captain Chamberlain asked Commodore Hume to speak to him about his dereliction of duty. Chamberlain noticed that while being addressed by the commodore, James stood with one hand in his pocket. Although the commodore seemed not to notice, the captain thought this most improper and rebuked James, who reacted with petulance. As a result, he found himself on two charges of insolence: one against the commodore and one against the captain.

The court-martial was held aboard Lord Nelson's legendary flagship *The Victory*, with proceedings announced by the firing of a cannon and the running up of 'the court-martial Jack'. The young man's punishment was relatively light; he was severely reprimanded and transferred from *Resistance* to HMS *Nile*. Nevertheless, it was a black mark on his record. Subsequently, his uncle wrote, 'Oppressed all day by thinking on the strange court-martial of J. R. Marsden for disrespect...'[2]. Rashdall thought a private rebuke would have been a more appropriate response.

Several days later a letter appeared in the local paper under the heading 'A Frivolous Court-Martial'. After outlining the case, the anonymous writer (quite possibly John Rashdall) concluded:

> We do not think the service will gain much by the example made of Mr Marsden. That he acted improperly there can be no doubt, but it was simply absurd to bring such a frivolous case before a court-martial. Had Captain Chamberlain acted wisely, he would have kept the matter in his own hands, and would have satisfied the claims of discipline by pronouncing a suitable admonition in a proper place.[3]

Dr Marsden's disgust with James was heightened by the fact that, following in the military tradition of his father and brothers, he had established the 11th Worcestershire Rifle Volunteers. As officer-in-charge of the corps at Great Malvern, he was incensed that his son and heir had flouted the same rules and respect for authority he was trying to instil in his recruits.

Malvern's hydropathic doctors were still providing a rich source of material for humorists. In 1863 a book was published under the title:

Health and Pleasure or Malvern Punch, compounded of Spirits and Water and Flavoured with things Geographical, Biographical Etc. The Whole Purified, Liquified, And Intensified

BY J. B. ODDFISH, ESQ., M.P., L.L.D, (Malvern Patient, Doctor of Laughs and Liquids)

The book included all manner of jokes and comic verse inspired by the water-cure:

Would you climb the rugged mountain,
Would you hear sweet warblers sing,
Come and taste the crystal fountain,
Nature's pure life-giving spring;
Breathe the tainted air no longer,
Leave your sickly painful couch,
Every bath shall make you stronger,
Nervous sufferers try the Douche.

In March 1864 the subject of the Paris trials was again aired in the English press. For both defence and prosecution camps, the Doudet affair had left an enduring sense of injustice, even among those who had been mere spectators. In the wake of a controversial criminal case in the French city of Aix, one of the governess's supporters recalled bitterly that she had been acquitted by a jury only to be found guilty by a Correctional Court tribunal. In essence, the article labelled the Marsden girls liars. It would not have made pleasant reading at Abbotsfield:

Trial by jury has never been more than tolerated by French authorities, and they resort to all sorts of evasions to escape the consequences of the institution. It is a common saying now in the Palais de Justice that the tendency of the day is to 'Correctionalise' everything – meaning to say that crimes are reduced to misdemeanors in order to obtain a certain conviction for a minor offence before a tribunal of correctional police. In many cases they try a prisoner before a jury first, and failing a conviction, bring him before the correctional police afterwards. This was done in the case of the unfortunate governess, Miss Doudet, whose trial I heard, and of whose entire innocence I was fairly convinced. She was accused of cruelty towards children of an English family, and if the children told the truth she must have been a fiend incarnate. Her counsel M. Nogent St Laurant pleaded that the children told lies, and the jury adopting that theory acquitted her. But subsequently an inferior court found her guilty on the very same evidence and sentenced her to five year's imprisonment.[4]

It was also in 1864 that John Rashdall left London, retiring with his young family to the village of Dawlish, 12 miles from Exeter on the south coast of Devon. He became Vicar of St Gregory the Great parish church. One positive effect of his scarifying breach with Mary and James Marsden was that during his ministry at Dawlish he became known as a peacemaker, adept at resolving conflicts and smoothing ruffled feathers within his congregation. However, soon after his move to Devon, Rashdall's skills of conciliation were required in a more personal sense. Old hurts were suddenly put aside when he was called upon by Dr Marsden to help during yet another family drama. Shockingly, James Jr had been court-martialled a second time and thrown out of the navy. He had been serving on the frigate *Royal Oak* while the ship was in dry dock at Malta. Rashdall's diary entry of Monday 7 November 1864 reveals his dismay at the news, and the fear that his godson had committed some truly dreadful crime: 'A tremendous blow this mgs. post – news from Malta – of court martial on J.R.M. [James Rashdall Marsden] and his dismissal from the service – Oh God sanctify it…I am overwhelmed & in consternation wait to read in 'Times' tonight the nature of the offence.'

It appears young James had sent word to his uncle himself, but the next day brought confirmation from Dr Marsden: 'Mg. [morning] brought a note from James L.M to tell me of his son's dism. from navy & that he believes the offence was – drunkenness! Strange to say – it was a relief to me – even this!' A week later Dr Marsden wrote again to say that no notice of the court-martial had appeared in the press, which Rashdall called 'a gracious amelioration'.

On 23 November Rashdall travelled to Malvern and had a long discussion with Dr Marsden regarding young James's future. It was felt that there were only three viable options, which Rashdall listed in his diary. The first two arose from the ongoing American Civil War and were certainly more suited to the young man's experience and temperament than the third:

1. Lieutenant in a blockade runner.
2. Lieutenant's commission in the American Army.
3. Colonist in Buenos Ayres [where] the Dr had a friend.[5]

Two weeks later James, home from Malta, suddenly appeared at Dawlish to stay with his godfather until things settled down. The pious atmosphere at the rectory would have been in stark contrast to the young man's rackety life in the navy. At just six years old, Hastings Rashdall was so saintly that his worried nursemaid had once gone to his mother saying, 'Master Hastings has been so long at his prayers, Ma'am, and I don't like to interrupt him.'[6] Perhaps the child, who loved to dress up and 'preach' like his father, managed to corner his big cousin and deliver an earnest sermon on the evils of alcohol.

James had either been too afraid to go home to Malvern, or had fled from Abbotsfield after a blazing row with his father. For Dr Marsden, the most galling aspect of his son's disgrace was that his brother Frederick's son, Frederick Jr, had excelled at Rugby public school and was studying to become a barrister at London's Inner Temple. On Christmas Eve, in the middle of the crisis, Sidney Marsden's widowed sister died, bequeathing Sidney and Frederick her £60,000 estate at Earls Colne in Essex. Dr Marsden could be forgiven for feeling that his brother, who now had an impressive country seat to complement his Order of the Bath, led a completely charmed life. What a bleak Christmas Day for Emily and her sisters at Abbotsfield, as they tiptoed around their father and fretted over the fate of their errant brother.

Whether James had any say in his future is unknown, but surprisingly it was decided to ship him off to distant Argentina with enough capital to establish himself as a farmer. As he would have known full well, there could only be two outcomes to the venture: redemption through hard work and financial success, or permanent exile if he should fail a third time. Unfortunately, the 22-year-old was entirely unsuited to the life of a colonist, being an ill-disciplined ex-sailor with a weakness for alcohol. Similarly exiled sons of the landed gentry at least had horsemanship skills and some knowledge of estate management.

Saying goodbye must have been a painful business for his sisters. When their brother was in the Royal Navy there had been the intermittent joy of seeing him arrive home on leave. On this occasion they knew it might be many years before they saw him again.

After arriving in Buenos Aires, James travelled 187 miles north-west to Rosario, and from there to the rough, frontier settlement of Frayle Muerto, in the Córdoba province. He joined a small enclave of British farmers who had arrived the previous year and were raising sheep and cattle. From Abbotsfield, Emily and her sisters kept him up-to-date with family news. In the spring of 1865 Mary Marsden and her daughter, Isabella, paid a visit to Alfred Tennyson on the Isle of Wight, reviving the poet's memory of his first attempt at mesmerism. On 9 August the same year, 84-year-old Harriet Marsden passed away while staying with her son Frederick at Earls Colne. The old lady's death was followed soon afterwards by that of Sidney Marsden. On 1 October 1867 a much happier event took place at Earls Colne when the widowed Frederick saw his daughter, Ellen, marry Charles Willis Godfrey, a well-educated young army officer. Ten months later Ellen gave birth to a daughter.

For Dr Marsden, hearing that his brother Frederick had become a grandfather emphasized the fact that his own daughters remained unmarried, though Emily and Rosa were now in their mid-twenties and Alice too had passed the age of majority. It had been more than ten years since the girls' alleged immoral habits had been so widely publicized, but no doubt there were matriarchs who made sure their sons did not form romantic attachments to the Marsden sisters. Why risk the snide remarks of acquaintances, or the horror of inherited deformities? Mary must have prayed her own daughter, 14-year-old Isabella, would not suffer by association.

James Jr would have found it difficult to respond adequately to his sisters' loving flow of correspondence. Life as a colonist was difficult and many subjects were best avoided. From the time he arrived in Argentina the country had been at war with neighbouring Paraguay. Thousands were dying from cholera, which spread from overcrowded army camps. At isolated Frayle Muerto there were regular and often fatal skirmishes between settlers and indigenous Indians during armed livestock raids. By 1868 many farmers had been forced to abandon cattle farming in favour of grain growing, which was less glamorous and far more labour-intensive.

In March 1868 John Rashdall received word from his sister Elizabeth that their 89-year-old mother was desperately ill at Cheltenham. She died soon afterwards and Rashdall's return for the funeral provided the opportunity for him to reunite with his Marsden nieces. Three months later he made a rare visit to Abbotsfield. Malvern held painful memories for the minister and he was understandably apprehensive about returning. But the old coolness between himself and Mary Marsden had disappeared and he was pleased he had gone. He reported that all was well with the family and that there had been a good report of his godson in Argentina.

However, young James was sending home rose-coloured accounts of his progress. In truth, after four years away he was not worth the cost of his passage home. A list compiled for the government in the first half of 1869 showed Mr Marsden as growing 50 acres of wheat, but those early crops were destroyed by locusts. There was a natural temptation for the colonists to drown their disappointment in whisky, or the local white rum called *cana*. Many settlers completely abandoned themselves to drink. A story circulated about two young Englishmen who took to their beds with a whisky bottle suspended from the ceiling, the idea being to swing it between themselves with minimum effort. One group famously slicked down their hair with white rum before staggering off to church to greet a new chaplain. Eventually it became clear the farming venture had failed, but returning home was not an option for James. He knew he would be judged harshly by Dr Marsden, particularly as his younger cousin Frederick had fulfilled the expectations of *his* father by being called to the bar.

Fortunately, John Rashdall remained ignorant of his godson's increasingly dire situation. Haunted by all that had befallen the young Marsdens, the domestic contentment Rashdall had found with Emily did not prevent a characteristically tormented entry in his 'diary of the soul' following his fifty-eighth birthday: 'Alas! for the past – how much to mourn over, & repent of: mercy, O Lord.'[7]

Surprisingly, his diaries make no mention of his surviving Marsden nieces' brave bid for independence that same year. During the summer Emily, Rosa and Alice left Abbotsfield and moved into Netley House in North Malvern, where they opened a private school. Emily was now twenty-eight, old enough to have acquired the air of authority necessary for keeping order among a group of flighty schoolgirls. On 4 July an advertisement in the *Malvern Advertiser* announced that Miss Marsden intended opening an academy for young ladies, '...in which the usual branches of a thorough English Education, with music and French, are taught'. The advertisement highlighted Célestine Doudet's particular, though grief-associated, legacy: the young women's strong grounding in music and the French language. Fees were to be made known on application, with the establishment's first term due to commence on 21 July.

Now a father of three, Rashdall's experiences with his nephew and nieces made him a naturally anxious parent. The previous summer he had sent his eldest son Hastings to Belmont, a preparatory boarding school at nearby Dartmouth. Before long he was writing to the school complaining that Hastings's spiritual development was being neglected. Despite assurances from the headmaster, Rashdall took his son's religious education into his own hands. In a letter home dated 30 January 1869, Hastings dutifully answered a list of theological questions his 'Papa' had set him.

Five days later John Rashdall suddenly fell ill. He died at the vicarage the following day, on 5 February. The cause of death was recorded as 'stomach derangement and rupture of a large blood vessel near the heart or brain'. He was buried in St Gregory's churchyard. On the day of the funeral the shopkeepers of Dawlish closed their doors as a mark of respect. The church service was conducted by the Dean of Exeter, a personal friend. It was later published in full in local papers. Despite having been vicar for less than five years, Rashdall had earned the love and respect of his parishioners. A public meeting was held to determine the most suitable way of commemorating his life. He was described by the chairman as a man who had been welcome in both the drawing rooms of the rich and the cottages of the poor.

As Rashdall had been about to found an institution for the benefit of working men, it was suggested a cottage hospital be established in his memory. However, Emily Rashdall feared the project would create local tension and said she would prefer a simple memorial stone for her husband. A fund had been established at the public meeting and, as word spread, members of Rashdall's former flocks in Exeter, London and Great Malvern expressed the desire to contribute. A local man was engaged to carve a tomb of white marble on a granite base, but meanwhile Emily Rashdall's anxieties over dissension came true. A group of 'Romish' women within the church took it upon themselves to plant a lavish garden on the freshly dug grave, erecting a tall, moss-covered cross as a centrepiece. Offended 'Protestants' repeatedly tore down the cross, leading to a dispute that made a mockery of Rashdall's legacy as a peacemaker. Soon afterwards, his distressed widow held an auction at which she disposed of virtually every item in the vicarage: rugs, culinary items, even the family bedding. She moved with her children to Cheltenham.

COURTESY OF DEREK WAIN, DAWLISH, 2010

The Reverend John Rashdall's grave, St Gregory's churchyard, Dawlish. The marble tomb was a memorial to the evangelical minister, funded by his many admirers

John Rashdall's death was an overwhelming blow for his nieces. He had been a constant and loving presence in their lives, frequently fulfilling the role of parent when their father had been too busy or too selfish to bother with them. He had known them during their infancy in Exeter, had been there for them when their mother died, and had given up the attractions of London to be close to them by moving to Malvern in 1851. Full of regret over the Doudet affair and the tragic loss of Lucy and Marian, Rashdall's concern for the welfare of the surviving girls led to his breach with their parents in 1855. How difficult it must have been for Emily and her sisters to write to James with news of his passing. A letter took over forty days to reach Buenos Aires and even longer to find its way upriver to the small community of Frayle Muerto.

Several months after Rashdall's death the *Malvern Advertiser* reported on a near disaster at Abbotsfield…the kitchen was almost blown sky high. As Dr Marsden's coachman was breaking up coal one morning, the cook began collecting the slack and throwing it into the stove. She complained of small explosions, and when the coal bin was checked a cartridge containing half a pound of gunpowder was discovered, presumably a leftover from mine blasting. The event gave Emily and her sisters some exciting news to include in their next letter to their brother, but unfortunately he would never receive it.

The vast distance between Argentina and England meant it was late November before word arrived, perhaps from Dr Marsden's friend in Buenos Aires, that 27-year-old James had died at the end of September. A short notice appeared among the death notices in the *Malvern Advertiser* and *Hampshire Telegraph*: 'MARSDEN – On the 28th September, drowned off Rosario in the Argentine Republic, James R Marsden, formerly Sub-Lieut, RN, only son of Dr Marsden, Great Malvern.'

Mystery surrounded the drowning, which occurred at some unknown point along the River Parana while James was returning to Frayle Muerto from Buenos Aires aboard the steamship *Lugan*.[8] He may have fallen overboard under the influence of alcohol or even taken his own life, depressed over his financial situation and the loss of his godfather. Rashdall could have been depended upon for support if James had been forced to return home. There are no records of a burial, suggesting his body was never recovered. After four years in Argentina he left the pitifully small sum of £82. James Marsden's fate was similar to many other gentlemen English settlers:

> Drinking, gambling, and horse-racing was the order of the day. The capital they had brought with them took unto itself wings... Many of these gentlemen ultimately were driven to take any menial work they could get; some died of delirium tremens, others self-despatched with their own revolvers.[9]

In a sense the Marsden girls had been mourning their only brother all their lives. They were heartbroken when 10-year-old Jimmy, dealing with boarding school and his father's remarriage, failed to respond to the letters his increasingly unwell and unhappy siblings sent from Cité Odiot. As an adult he remained physically and emotionally remote, either serving on ships in the Royal Navy or struggling to survive in the lonely colonial outpost of Frayle Muerto. His untimely death robbed them of any chance of reconnecting. It is impossible to calculate the effect the double loss of their uncle and brother had on young women who had already coped with so much.

21. Dangerous Liaisons

❧

During the summer of 1870 Great Malvern was the subject of an article in the medical journal *The Lancet*. In what was the first, ominous sign that all was not well in the famous spa, the author wrote that the town's water supply was severely diminished. More alarming for a health-cure centre was news that there had been fatal cases of diphtheria and unidentified 'fever'.

Dr Marsden, due to his Turkish bath complex, was one of those badly affected by the water shortages. He was also becoming disenchanted with Great Malvern on other fronts. His influence and authority were being challenged by newcomers, although he still captained the volunteer rifle corps and sat on a myriad of committees, including the Town Board, the Educational Board and the Fire Brigade Committee. In February 1870 he became embroiled in a row over the Rhine band. The trouble began after a carriage horse was startled by music outside Dr Gully's Tudor House, leading to the injury of a bystander. The Town Board proposed the band be restricted to the Promenade Gardens and St Ann's Well. Dr Marsden strongly opposed the motion, arguing that the German musicians contributed to the prosperity of Malvern and that such a restriction might force them to leave. He said he and Dr Gully had brought more people to the town than six other men and were each contributing £50 per annum to support the band. Never one to 'hide his light', he added that his own medical practice attracted more people than Malvern College, giving him the right to a say in the matter. To his chagrin, he was defeated six to three. In May, before the issue was resolved, he and Mary left town for almost twelve months, sub-letting Abbotsfield.

A letter from Dr Marsden in July accepting the rank of Major in the rifle corps reveals the couple were visiting the German spa town of Swalback [Schwalbach]. As they socialized within the town's English community, life for Mary and Isabella would have been little different to that in Malvern; their days filled with letter writing, needlework, walks and carriage rides. Dr Marsden may have combined a change of air with an opportunity to assess Malvern's competition. Foreign travel was becoming easier and English spa towns had begun to lose clients to more sophisticated Continental resorts.

It was American visitors who kept Malvern's boarding houses full, including a young writer from a wealthy background by the name of Henry James. James arrived in March 1870, hoping to alleviate a range of complaints including fatigue, constipation and back pain. Cold douches and enemas may have coloured his self-confessed peevish view of Malvern ladies, which he expressed in a letter to his brother. One hopes it was not the three Misses Marsden who inspired him to write, 'I am tired of their plainness & stiffness & tastelessness – their dowdy heads, their dirty collars and their Lindsey Woolsey trains.'[1] Mr James also despaired of finding intellectual companionship among his fellow patients, complaining their conversation was unimaginative and that they took the beauty of their surroundings for granted.

By now, Malvern was establishing a reputation as a centre of education. However, all was not well at the Netley House academy for young ladies, and after little more than two years the venture failed. Could it be that the old rumour mill began to turn, producing mothers who feared the Doudet connection might harm their daughters' reputation? Worse, were there those who worried their children might be sexually perverted by Miss Marsden and her sisters? There was no announcement that the school was about to close, but regular advertisements in the *Malvern Advertiser* ceased early in November 1870. By the middle of the month Emily and her sisters were no longer residing at Netley House. Their parents and Isabella were still in Germany and perhaps the young women joined them before returning to Abbotsfield. None of the family appear in the 1871 census.

During Dr Marsden's year-long absence from Malvern there was a remarkable development in the life of his old friend Dr Gully. At sixty-three, Gully metaphorically crossed his own establishment's famous 'Bridge of Sighs' by falling in love with a patient young enough to be his granddaughter. Florence Ricardo, aged twenty-six, had arrived at Malvern at the end of April 1870, in a state of mental distress due to her wealthy young husband's alcoholism. Alexander Ricardo joined his wife, promising to undertake the 'cure', but was soon back in his London drinking haunts. Dr Gully was full of sympathy for Florence and, despite the disparity in their ages, she became infatuated with him. Before long the pair were enjoying cosy little get-togethers at Gully's home. Mrs Ricardo was an acknowledged beauty. Little wonder that the portly, bald-headed Gully was flattered and that he should develop quite a spring in his step. On 5 June local boarding-house keeper Jane Curzon noted warmly in her diary, 'I saw Dr Gully when he came to Miss Ropes [one of Miss Curzon's boarders] and he looked wonderfully well.'[2]

By the time the Marsdens returned home in May 1871, Alexander Ricardo had died from the effects of alcohol and Florence and Dr Gully had begun a sexual relationship. This was not as incongruous as it may appear. Gully was a charming, cultivated man, very possibly a more experienced and sensitive lover than the dissipated Ricardo. There is no

Dr James Manby Gully. The physician was liked and respected by such eminent Victorians as Thomas Carlyle and Charles Darwin, but his career would end in disgrace

COURTESY OF BRIAN ILES, GREAT MALVERN

199

reason to suppose Dr Gully had been celibate during the long separation from his wife. Prostitution thrived beneath the veneer of Victorian prudery and the doctor spent a good deal of time in London and abroad.

When the prematurely widowed Mrs Ricardo left Malvern to settle in London, a lovesick Gully followed, giving up his thirty-year practice at Great Malvern. He fully intended that they should marry when old Mrs Gully died, although Florence's parents were so upset by the affair that they broke off all relations with their daughter. The people of Malvern, blissfully ignorant of the real reason behind their beloved Dr Gully's 'retirement', farewelled him with an outpouring of affection and gratitude. Charlotte Dyson, however, could not bear the thought of life without her old friend's society. She and her sister moved to London in his wake.

Coincidentally, Dr Gully's adulterous passion was running white-hot at the very time when Dr Marsden was experiencing his own midlife crisis. He had suffered a humiliating loss of face over the issue of the Rhine band. His beloved Malvern was becoming the last hope for the dying rather than a resort for fashionable hypochondriacs and wealthy dyspeptics:

> We have no royalty this year to draw a crowd – only an Earl and two or three Countesses…Some are very ill. A very feeble Earl went past my window just now drawn by a donkey in a low wheeled chair, very convenient for invalids. There was the mild donkey, the rough donkey-driver, the poor sick Earl a shadow of himself, so thin, so wan, so ghostlike, and his tall ruddy chaplain walking beside him. The air of the hills may revive his Lordship, but I fear not. When people can live nowhere else they are sent to Malvern.[3]

More personally, Mary Marsden was now over fifty. She was no longer the attractive young woman who had stirred the doctor's loins when she arrived for treatment at Cotswold House in the autumn of 1851. In fact, there may have been problems with the physical side of their marriage for many years. After the premature birth of the couple's stillborn son in 1856, there were no more children. This was unusual in an era when the only reliable method of contraception was abstinence, which Mary may have insisted upon. The doctor's eye began to rove. We might conjecture that his sense of responsibility lessened after the death of his 'moral conscience' John Rashdall, followed within months by the drowning of his son and heir in Argentina.

If Dr Gully did not divulge his love affair to his old friend and colleague, Dr Marsden would soon have heard of it through the close fraternity of the medical profession, particularly when the lovers' indiscretions created a scandal in London. Did Gully's adulterous affair influence Dr Marsden, or was it mere coincidence that he too became involved with a much younger woman?

A clue to how the attachment came about can be found in the 1871 English census, with an entry for the Welch family of Pump Street, Malvern. The head of the household was labourer James Jervis Welch, but significantly his wife Mary was described as a bath attendant. Perhaps she was employed at Hardwicke House, or at Dr Marsden's Turkish baths. In the event it was not Mrs Welch who attracted the doctor's attention but her daughter, Sabina Amanda, the second eldest of four children. She was nineteen years old at the time of the census and her occupation was recorded as 'servant'. The family were long-time residents of Great Malvern. Sabina's parents were the James and Mary Welch married by the Reverend John Rashdall at the Priory Church in 1851.

Pump Street was a narrow, hillside thoroughfare in north Malvern comprising tiny workers' cottages. A few doors away was a blacksmith's shop and at the top of the lane a donkey station created even more noise, mess and odour. It was a far cry from the serene splendour of Hardwicke House and Abbotsfield. Little wonder Sabina was flattered by Dr Marsden's attentions, although their romance must have been fraught with difficulty. As Florence Ricardo's doctor, James Gully had been able to visit his lover without undue comment. It was far more difficult for a man in James Marsden's position to conduct an affair with a servant girl in a small, close-knit community. For this reason, he too began planning a move to London.

Meanwhile, Dr Gully and Florence Ricardo discovered there was a heavy price to pay for illicit sexual pleasure. In the early autumn of 1873 the couple travelled to Kissingen, a German spa resort. Soon after they returned, Florence began to suffer from nausea, which she initially put down to the effects of the spa's hot mud baths. However, as the weeks went by the horrifying truth dawned…she was pregnant! When all other measures failed, Dr Gully performed an abortion, but there were serious complications and Florence nearly died. She was nursed back to health by her discreet companion, Mrs Jane Cox.

By the summer of 1874 Dr Marsden was beginning to withdraw from his civic duties, preparing the ground for a permanent move from Malvern. In 1844 he had claimed delicate health rather than personal ambition as the precipitating factor for the removal of his family from Exeter. Thirty years on there was a sense of *déjà vu* when the *Malvern Advertiser* announced Dr Marsden would be resigning from the Malvern Local Board: '…in consequence of a recent illness it would be necessary for him to husband his health so much that attention to his duties as a member of the board would be impossible'.[4]

In December the family shifted from Abbotsfield into temporary quarters at Tintern House, a nearby boarding house. On 6 March 1875 a report in the *Malvern Advertiser* noted Dr Marsden's imminent departure. It was accompanied by a glowing testimonial: 'Malvern will lose a gentleman to whom it is in many ways indebted, and, not the least, in respect of his untiring exertions to establish and consolidate our local rifle volunteer force, of which he is still the Major.' There was an acknowledgement of Marsden's work as a Town Commissioner and of the contribution he and Dr James Gully had made to hydropathy by their '… rare combination of medical skill and literary ability [that had] lifted the new treatment to a pedestal'. What the article did not mention was that both men had toppled from the pedestal of moral propriety.

Dr Marsden would maintain a professional connection with Malvern through his continued ownership of Hardwicke House and neighbouring Elmsdale. The Turkish baths were still in operation, although Hardwicke House had been let as a boarding house and Elmsdale as a private boys' school. At the time the properties were returning the substantial annual rent of £545.[5]

It must have been difficult for Mary Marsden and her daughters to leave close friends and neighbours for the sprawling, impersonal metropolis of London. Of all the family, Isabella was the most likely to have welcomed the move. At twenty-two she was still young enough to dream of finding a husband in the social whirl of the capital. However, given Dr Marsden's professed 'ill health', the family, as well as the townspeople, must have questioned his decision to move to a crowded, smog-bound city after spending decades trumpeting Malvern as the healthiest place on earth.

Dr Marsden was not the only member of the family with health problems. Rosa required medication for a chronically bad digestion. Alice had inherited her father's weak chest and was plagued by crippling rheumatic pain. It is possible there were underlying psychological issues. Although the young women suffered from complaints said to respond particularly well to the water-cure, the regime had failed miserably. One wonders whether the doctor defended his therapies by attributing his daughter's afflictions to their alleged self-abuse as children.

22. Burgundy and Mrs Cox

﹏⁓❧⁓﹏

After moving from Malvern in the spring of 1875 the Marsden family became residents of exclusive Mayfair. Dr Marsden leased an elegant townhouse at 29 Lower Grosvenor Street, a few doors along from the Earl of Abingdon. There was a particular satisfaction for Dr Marsden in moving to the street. Ten years earlier a homeopathic chemist had moved in, but met with overwhelming opposition:

> Mr Walker, one of the oldest of our homeopathic chemists, had last year removed into Grosvenor-Street. Now Grosvenor-Street is undoubtably very aristocratic, and few are allowed to carry on business in it. Mr Walker, however, had permission from the owner of the house he took to carry on business there. For about a year all went well; many of the noble families in the street welcomed homeopathy and patronized it; but unfortunately an unusually large number of allopathic physicians and surgeons dwell in Grosvenor-Street, their number according to the last Directory being not less than twenty-two, a dozen surgeon-dentists not included. Those gentlemen could not bear to see the hated symbols of homeopathy in their midst.[1]

The 'drug' doctors found a loophole in Mr Walker's lease and forced him to close shop. What on earth did they make of Dr Marsden, who complemented his homeopathic remedies with sitz baths, ascending douches, and wet-sheet windings? Whatever the case, it would certainly have taken a brave band of men to try to oust him.

London had changed a great deal since the Marsden siblings stayed with their Uncle John Rashdall in 1862. Sir Joseph Bazalgette's 83-mile sewerage system had just been completed, greatly improving the sanitary conditions of the capital. The city's underground railway had been in operation for over a decade and Mr Arthur Liberty had just opened his vast 'oriental bazaar' on Regent Street. Construction of the Royal Albert Hall, the vision of the late Prince Albert, had added to the city's vibrant cultural life. The Victorians loved to be entertained and there was a constant and bewildering selection of plays, concerts and exhibitions. When the Marsdens arrived, the celebrated actor Henry Neville was appearing in *The Two Orphans* at the Olympic Theatre. A comic opera was being performed at the Criterion, and at Madam Tussaud's waxworks, models of every British monarch from William the Conqueror to Queen Victoria could be seen for the price of a shilling.

Creating a stir within literary circles was the serialization of Anthony Trollope's new novel *The Way We Live Now.* The cutting social satire was based on the culture of greed, and inspired by a number of recent financial scandals. Emily and her sisters would have been a little embarrassed to find that one of the book's main characters, the shady Augustus Melmotte, had tried to secure his place in London society by buying a mansion in Grosvenor Square.

It was important for Mary and her daughters to be accepted by the matriarchs of Mayfair. Each new social connection could lead to a suitable husband for Isabella. No doubt the women ran a critical eye over their wardrobes. Outfits admired in Malvern might not 'do' in London, where the slightest change of fashion was reported, discussed and slavishly followed. That summer the mania was for all shades of red, in particular *lupin* red, named in honour of Monsieur Lupin whose horse had won the Paris Grand Prix. Meanwhile, the continued popularity of pronounced bustles and long trains prompted one wit to ask when the craze for camel humps and mermaid tails would ever end.

As they settled in at No. 29, Mary Marsden waited anxiously for calling cards to arrive. But even if their immediate neighbours should snub them, they could rely on the company of old Malvern friends living across the Thames. Foremost was their beloved Dr Gully, who had moved into a house called Orwell Lodge, in suburban Balham. The house was a convenient five-minute walk from his wealthy mistress, Florence Ricardo. Florence had leased The Priory, a Gothic-inspired mansion set in 10 acres of garden on Balham's Bedford Hill. Charlotte Dyson and her sister Fanny were living not far away at Ferndene, in London Road, Streatham. If Mary and her daughters found Dr Gully's attachment to Mrs Ricardo a little untoward, Charlotte Dyson would have explained that Dr Gully had been very kind to the young widow at Malvern, and was continuing to take a fatherly interest in her welfare.

Soon, unknown to Mary Marsden and the Misses Dyson, another ex-Malvern resident would arrive in south London. After delaying long enough to allay suspicion, Dr Marsden arranged for Sabina Welch to move to Brixton. It can hardly have been a coincidence that Dr Marsden should choose to set up his love-nest within a stone's throw of Dr Gully in neighbouring Balham. As a close friend and fellow adulterer, Gully would have been the one person Dr Marsden felt able to confide in. Orwell Lodge's proximity to Brixton provided the perfect cover for the doctor's visits to Sabina: 'You take the girls to the theatre, Mary, I've promised to spend the evening at Orwell Lodge with poor old Gully.' Mary Marsden had no reason to doubt her husband's concern for his friend. By the autumn of 1875, everyone in Gully's circle sensed the old fellow was lonely and unhappy, though few understood why.

It was, of course, a matter of the heart. Although Florence Ricardo was still very much attached to Dr Gully, she had been traumatized by her pregnancy and by the botched abortion that almost claimed her life. The couple's relationship had become platonic. Nevertheless, a devoted Gully hoped that time and gentle love-making would set things right. However, everything changed in October 1875 when Florence met young barrister Charles Bravo. The 30-year-old had no money of his own, but his offer of marriage provided an opportunity for Florence to restore her tarnished reputation and to reconcile with her parents. She agreed to marry Bravo, telling a heartbroken Dr Gully they must never see each other again. Despite some misgivings on Florence's part regarding property settlements, she and Bravo married in London on 7 December. In retrospect it might have been a bad omen that for days afterwards the city was enveloped in one of the suffocating black smogs that made the asthmatic Alice Marsden's life a misery.

By the time the newlyweds returned from their honeymoon the papers were devoting advertising and editorial space to Christmas:

> Death warrants go out amongst the ducks of Lincolnshire and the turkeys of Norfolk. The butchers, somewhat daunted of late by the devotion of a fickle public to Australian beef and mutton, recover their spirits. Who could dine of aught but a true British

sirloin at Christmas? Even now we seem to sniff its savoury odours, to behold the attendant mince pies and crown of the Christmas dinner – the traditional holly-stuck plum pudding.[2]

With Rosa's delicate stomach in mind, the cook at Grosvenor Square may have been instructed to produce a rather unusual plum pudding, especially if there had been a recent snowfall:

HYDROPATHIC CHRISTMAS PUDDING

Mix together a pound and a quarter of flour or meal, half a pint of sweet cream, a pound of stoned raisins, four ounces of currants, four ounces of potatoes (mashed), five ounces of brown sugar, and a gill of milk. When thoroughly worked together add eight large spoonfuls of clean snow; diffuse it through the mass as quickly as possible; tie the pudding tightly in a bag previously wet in cold water, and boil four hours.

The theory behind the addition of snow was that it contained 'atmospheric air'. This was released as the flakes melted, lightening the pudding and making it more digestible.

As the staff prepared the house for the festive season, Mary Marsden and the girls would have been thinking of friends and family at Malvern and Cheltenham, addressing Christmas cards in what was becoming a popular tradition:

> *When the ruby-eyed holly bush*
> *Gladdens the sight,*
> *And the pearls of the mistletoe*
> *Sparkle with light,*
> *Think of one whose fond heart with*
> *Affection is beating,*
> *Who now sends with love this new postal greeting.*

It was the family's first London Christmas, and possibly their last.

At midnight on 31 December, church bells pealed throughout the city in celebration of the New Year. It was a time of renewal, and hope for the future:

> *Ring out the old, ring in the new,*
> *Ring out the false, ring in the true.*

Mary Marsden and her daughters had put Great Malvern behind them and settled into their new life. Unfortunately, at The Priory in Balham past history and old habits were creating problems for the newlywed Bravos. Before her marriage Florence had confessed her relationship with Dr Gully. Charles had appeared to understand, admitting to having 'kept a little woman' at Maidenhead. However, as the glow of the honeymoon faded he began to taunt Florence about his elderly predecessor. His jealousy was fuelled by the fact that James Gully was living under his nose at Orwell Lodge. Bravo also criticized his wife for drinking too much. In turn, Florence began to suspect she had been married for her money. She considered her new husband ill-tempered and mean, especially when he threatened to dismiss her companion and close confidante, Mrs Cox. Tension increased markedly after Florence suffered two miscarriages in quick succession. She began to find every means possible of avoiding sexual relations.

At 9.30 p.m. on Tuesday 18 April Charles Bravo again chastised his wife for excessive drinking, then retired for the night. Florence, still pleading illness, was sleeping in another room. Soon afterwards Bravo appeared in his nightdress in great distress, shouting for his wife to bring him hot water. It would be discovered that he had ingested a fatal dose of tartar emetic (containing the poison antimony). After suffering in agony for three days, Bravo died on 21 April, just four months after his marriage. He had remained conscious for most of the last three days of his life, but according to his doctors he neither confessed to taking poison himself nor accused anyone else.

On 25 April an informal inquest was held in the dining room of The Priory. Florence was not required to give evidence and the coroner, a friend of the family, found that the dead man had taken his own life. As was often the case, he obligingly returned an open verdict, sparing the family the scandal associated with suicide. However, dissatisfaction with the coroner's decision led to a second, far more exhaustive, enquiry. It took place in the billiard room of the nearby Bedford Hotel. Hotels were commonly used for inquests as there were few other premises with a room large enough to accommodate lawyers, jury members and witnesses, not to mention the general public. Until the end of the nineteenth century there were few purpose-built coroner's courts.

This time, every sordid detail of Florence's affair with Dr Gully would be revealed. Had jealousy over the doctor driven her husband to suicide, or was it murder? It was possible that someone had added poison to the bottle of Burgundy that Bravo consumed at dinner, or had placed it in his bedside carafe of water. When dissolved, tartar emetic is almost odourless and tasteless. The case had all the elements to capture the imagination of the public: money, a mysterious death, and an upper-class sex scandal involving a charismatic doctor and a beautiful young woman. There was also the macabre spectacle of Bravo's body being exhumed. The press published illustrations of jury members at Norwood Cemetery, viewing the dead man's rotting torso through a glass sheet inserted in his coffin.

When Dr Gully was questioned at the inquest he was forced to admit to having had a 'criminal intimacy' with someone half his age. Worse still, Mrs Cox left the jury (and the public) in no doubt that he had performed an abortion on his lover:

> In November 1873, early in the month – it was after her return from Kissingen – she [Mrs Ricardo] had an illness, and Dr Gully attended her. I made an inquiry as to what that illness was, and was told by Mrs Ricardo that it was 'an unusual natural illness'. Dr Gully said the illness arose from 'a kind of tumour', which, he said, was removed.[3]

Gully was cast as a possible murderer after details emerged that his coachman George Griffith purchased tartar emetic at Malvern several years earlier.

The poison book kept by Mr Clark, the chemist at Great Malvern, was produced, showing an entry dated 11 July 1869:

> Name of Purchaser – Dr Gully
> Name and quantity of poison sold – 2 ozs emetic tartar
> Purpose for which required – Horse medicine
> Signature of purchaser – George Griffith[4]

Griffith admitted 2 oz was enough for 400 doses. Asked why he purchased so much, he said he originally intended keeping a supply on hand for several years. However, he said he used some and threw the rest away. He denied making the purchase at Dr Gully's request, though when pressed he agreed he may have given the chemist a note from his employer.

The press had a field day. It did not escape notice that Dr Gully's lawyer was Mr Sergeant Parry. In 1859 Parry had defended the water-cure doctor Thomas Smethurst, convicted of poisoning his lover with arsenic.

As at the Doudet trials twenty years earlier, English matrons attended the inquest in droves:

> There has been a great unearthing of scandal, and the audience is as merry and exhilarated as if at a play, laughing at anything funny and buzzing applause. The ladies are especially lively, and they came in such numbers and made so much noise that the coroner a few days ago decided not to admit women anymore and they are now rigorously excluded.[5]

The ladies may well have been enjoying themselves, but the reporter had misinterpreted the coroner's directive. Women and children were excluded due to the indelicate nature of the evidence. Ultimately, there was not quite *enough* evidence, indelicate or otherwise, to send the matter to trial.

On 11 August the jury returned its verdict:

> We find that Mr Charles Delauney Turner Bravo did not commit suicide; that he did not meet his death by misadventure; that he was willfully murdered by the administration of tartar emetic; but there is not sufficient evidence to fix the guilt upon any person or persons.[6]

The case remained the subject of intense speculation. Little wonder that on 9 September 1876 *The Worcester Journal* reported that Dr Gully had left England for France. By that stage, portraits of everyone involved in the 'Balham Mystery' were on sale. Of course it was Florence Bravo who remained the strongest suspect, with her companion Mrs Cox as a likely accomplice. The case, and the tantalizing idea of the beautiful Florence as poisoner, inspired the following piece of doggerel:

> *When lovely woman stoops to folly*
> *And finds her husband in the way,*
> *What charm can soothe her melancholy,*
> *What art can turn him into clay?*
>
> *The only means her aims to cover*
> *And save herself from prison locks,*
> *And repossess her ancient lover,*
> *Are Burgundy and Mrs Cox.*

Reading the salacious newspaper accounts of the inquest, Sabina Welch must have shuddered at the thought of her own situation being exposed. If she were to lose the protection of Dr Marsden, she would be faced with two unpalatable options: returning to Malvern in disgrace or being reduced to accepting a lowly servant's position in London.

Nowhere would the Balham inquest have had greater impact than at 29 Grosvenor Street. For Emily and her sisters, the confessional evidence revived memories of the Paris trials. Regardless of their disgust at the admissions of Florence Bravo and Dr Gully, they could relate to the shame and humiliation of the very private becoming public. When reading of the coroner pinning Florence down in relation to her 'criminal connection', Rosa must have re-lived the moment when she became the object of the President's attention at the Court of Assizes: '… in a letter dated from Chaillot written by you, Miss Rose, there is the following sentence: – "My aunt was very indecent this morning at her toilet." Why did you write that?' Guilt, whether justified or not, can rarely be erased. It is a destructive force lurking just below the surface, and in the worst scenario it can completely overwhelm a troubled spirit.

At Ferndene, Charlotte Dyson's distress over Dr Gully was so intense that her relatives worried about her welfare. In a letter to her cousin Mary dated 17 August 1876, the novelist Charlotte Mary Yonge wrote:

> Poor Charlotte Dyson [a friend's niece] is perfectly broken hearted and bewildered about that wretched Dr Gully, whom she had looked on all her life as people used to do on Uncle James, leaning on him for everything, and her aunt is very anxious as to the effect it may have on her health. She would believe nothing against him at all, till his own words left no doubt.[7]

The same thing could have been written in respect of Emily, Rosa and Alice Marsden. During questioning about her relationship with Dr Gully, Florence Bravo had said she first met him at the age of fourteen, while visiting Malvern with her mother. It had been a relatively brief stay, but the doctor left a strong and positive impression. Florence said he had been very kind to her and her sisters, taking notice of them and inviting them to tea. The Marsden girls had benefited from the doctor's kindly interest from the time they were infants. He was a sympathetic presence during the many tragedies in their lives, most recently the drowning of their brother James and the loss of their Uncle John. One of the saddest aspects of the Bravo inquest was that this gentle, sensitive man became a social pariah, and thus an unsuitable friend for Emily and her sisters.

Dr Gully's fall from grace also had a lasting effect on his patients, even those he had treated many years previously. A book written by James Fraude after the death of his friend Thomas Carlyle included the following anecdote:

> It will be remembered that he [Carlyle] had once stayed at Malvern with Dr Gully, and that on the whole had liked Gully, or had at least been grateful to him. Many years after, Gully's name had been before the world again, in connection with the Balham mystery, and Carlyle had been shocked and distressed about it. We had been out at Sydenham. He wished to be at home at a particular hour. The time was short, and I told the coachman to go back quickly the nearest way. He became suddenly agitated, insisted that the man was going wrong, and at last peremptorily ordered him to take another road. I said that it would be a long way round, and that we should be late, but to no purpose, and we gave him his way. Bye-and-bye, when he grew cool, he said, 'We should have gone through Balham. I cannot bear to pass that house.'[8]

And what did Charles and Emma Darwin make of Dr Gully's behaviour? Their reaction is not recorded but the knowledge that the doctor had performed an abortion on his lover surely tainted their memories of young Annie's final weeks under his care. Coincidently it was that very year, 1876, that Darwin expressed the couple's unabated sorrow over Annie's death in a private autobiography: 'We have suffered only one very severe grief in the death of Annie at Malvern on April [23] 1851, when she was just over ten years old.....Tears still sometimes come into my eyes, when I think of her sweet ways.'[9]

At Grosvenor Street, the shock of Dr Gully's involvement in the Bravo affair had scarcely begun to fade when the Marsden girls were hit with news of their father's relationship with a servant girl from Great Malvern, someone even younger than their half-sister Isabella.

23. Reduced Circumstances

E xactly when Mary Marsden became aware of her husband's adultery is unknown, although there is evidence the couple were living apart by the first months of 1877. Perhaps Mary caught her husband out in a lie, or was tipped off by a 'well-meaning' friend. The Dyson sisters, their naivety destroyed by Dr Gully's disgrace, could have spotted Sabina Welch in south London and put two and two together. In similar manner, gossip about the Bravo case in Malvern may have reminded someone that the comely Sabina had left town soon after Dr Marsden.

One suspects Mary was protected emotionally by moral outrage and by the intense Highland pride that led to her sustained breach with the Rashdall family in 1855. It was a different matter for her daughters, particularly her vulnerable stepdaughters. How were they to cope with their father's hypocrisy and betrayal following so soon upon the scandal surrounding Dr Gully? Above all, Dr Marsden's behaviour was a desecration of the memory of their sisters Marian and Lucy, whose childhood deaths were linked to the perception that *they* had been morally impure.

It is doubtful whether the doctor had any desire to reconcile with his wife or to maintain a relationship with his daughters. His vision of raising children who would reflect the benefits of his medical theories had ended with the scandalous Paris trials, followed by his son's dismissal from the Royal Navy. In his mind their behaviour provided a convenient justification for his relationship with Sabina Welch. He may also have assuaged his guilt by blaming Mary for the Doudet affair, attributing his daughters' immoral habits to anxiety over his remarriage.

Lieutenant Colonel Frederick Marsden CB, Justice of the Peace and pillar of society, would have viewed his brother's messy private life with dismay. Frederick's estate at Earls Colne was listed among the principal seats of Essex and by 1876 his name appeared in Kelly's Directory of the Upper Ten Thousand, a list of the ruling elite judged to control the country's political and financial systems. For James to have dishonoured the Marsden name was bad enough, but his conduct also cast a shadow over an important family celebration. Frederick Marsden Jr, on leave from his position as a magistrate in Calcutta, was married at the British Embassy in Rome on 11 March 1877. It would be interesting to know whether his Uncle James was invited to the ceremony.

Mary Marsden and her daughter were fortunate in that Mary was financially independent, protected by her 1852 marriage settlement. Despite the Married Women's Property Act of 1870, many women had little choice but to continue living with men who humiliated them with barely concealed affairs, were drunkards, or prone to physical violence. Having decided to leave her husband, Mary chose not to return to the Campbell clan in Scotland but to join her sisters Isabella and Augusta on the south coast at Bournemouth. Divorce was not an option. A man's adultery (unlike a woman's) did not constitute grounds for legally dissolving a marriage. Separation was tolerated, although it represented social suicide. Mary's removal from Grosvenor Street virtually destroyed her daughter Isabella's marriage prospects.

Emily and Rosa were faced with the practical issue of how to support themselves and the invalid Alice if they were to completely break with their father. Possessing neither the capital nor, following the failure of Netley House, the confidence to open another school, their only viable option was to emulate Mademoiselle Doudet and become governesses. But the profession was then hugely oversupplied. In 1874 a home for unemployed governesses in London with accommodation for 99 women received 676 applications for admission. With their proficiency in French, crossing the Channel was a possibility, but there were already some 2,000 English girls either working or seeking work as teachers and milliners in Paris:

> Many of them are in a very forlorn and desolate condition…It is melancholy to learn (the statement is made by a chief official of the Paris Police) that most of the bodies found in the Seine and exposed, though rarely recognized, at the morgue, are those of homeless and friendless English girls.[1]

Given the Marsden sisters' state of mind and their heartbreaking associations with Paris, they would have been more susceptible to self-harm than their peers.

In the end, the young women threw in their lot with their stepmother and half-sister. And no matter how much they despised their father, there was no alternative but to swallow their pride and accept an allowance from him. The amount they received was far from generous. Like the Standbury sisters in Anthony Trollope's novel *He Knew He Was Right*, they must have felt their fate would be '...to eat and drink, as little as might be, and then to die'.[2]

If there was a positive in the move from London it was that Alice's health could be expected to improve. Bournemouth was a well-established health resort due to its sea air and temperate climate. In the early part of the century two local landowners had planted hundreds of pine trees, including an avenue leading to the seafront known to this day as 'Invalids' Walk'. The astringent aroma of the pines was thought to benefit patients with chest complaints such as asthma and consumption. More importantly, sea-bathing was promoted as a means of relieving arthritic and rheumatic pain. How satisfying it would be if the invalid Alice was restored to health by bathing in the ocean when all her father's water-cure therapies had failed.

Used to undergoing medical treatment in the privacy of her own home, Alice would have appreciated the modesty afforded by the Victorian bathing machine, a small, four-wheeled carriage that was rolled into the sea. Its occupant could discreetly change into a bathing costume before slipping into the waves unobserved from the shore.

Unfortunately, within a few months the newly formed household in Bournemouth split up. By the early spring of 1877 Alice and Rosa had moved into lodgings at Eastbourne, nearly a hundred miles along the coast in East Sussex. Living independently meant serious financial sacrifice. For the first time in their lives the pair would have no lady's maid and Rosa became her sister's sole carer. After the spaciousness of Abbotsfield and 29 Grosvenor Street, they were now confined to several small rooms as paying guests. Emily, who remained with her stepmother, would later say that her sisters had moved 'for their health', which seems illogical given all that Bournemouth had to offer. It is more likely that tensions arose between the women as they tried to rebuild their lives. Alice had lost her position as 'baby' of the family in 1853, during the most traumatic year of her life. It would be understandable if, after another year of emotional turmoil, old resentments towards her stepmother and half-sister bubbled to the surface.

By April the pair had moved again, this time further east to Hastings, where they found lodgings close to the seaside in Plynlimmon Terrace at the home of Mrs Selina Campeney. The young women were obsessive about their health, with their most frequent visitors being the doctor and the chemist's delivery boy. At the end of September there was yet another move, to the virtually conjoined town of St Leonards-on-Sea, where the air was said to be more bracing. By now there was a disturbingly restless and neurotic aspect to their lives. In Bournemouth, Mary Marsden was able to link into her sisters' existing circle of friends and acquaintants, but Rosa and Alice faced social isolation, especially as the year wore on and the weather became colder. There would have been many days when it was impossible for them to venture out, throwing them back on their own resources.

Describing the twin resorts of Hastings and St Leonards in 1863, a visitor remarked on the rapid expansion of the area: 'And what attracts all these people here? you ask. Why, my friend, some come to dance and some to die. The place has its festive side and its funereal side.' On the subject of invalids, the author wrote that the famous British reserve could lead to loneliness:

> Great as is the benefit which, without a doubt, is frequently derived from the air here, that benefit is often neutralized to a great extent by the fact that the visitor frequently exchanges a spacious house for a few apartments and, instead of many friends, finds himself, save from accidental circumstances, destitute of society.[3]

On 15 December 1877, as Christmas approached, a London journalist wrote a seasonal piece for the *New York Times*. It was a time, he said, when cares and troubles should be banished and when brave and hopeful hearts should prepare to welcome Father Christmas:

> 'Hurrah for Christmas' seems to be the general sentiment of the hour. Children know it is peculiarly their season. They are

dreaming of holidays, presents, puddings, mince-pies. The toy-shops of London are crowded from morning till night. Great wagon-loads of holly and mistletoe come in from country lanes and Western apple orchards. The fruit shops have enormous stores of oranges, lemons, figs, and grapes. Raisins cram the grocers' windows. Festival candles of every colour (a relic of Catholic days) decorate the Italian warehousemen's cases. Tailors and dress-makers are busy.[4]

In St-Leonards-on-Sea, the first Christmas market was being held in the old town and the shops and churches were decorated with laurel, holly and ivy. Nevertheless, perhaps due to unseasonably mild and muggy weather, the jollity of the *Hastings and St Leonards Observer* editorial appears a little forced:

> It is Christmas, unmistakably Christmas. Frost and snow have found more congenial climes; the sun shines brightly overhead: there is slush and mud, almost warm beneath one's feet; but it is Christmastide for all that. Even if the Almanacs did not tell us, we might see it in the gaily-decked trappings of the shops... Come in what garb it will – in showers of freezing rain, in cold biting frost and falling snow, or in misty muddy mugginess – it is always welcome...[5]

With its emphasis on home and family, Christmas has always been a difficult time for the poor, the lonely and the depressed. Miss Mary Roberts, aged seventy-one, had, like the Marsden sisters, recently arrived in St Leonards where she was living with a paid companion. On the night of Thursday 20 December she retired to bed and her companion went back downstairs to the kitchen. Soon afterwards there was a thud in the courtyard, described as sounding like the fall of a rolled-up carpet. Upon investigation, the body of Miss Roberts was found in a crumpled heap. Although it was the winter solstice, the shortest day of the year, an eerie glow from a full moon revealed a sight those who witnessed it would never forget.

At the inquest held the next day at the British Hotel it was revealed that Miss Roberts had jumped from her bedroom window, a height of between

30 and 40 feet. She had multiple fractures, but it was a terrible head wound that killed her. The coroner, Mr Davenport-Jones, concluded that although the woman had taken her own life she had done so while in an unsound state of mind. This was a common finding in such cases, protecting both victim and family members from the stigma of suicide.

The full moon has long been associated with derangement of the mind and abnormal behaviour. In St Leonards, the old myth would gain more credibility when residents discovered that, as Mary Roberts plunged to her death, another drama was being played out just a few streets away at No.1 St Margaret's Terrace.

24. As Easy as ABC

❦

Early in the morning on Wednesday 19 December, Emily Marsden rugged up against the cold, said goodbye to her stepmother and Isabella, and set off on the journey to St Leonards. She was carrying a small travelling case, intending to be away for a number of days. The most convenient and quickest means of transport between Bournemouth and St Leonards was by train, although competing companies controlled the lines along the south coast and connections were difficult. It was probably simpler for Emily to travel to London first, then change to the Hastings line – still a tiring, all-day journey.

There was ample time for Emily to contemplate what promised to be an unusually subdued Christmas with her sisters. It would surely have made more sense for Rosa and Alice to return to Bournemouth, but they had insisted on remaining at St Leonards. Rosa had explained this was because they were once again on the point of moving. A flight of steps led from their current apartments down to the parish church and the seafront, and perhaps one of the lodging houses around Warrior Square had been deemed more convenient for the invalid Alice. The timing of the move, their third in less than twelve months, was odd to say the least, but the bustle involved would be a welcome distraction at a time when it was all too easy to dwell on the past.

When Emily arrived at St Margaret's Terrace that evening she would have been disappointed to discover how little her sisters had benefited from what was now a nine-month 'change of air'. The young women were preoccupied with their aches and pains, and in the attic bedroom Emily was to share with Rosa, the dressing table was cluttered with medicine bottles.

THE WATER DOCTOR'S DAUGHTERS

No. 1 St Margaret's Terrace, St Leonards, where Rosa Marsden cared for her invalid sister, Alice, in severely reduced circumstances

The next morning Alice supervised from her chair as Emily and Rosa began the complicated process of packing: dusting off trunks and cases and sorting out clothes, books, toiletries and keepsakes. Busy hands and occupied minds keep dark thoughts at bay, and it was only when the sisters finally sat down to supper that the atmosphere became a little strained. There were so many painful subjects to be avoided, and Emily had long since exhausted the news from Bournemouth. Coincidentally, she had travelled to St Leonards on their Uncle John Rashdall's birthday. How shocked and distressed he would have been by the behaviour of Dr Gully, and more particularly by their own father's adultery.

By the time the landlady's niece, Mary Kerry, came in to clear away the dishes the conversation had almost ground to a halt. Soon afterwards Rosa excused herself, complaining of her old stomach trouble. Her sisters sat for a little while longer before Alice admitted she was tired and Emily helped her to her room. At about nine-thirty Rosa called goodnight to them from the sitting room and made her way up to bed.

Some fifteen minutes later Emily and Alice heard their sister crying out in obvious distress. Emily rushed upstairs to find Rosa standing undressed in the bedroom doorway, ashen-faced and clutching a white chemist's bottle. She had great difficulty speaking, but managed to make Emily understand that the medicine she had taken for her indigestion had made her sick. She began to vomit, which Emily interpreted as a good sign. As a doctor's daughter she knew how important it was that whatever was causing her sister's illness was expelled as quickly as possible. When the retching stopped, an exhausted Rosa was helped to bed. It was hoped the crisis was over and that after a good night's sleep she would suffer no ill-effects. However, within a few minutes her condition worsened and her whole body began to contort. Alarmed, Emily sent for the nearest physician, Dr Heath from Warrior Square.

Irish-born Dr Heath was just twenty-five years old, a recent graduate of Queens University in Belfast. By the time he arrived at St Margaret's Terrace at about ten-thirty he could find no pulse at Rosa's wrist, although she was fully conscious. He noticed that her pupils were wildly dilated and that her extremities were cold. Although she was writhing on the bed she told the doctor she was in no pain, but felt 'dreadful'. One of her sisters (probably Emily) explained that Rosa had taken indigestion medicine that was old and had 'gone bad'. But to Dr Heath, her symptoms suggested something quite different and he asked to see the bottle. It was clearly labelled 'The Mixture; a sixth part to be taken every four hours, if necessary. Miss R Marsden.'[1] The name of a dispensing pharmacist from Hastings also appeared. But the moment Dr Heath smelled and tasted the contents he knew his suspicions were correct: Miss Marsden had swallowed deadly belladonna liniment. He was shocked that the poison had found its way into a medicine bottle, but there was no time to think about how such a thing could have occurred. His immediate concern was trying to save his patient's life.

Belladonna (also known as deadly nightshade) is a perennial woodland plant containing the chemical substance atropine. All parts of the plant are highly toxic, especially the root. It produces black berries which are sometimes eaten by children in mistake for cherries. Just five berries can be enough to kill a young child. The name belladonna or 'beautiful woman' arose from the ancient practice by Italian women of enhancing their eyes with drops of the plant's essence, hence Rosa's dilated pupils. Her difficulty in speaking was caused by a characteristic dryness of the mouth and constriction of the throat; in the Victorian language of flowers, the plant stands for 'silence'.

As a liniment, belladonna was considered to be beneficial in relieving joint pain, and what Rosa had taken was Alice's rubbing liniment, a popular preparation sold under the brand name of ABC Liniment, due to its three main ingredients of aconite (another dangerous toxin often dubbed 'the queen of poisons'), belladonna and chloroform. Despite its potency, fatalities from belladonna poisoning were rare in adults, but the doctor feared the worst when Rosa told him she had swallowed a double dose, equating to 2 fluid ounces. He administered the usual remedies, which would have included an emetic in case there were still traces of poison in her stomach. Another treatment was catheterization; belladonna suppresses the production of urine, allowing more poison to be absorbed.

Against all odds, Rosa began to improve, but after insisting that Alice get some rest Emily maintained an all-night vigil. Dr Heath stayed until about a quarter-past four in the morning, by which time Rosa's breathing was regular and she had a perceptible pulse. He felt it was safe to leave her for a few hours and when he returned at 9 a.m. the next morning it seemed his patient was miraculously free of the poison. Her limbs were no longer in spasm and she could speak more freely. Everyone breathed a sigh of relief, but unfortunately their optimism was misplaced. Almost imperceptively the sinister belladonna began a second offensive, attacking Rosa's nervous system. By the middle of the afternoon her lungs began to fail and she continued to deteriorate until once again her pulse faltered. At 10 p.m. Dr Heath warned Emily and Alice that he did not think their sister could last much longer and that they should make their final farewells. Rosa died at 11.30 p.m. that night, essentially due to respiratory paralysis. The young doctor left the house feeling there was something untoward about the whole tragic business. Earlier in the day, when his patient had appeared to be recovering, he had questioned all three Marsden sisters as to how the liniment came to be in Miss Rosa's medicine bottle. He was not at all satisfied with their responses, particularly with a remark made by the dead woman's younger sister, Alice.

25. A Broken Bottle

In the midst of overwhelming grief it must have been of some comfort to Emily and Alice to be told that Rosa's body could be prepared for burial. Dr Heath had explained grimly that he did not consider a postmortem necessary as the amount of belladonna the dead woman had swallowed was sufficient to kill half a dozen people. However, the circumstances of Rosa's death, particularly the mysterious transfer of the poison, meant there would be a formal investigation. The doctor notified coroner Davenport-Jones, who had only just wound up the inquest into the elderly Mary Roberts's death.

Christmas was now just three days away and arrangements for what promised to be a complex inquiry were made with even more haste than usual. There was a flurry of activity the next day as witnesses were summoned and jurors selected and sworn in. Members of the jury were taken to view the body at St Margaret's Terrace before the inquiry opened that evening at the Norman Hotel in Warrior Square. As Charles Dickens wrote in *Bleak House*, 'The Coroner frequents more public-houses than any man alive. The smell of sawdust, beer, tobacco-smoke, and spirits, is inseparable in his vocation from death in its most awful shapes.'[1]

With their sister Rosa dead for less than twenty-four hours, Emily and Alice would not only be required to attend the inquiry, but to appear as principal witnesses. All this as they struggled to fulfil the complex social and religious customs surrounding a Victorian death.

Mr Walter Dean, a local piano teacher from Hastings, was appointed foreman of the jury. Another of its members was Mr James Fox Wilson, a private tutor and bookseller. However, the most vocal juryman would be 60-year-old James Haisell, the proprietor of public dining rooms in Hastings' Pelham Street. Mr Haisell's misguided determination to place blame on the chemist who had dispensed the belladonna liniment would waste valuable time and deflect attention from far more relevant issues.

Dr Heath was the first to give evidence. He described the scene that met him when he arrived at St Margaret's Terrace, and the action he took after realizing his patient had been poisoned. Of course, unknown to the coroner and the jury, Rosa Marsden and her sisters were infinitely more familiar with belladonna than the doctor…or almost anyone else in the country for that matter. It had been the main agent in their father's first and much vaunted homeopathic cure of a horse at Exeter in the 1840s, and he had been prescribing it in various forms for his human patients ever since. On countless occasions his daughters would have collected supplies of the drug from Mr Clark, the Malvern chemist, and probably even helped their father prepare doses. Alice's regular treatment with ABC Liniment represented only a tiny percentage of their collective familiarity with the poison.

The doctor said that on the following morning, when he felt his patient was out of danger, he tried to determine how the belladonna came to be in the medicine bottle. Rosa managed to tell him that she could not account for it at all, but according to Dr Heath, Alice then admitted it was *her* doing. She said she had transferred the liniment when it arrived at their lodgings in Hastings several months earlier, because the delivery boy had broken the bottle. According to Dr Heath, Alice went on to reveal that instead of relabelling the bottle, she had simply 'trusted to remembering' the change. Rosa, conscious and in full control of her mental faculties, did not refute Alice's startling admission. Nor did she or Emily direct any words of recrimination towards their younger sister.

Emily was the next to be called. In answer to a series of questions from the coroner, she stated:

> I am deceased's sister. Deceased was thirty-four years of age. I reside with my stepmother. Deceased has been residing here since last April, and came here with my sister Alice, who is an invalid. I came from Bournemouth on Wednesday. My sister had been staying at Eastbourne in the spring.

Describing the events of Thursday night, she told the jury:

> Previous to my sister going to bed, she had been in the sitting-room alone, and, I think, took some medicine. About ten o'clock my sister's loud cries attracted me upstairs…I went upstairs, and found

deceased just at the door of her room. She had the bottle in her hand. She spoke with difficulty, and said she had taken something out of the bottle. Deceased thought the medicine was bad.

Emily explained where the bottle of ABC Liniment would have been located on the day of Rosa's death, 'As we were moving to fresh apartments, I and my sister [Rosa] collected the various medicine bottles, to the number of thirty or forty, which were put into a black bag downstairs.'[2]

Even for the health-obsessed Marsden sisters, the number of bottles sounds extreme, but the Victorians were enthusiastic self-medicators and the newspapers were full of advertisements for patent medicines. Alice and Rosa would have had a large collection of ointments, pills and lotions as well. When The Priory at Balham was searched for possible poisons in the Bravo case, about a hundred bottles and other medicine containers were collected. Emily said that Alice had told her about a liniment bottle being broken at the time it was delivered to Plynlimmon Terrace. However, she then directly contradicted Dr Heath's evidence: 'I am positive my sister Alice said that she did not know who changed the liniment into the present bottle.'[3]

At the conclusion of Emily's testimony, proceedings were adjourned. The next day being Sunday, the inquest would not reopen until Monday afternoon – Christmas Eve. It was a sombre scene at St Margaret's Terrace. Instead of candles placed on windowsills to celebrate the season, Emily lit funeral tapers around Rosa's body. And instead of sending out colourful greetings cards, she was obliged to write notes advising friends and family of this latest tragedy. Passers-by noticed the curtains of the house were drawn and that the front door was hung with a circle of black-ribboned laurel instead of the usual gay wreath. It was all a grotesque mockery of the most joyful event in the Christian calendar.

On Monday, as participants in the coronial inquest made their way through Warrior Square, locals were buying last-minute gifts and festive foods at the Christmas market, drinking mulled wine, exchanging good wishes, and listening to carol singers. Few were aware of the human drama being played out in the Norman Hotel.

In the makeshift courtroom the chemist who had dispensed the belladonna liniment was called. He was Mr James Alfred Bell, a fully qualified chemist who had been in business in Hastings for ten years.

Under the Pharmacy Act of 1865, belladonna was judged a level one poison, in company with other dangerous substances such as arsenic, tartar emetic, cyanide and opium. Such compounds were not to be sold unless prescribed by a physician and clearly labelled as poison. The pharmacy profession had taken various other measures to reduce the number of accidental poisonings. Because many people were illiterate in the nineteenth century it was decided to use colourful bottles to distinguish poisons, usually green or cobalt blue. Another problem was that people tended to fumble for their medicine in the dark or by candlelight, leading to fatal errors. For this reason bottles were made with moulded symbols such as a skull and crossbones, distinctive ribbing, or raised lettering spelling out 'Poison, Not To Be Taken'.

Mr Bell told the court he had dispensed the liniment on 21 May after it had been prescribed by a Dr Pelham. In accordance with regulations it had left his establishment in a blue bottle, with appropriate words of warning moulded into the glass. It was delivered by 12-year-old George Morris. The boy was employed by a local milliner, but occasionally earned a few extra pennies running errands for Mr Bell. The chemist admitted that the boy had broken the bottle, but said he had not been informed of this until several days later. Because the Marsden sisters had not returned the bottle, he assumed the breakage was not serious. At this point one of the jurors, Mr Haisell, interjected:

> Do you not think, Mr Coroner, that Mr Bell, knowing he had supplied a deadly poison, and hearing of the bottle being broken a few days afterwards, it was his duty to send to the parties and ascertain if they required a fresh bottle to put what was left of the belladonna in?

Before the coroner could comment, the chemist responded:

> 'I was not to know how far the bottle was broken. It might have been dropped and only nipped. Had the ladies told me they should have liked it to be put into a fresh bottle, I should have sent for it immediately.'
> **Mr Haisell** – 'Had it been my case I should have sent for it and given them a fresh bottle, especially as you were told it was broken. Therefore I think there is some negligence on your part.'[4]

The word 'negligence' struck fear into Mr Bell's heart and he felt obliged to defend his reputation: 'Ever since I have been in business I have not had any complaint of a mistake.'[5] Criminal negligence in the dispensing of poisons was a serious matter, demonstrated by a case involving the Sheffield Infirmary. In 1848 a 76-year-old patient died after ingesting extract of belladonna instead of applying it to a plaster for external use. Due to staff shortages at the infirmary the medication had been dispensed by a hospital porter, who had given the patient only oral instructions for its use. At the inquest the coroner informed the jury that if belladonna had caused the patient's death, and the porter

> in sending out that poisonous medicine without proper printed or written instructions, showed such negligence and disregard for human life as will in your judgment render it necessary that this case should be sent to a higher tribunal, I am afraid it will be your duty to find him guilty of manslaughter.

The porter only escaped prosecution because the elderly man had several pre-existing conditions. Therefore, it could not be proved beyond reasonable doubt that he died from belladonna poisoning. Nevertheless: 'The Jury fully concurred with the Coroner as to the loose manner in which medicines had been sent from the infirmary; and they recommended the instant dismissal of the porter.'[6]

With Haisell warming to his task and seeming to fancy himself as a criminal prosecutor, Mr Bell was fortunate that the coroner was a man of common sense:

> **Mr. Haisell** – 'Dr. Heath said no chemist should supply such a deadly poison.'
>
> **The Coroner** – 'Without the prescription, and here is one.'
>
> **Mr. Haisell** – 'He said, "Unless by a medical man's prescription".'
>
> **The Coroner** – 'Well, here is the doctor's prescription. Mr Bell was quite right. He states that Dr Penhall came into his establishment and wrote out a prescription. Mr Bell was quite right in supplying the belladonna: indeed, he would have been wrong if he had not done so.'

But Mr Haisell was determined to find fault with the chemist's actions. A little later he returned to the matter of the broken bottle:

> **Mr. Haisell** – 'The question is whether it was not his [Mr Bell's] duty to send back for it, knowing that the bottle was broken.'
> **A juryman** – 'Mr Bell has explained that as reasonably as any man could explain it.'
> **Another juryman** – 'By that arrangement he would have to send to every patient to see if the bottle was broken.'[7]

Perhaps it was men like Mr Haisell who prompted an article in a contemporary medical journal, arguing strongly against coroner's courts:

> The jury in ordinary cases consists of the lowest class of tradesman, or of mere loafers and bystanders, they sometimes make use of their brief authority to annoy a responsible witness, medical or not, and to throw out insinuations of neglect or misconduct. The author of 'Evils of England' points out, amongst other flagrant instances of waste, the waste of time caused by summoning juries away from their own affairs, to determine questions which were far better left in the hands of an educated and impartial judge.[8]

The question of what happened to the contents of the broken liniment bottle was finally resolved when Mrs Selina Campeney, the landlady at Plynlimmon Terrace, was called. She said she remembered the boy delivering it in May and that Miss Alice had asked *her* to pour the contents into another bottle. She said she did so, but was positive she had transferred it into a small blue poison bottle which had previously held mustard liniment prescribed for Alice. More importantly, this container had remained in her home when the Marsden sisters moved to St Leonards. It had only recently been retrieved by the police, and was produced in court. Mrs Campeney added, 'I thought the liniment was used, because when I took the bottle up the other day there was only a very little in it.'[9] This remark passed without comment but it suggests the belladonna found in Rosa's medicine bottle had been dispensed to Alice at a later date, and that all Mr Haisell's huffings and puffings about the broken container were irrelevant.

With no logical reason for transferring the belladonna liniment prior to Rosa's death, the jury now had to consider the shocking possibility of foul play. Before Mrs Campeney stepped down, Hastings' Chief-Constable, Mr William Glenister, hinted at a possible suspect by questioning the landlady about the relationship between Rosa and Alice. She assured him that the sisters had appeared very much attached to each other. Emily had been asked the same question the day before, and she too had assured the court that her sisters were very close.

Alice Marsden was then called. In contrast to Mr Bell she was treated very gently. Even Mr Haisell remained silent, no doubt constrained by the witness's status as a gentlewoman in delicate health, and sensitivity to her bereavement so close to Christmas. It was the coroner who challenged her about having admitted to transferring the belladonna: 'Dr Heath said that you said you had changed the liniment from one bottle to the other.'[10] Alice told him the doctor was mistaken. However, far more relevant was her comment that Rosa frequently rubbed her down with the liniment. This meant that unless the transfer had occurred very close to the time of her death, Rosa would have been familiar with whatever container the belladonna happened to be in. Frustratingly, Alice was not asked *when* Rosa had last applied the liniment, or whether it had then been in a blue poison bottle or a white mixture bottle. In response to another question by the coroner, she insisted she had no idea how the belladonna found its way into a medicine bottle.

The final witness called was the servant Mary Ann Kerry, niece of the landlady at St Margaret's Terrace. Miss Kerry confirmed that on the night of the poisoning she had handed Dr Heath the bottle from which the deceased had taken 'indigestion mixture'.

The Hastings Observer gave the most detailed account of Mr Davenport-Jones's final address to the jury:

> The Coroner then summed up the evidence, which, he said, he considered most unsatisfactory. There was no evidence to show how the poison got into the mixture bottle. He would go through the whole of the evidence, and make one or two remarks upon it, and then the jury must decide on their verdict. The question for them to consider was − How did deceased come by her death? That would be very clear − by poison. The next was − Who

administered it? That was also quite clear. They would then have to consider how it came into the bottle. It might have been done designedly or carelessly. If it was done designedly, then the party who made the change would be guilty of wilful murder...[11]

Theoretically, either Emily or Alice could have poisoned Rosa, although it is difficult to find a motive. Certainly they had suffered intense emotional stress throughout their lives, but could the resulting psychological damage have been severe enough to drive one of them to homicide? One possibility is that the claustrophobic relationship between Rosa and the dependent Alice created smouldering resentments. Evidence presented during the Paris trials suggests that Alice was more intense and impulsive than her older sisters. For example, there was a claim by Mademoiselle Doudet, uncontested by the Marsdens, that a scar on Rosa's shoulder had been inflicted by Alice with scissors or a knife. Further, young Alice's allegations that the governess cut her fingers, tried to pull out her tongue, and forced her to drink her own urine were far more outlandish than the charges made by Emily and Rosa. But could Alice have developed into someone unbalanced enough to kill her sister?

There is another problem with the hypothesis of foul play. Rosa, unlike the elderly patient at the Sheffield Infirmary, would have recognized the smell of liniment immediately, having been applying it to Alice on a regular basis. If either of her sisters had wanted to harm her it would surely have made more sense to disguise the smell and taste by adding it to strongly flavoured food or drink.

After canvassing the possibility of murder, coroner Davenport-Jones went on to say: 'If it [the poison] was put in in a careless manner, so that it should come in a person's way, not caring whether a person took it or not, then the charge would resolve itself into manslaughter.'[12] He reminded the jury that although the previous landlady testified to transferring the liniment from the broken bottle, she was positive it had *not* been put into a mixture bottle. He also absolved the dispensing chemist of blame, saying he did not consider it a pharmacist's responsibility to replace a damaged bottle unless specifically asked to do so. It was clearly Alice, due to initial admission to Dr Heath, who was most at risk of being sent to trial for manslaughter.

Curiously, the only scenario the coroner did not put to the jury was that Rosa Marsden had taken her own life. This seems stranger still when he had come straight from the inquest into the death by suicide of the unfortunate Mary Roberts. Not once was the possibility of suicide raised during the inquest and yet Rosa had many reasons to be morbidly depressed. She was a despised and unfulfilled spinster with a tragic history. More recently she had suffered the humiliation of coping in severely reduced circumstances. Rosa had spent the last nine months in a succession of cheerless lodging houses, nursing her invalid sister and dwelling on the betrayal of her father and Dr Gully. She may even have been directly influenced by the Bravo poisoning, as the similarities were striking. Like Charles Bravo, she had rushed from her room after dinner with the news that she had inadvertently swallowed a harmful substance. Like Bravo, she died with a strangely calm acceptance of her fate. But there was one important difference. The element of sexual jealousy in the Balham case meant that Charles Bravo, even as he writhed in agony on his deathbed, had been interrogated by his doctor over whether he had deliberately taken poison.

If Rosa did commit suicide she may have tried, albeit ineptly, to protect the feelings of her sisters by pretending she had ingested spoiled indigestion mixture. With all the medicines in the house gathered together, it would have been a simple matter for her to slip away and transfer the liniment. Emily had testified: 'Previous to my sister going to bed, she had been in the sitting room alone, and, I think, took some medicine.'[13] What had led Emily, then in another room, to this belief? Did she hear the chink of glass? If so, what she may have heard was her sister transferring the belladonna into a white mixture bottle. Alice, in response to a question from the coroner, had also said, 'I think deceased must have got the bottle produced from a bag, which contained several bottles.'[14]

When Dr Heath arrived, Emily and Alice presumably tried to shield their sister from a charge of attempted suicide by repeating the story of spoiled medicine. It was only after Dr Heath checked the bottle and identified belladonna that Alice suddenly changed tack and said she had transferred the liniment 'months ago' without altering the label. Her admission was made when it seemed likely her sister would recover. After Rosa died, Alice realized she was in serious trouble and hastily retracted her 'confession'.

That Emily had initially dismissed Rosa's story of 'spoiled' medicine was revealed when Alice was giving evidence. In the stressful atmosphere of the inquest she apparently forgot the version of events she and Emily had rehearsed. Shown the medicine bottle containing the poison, she said, 'I recognize the bottle produced. I first saw it on Thursday night. My sister Emily rushed downstairs with it, and said that deceased had taken the wrong medicine; she asked me if I could give an explanation, and also asked to see what was written on it.'[15] Note the use of the expression 'wrong medicine', not 'bad'. Clearly Emily had recognized the smell of the liniment and was confused as to how it came to be in Rosa's medicine bottle.

It could be argued that Rosa would not have raised the alarm if she had intended to end her life, but suicides often panic after taking the fatal step. More importantly, she would have been aware that belladonna is a fast-acting agent and that she was already beyond help. To have knowingly caused her sisters such shock and grief at Christmas is hard to understand until it is remembered that Emily's presence ensured that Alice would not have to cope alone. Similarly, the proposed move to new apartments meant that everything was packed up neatly for Emily to deal with. It raises the troubling possibility that Rosa may have been planning her death for some time.

In November the previous year, a case of near-fatal poisoning by belladonna received wide publicity. The woman involved had swallowed one tablespoon of rubbing liniment in mistake for medicine. Her physician explained that the patient appeared to be drunk, or '…in a state of somnambulism'. The hallucinogenic effects of belladonna were in stark contrast to the agony experienced by Charles Bravo after he ingested tartar emetic. Anyone contemplating suicide might have considered that if two (or in Rosa's case four) tablespoons of liniment were taken, a relatively painless death would ensue.* An article on the case published in the *British Medical Journal* also highlighted the scandal attached to suicide. When the attending doctor was asked by the family if he thought the victim would recover, he said yes, noting, 'I need hardly say how satisfactory it was to be able to give an assurance of this sort in a house

---

* Evidence that ABC Liniment was a logical choice of poison for the well-informed suicide can be found in the death of Scottish history lecturer Dr Henry Bellyse Baildon in 1907. Dr Baildon had previously trained and worked as a chemist. The 58-year-old had been suffering from 'an intense depression of the spirits'. One day he failed to return from a walk and his body was later found in a quarry. An empty bottle of ABC Liniment was found beside him. Dr Baildon's death certificate showed the cause of death as 'Melancholia. Poisoning (ABC Liniment)'.

where all were in consternation, and visions of "Crowner's quest", as the master put it, were looking in apparent close proximity.'[16]

The inquest into Rosa's death was remarkable for the many issues it did not address: her emotional and mental state, her familiarity with belladonna, the quantity of poison she swallowed, and the contradictions in Alice's evidence. From the newspaper reports of the inquiry it appears the jury were also unaware that the Marsden sisters were the daughters of a doctor. Nor, presumably, did they realize that Rosa had particular reason to be interested in the recent Charles Bravo poisoning due to the family's long and close connection with Dr Gully.

After deliberating on the limited evidence and taking into account the coroner's direction, the jury returned an open verdict. It was reproduced almost word for word on Rosa's death certificate: 'Deceased came to her death by taking a quantity of Belladonna and Aconite liniment in mistake for medicine, which was placed in a mixture bottle, but how the liniment came to be so placed, there is no evidence to show.'[17]

© GENERAL REGISTER OFFICE ENGLAND

Detail from Rosa Marsden's death certificate, which recorded the suspicious circumstances surrounding her death by belladonna

At the conclusion of the inquest, the jury members dispersed, probably ending up in the public bar of the hotel, where they could continue to argue the point with the obstinate Mr Haisell over a few pints. Coroner Davenport-Jones and Dr Heath, equally dissatisfied over the outcome, were free to go home and spend Christmas with their young families. Emily and Alice's Christmas Day does not bear thinking about.

26. Make Her Grave Straight

Rosa's funeral was held on Boxing Day, organized by Emily between her appearances at the inquest. Whether anyone other than Emily and Alice attended is unknown. Perhaps Mary Marsden and Isabella came from Bournemouth and Fanny Rashdall from Brighton. What a shocked and sorrowful little gathering it must have been. Only the open finding of the inquest provided a degree of solace. No one was to be charged over the death and, like the drowned Ophelia in Shakespeare's *Hamlet*, Rosa would go to her grave untainted by the sin of self-murder:

> *'Is she to be buried in Christian burial that seeks her own salvation?'*
> *'I tell thee she is, therefore make her grave straight, the crowner hath sate on her, and finds it Christian burial.'*
> *'But is this the law?'*
> *'Aye, marry is't, crowners quest law.'*

Dr Marsden was a mere two hours away by express train from London, but evidence suggests he was not among the mourners. This may have been due to awkwardness over the family break-up, or that he was out of contact, spending Christmas with Sabina in Brixton.

What words did St Mary Magdalen's Reverend William Wheeler Hume find for Rosa, the quiet young woman who had attended his church for the past few months and who had showed such loving care for her frail sister? Did her name spark memories of the infamous Doudet case, or was the minister ignorant of the Marsden sisters' traumatic past? A fitting farewell for Rosa would have been the poem 'Sleep Brings No Joy To Me' by Emily Brontë, who lost three siblings in circumstances strangely similar to the deaths of Marian, Lucy and James Marsden. Elizabeth and Maria Brontë's childhood deaths were hastened by harsh conditions at

Cowan School and Branwell Brontë died aged thirty-one, addicted to alcohol and laudanum:

> *Sleep brings no joy to me,*
> *Remembrance never dies;*
> *My soul is given to misery*
> *And lives in sighs.*
>
> *Sleep brings no rest to me;*
> *The shadows of the dead*
> *My waking eyes may never see*
> *Surround my bed.*
>
> *Sleep brings no hope to me;*
> *In soundest sleep they come,*
> *And with their doleful imagery*
> *Deepen the gloom.*
>
> *Sleep brings no strength to me,*
> *No power renewed to brave,*
> *I only sail a wilder sea,*
> *A darker wave.*
>
> *Sleep brings no friend to me*
> *To soothe and aid to bear,*
> *They all gaze, oh, how scornfully,*
> *And I despair.*
>
> *Sleep brings no wish to knit*
> *My harassed heart beneath;*
> *My only wish is to forget*
> *In the sleep of death.*[1]

It was now more than twenty years since John Rashdall had made his anguished and prophetic comment about the young Marsdens in 1855: 'What a fatality seems to rest upon these children! God set things right: it is beyond human skill.' Of Dr Marsden's seven children to survive infancy, four had died prematurely of what might be deemed unnatural causes.

Rosa's funeral plot in Hastings cemetery was paid for by Emily, who arranged for a stone cross to be erected on her sister's grave. Regrettably, it was removed in 1970 along with many other headstones, though staff at the borough council have been unable to discover why. Rosa had not made a will and ironically it was Dr Marsden, as her 'natural and lawful father and next of kin', who was granted Letters of Administration. His daughter's estate was valued at under £300. The doctor's residential address on the probate form (dated 23 January 1878) was 29 Grosvenor Street, London, although he was maintaining the household in Mayfair purely for the sake of respectability. Since his marriage break-up he was spending most of his time with Sabina in south London.

On 26 December the *Birmingham Daily Post* reported Rosa's death under the headline 'A Singular Case of Poisoning', noting that the victim had taken enough poison to kill six people and that the deceased's sister had told Dr Heath, '…that she remembered some time back putting the belladonna into the bottle, the mouth of the original bottle having been broken, and that she trusted to her memory to avert any evil arising from the transfer'. At best, the *Post*'s readers would have thought Alice a very careless young woman!

Three days later, Rosa's death notice appeared in the *Malvern Advertiser*. The townspeople, still reeling after the spectacular downfall of Dr Gully, must have been shocked to read that one of the Miss Marsdens had died so soon after leaving them. The wording of the notice contained a reminder of the earlier loss of her sisters: 'MARSDEN – At St Leonards-on-Sea, suddenly, Rosa Sydney Marsden second surviving daughter of James Loftus Marsden Esq M.D. Aged 34'. In the next issue there was a brief report of the inquest, and the revelation that Rosa had died from belladonna poisoning. With their intimate knowledge of the Marsden sisters' history, many residents would have drawn the conclusion that Rosa had committed suicide. Hester Candler was still alive and living in Malvern at the time. Did she feel a stab of regret, even guilt? Or was she quite comfortable in the belief that she had done her duty all those years ago? By now, gossip had also ensured that many people in Malvern were aware of Dr Marsden's relationship with Sabina Welch and the fact that he had recently separated from his family.

The scandal of Dr Marsden's adultery meant that, like Dr Gully, he could never return to Malvern. How could he face the well-wishers who farewelled him with such fine sentiments in 1875 – neighbours, patients, and above all the young men he had mentored in the rifle corps? Hardwicke House and Elmsdale had been let well before the doctor left Malvern, but it was only after his separation from Mary that he relinquished control of his beloved, state-of-the-art baths. The following advertisement appeared in 1877:

GREAT MALVERN – Hardwicke Baths – A very pretty Building – TO LET. £50 a year. Comprising four habitable rooms. Turkish Bath, a Caplin Electrical Bath, Hot and Cold Douches, Sitzing Baths of all Kinds, Hot and Cold needle baths, a large Exercise room with ordinary and kinesipathic apparatus, and a chemical laboratory. The proprietor, Dr Marsden, having left Malvern for London.[2]

It read well, but the water-cure had continued to decline and in 1879 it was the Freemasons who took up the lease of the baths as headquarters for their lodge.

On 17 September 1878 Florence Bravo died at Southsea, aged thirty-three. There was speculation that she killed herself, consumed by guilt over her husband's death. In fact, she *was* a victim of self-administered poison, but in this case the agent was alcohol. In her final days she had refused medical attention because she felt her private life was being talked about and she did not want to invite more gossip. But death did not protect Florence from public scrutiny. A postmortem conducted prior to an inquest revealed diseased kidneys and what was described as 'a drunkard's liver'. Florence left a legacy of £1,000 to her goddaughter and namesake, Dr Gully's little granddaughter. The old doctor's grief was compounded by the fact that he was widely condemned as having contributed to the young woman's death. Press reports were witty, but merciless:

Meantime, by means of cold water and cool temperament, a fellow delinquent still enjoys a frosty and kindly old age. Dr Gully, at whose door in reality lies this wretched death, trots up and down in health and vigour, the sun shining benevolently on his white head and ruddy face.[3]

Florence was buried in St Mary's churchyard in the village of Buscot, the Oxfordshire home of her heartbroken parents. The gossip and innuendo surrounding her had remained so strong that she was interred at midnight, in an unmarked grave.

27. Ellen Amy

⟨ formula ⟩

The timing of Rosa's death was especially difficult for Emily and Alice. For the rest of their lives Christmas would bring memories of watching their sister slowly succumb to poison, and of testifying before a jury as her barely cold body was laid out in their lodgings a few streets away. In this respect the coronial inquest at St Leonards would have been more stressful than the Paris trials, held almost two years after the deaths of Lucy and Marian when time had blunted the pain. Additionally, Mademoiselle Doudet's humiliating accusations against the girls had been ameliorated by her eventual conviction, whereas the inquest's open finding left an unpleasant shadow of suspicion over Alice.

Rosa's death left Emily with divided loyalties. If Alice did not wish to live with her stepmother and half-sister, Emily would have to replace Rosa as her carer. This appears to have been what happened. By the 1881 census all four women were living on the Isle of Wight, though in separate establishments. Mary Marsden and Isabella had taken apartments at Montrose House, in the health resort of Ventnor. Emily and Alice were lodging with a carpenter and his family in the village of Newchurch, 5 miles to the north. It was a noisy, chaotic household in which there were seven children aged from one to fifteen – a strange choice for two retiring maiden ladies, especially given Alice's delicate health.

In the autumn of 1878 Sabina Welch discovered she was pregnant. With her lover separated from his family, she felt secure enough to give birth to the child. For Dr Marsden, Sabina's pregnancy offered perhaps his last chance at immortality through the continuation of his genes. His son and heir was dead and there was little likelihood that his surviving daughters would marry. Frustratingly, he would be unable to give the child his name unless he outlived Mary and married a third time. If he hoped for a son, he was to be disappointed. Sabina gave birth to the doctor's seventh daughter, Ellen Amy, on 30 June 1879. Sabina pretended that Welch was her married name, recording the child's father as James Welch of No. 1 Grenada Terrace, Stockwell Park Road, Brixton. Faced with providing a maiden name, she came up with the unimaginative if time-honoured alias of Jones. The baby was christened on 23 July 1879 at St Andrews Church, Stockwell. What would the future hold for this child, born illegitimately with an elderly father who was unlikely to see her reach maturity?

The 1881 census shows that Sabina and her child had moved to Felix House, a property James Welch, aka Dr James Marsden, had leased at 57 Brixton Rise, Lambeth. As 'Mrs Welch', Sabina became landlady of a genteel boarding house, employing a nursemaid for the now 18-month-old Ellen. Her lodgers were from the respectable middle classes: a manufacturing iron merchant and his wife, a young doctor and his sister, and the wife of a commander in the Royal Navy. Meanwhile, Sabina's parents had moved 4 miles from Great Malvern to the village of Leigh, in the Malvern Hills. Mary Welch was no longer a bath attendant; she and James were now earning their living as tea and coffee vendors, catering to Malvern's dwindling water-cure clients. Dr Marsden does not appear in the census, but his servants at 29 Grosvenor Street included a maid, a cook and a middle-aged housekeeper by the name of Ellen Elizabeth Physick. Miss Physick would eventually become an important presence in little Ellen Amy's life.

In the summer of that year Dr Marsden attended the 7th International Congress of Medicine, held in London. He was in illustrious company as among the 3,000 delegates were Louis Pasteur, Joseph Lister and Charles Darwin. One of the most novel and popular features of the Congress was its museum of 'living exhibits'. Attending doctors struggled to be heard above the crush of spectators as they discussed the condition of surprisingly amenable sufferers of conditions ranging from leprosy and lupus to inherited syphilis. Dr Marsden had his own moment in the sun, presenting a case of cystitis. It was a reminder of those early, promising years when he had made his mark at West Country seminars. But he must also have felt a growing sense of his own mortality. Having reached the biblical 'three score years and ten', men of his generation were beginning to pass away.

On Friday 21 April 1882 *The Times* reported the death of Charles Darwin, who suffered a heart attack at his home, Down House:

> Yesterday, at his quiet Kentish home, one of the greatest of our countrymen passed away. Suddenly and almost without warning the long and noble life of Charles Darwin came to an end... Today, and for a long time to come, he will be mourned by all those in every land who can appreciate his vast service to knowledge and who honour a lifelong devotion to truth.

Alice Marsden had been barely four years old when her siblings and the young Darwins played together in the spring of 1849, but for Emily the great man's death would have brought back a host of memories, including the death of Annie Darwin at Great Malvern in 1851.

In 1887 Francis Darwin edited his father's autobiography. He included some reflections by one of his sisters (probably Etty) on their famous parent's love and affection when they were growing up:

> Another characteristic of his treatment of his children was his respect for their liberty, and for their personality. Even as quite a girl, I remember rejoicing in this sense of freedom. Our father and mother would not even wish to know what we were doing or thinking unless we wished to tell. He always made us feel that we were each of us creatures whose opinion and thoughts were valuable to him, so that whatever that was best in us came out in the sunshine of his presence.[1]

Many years later Darwin's great-great-grandson Randal Keynes would visit Annie Darwin's grave in the churchyard at Malvern. The sight of Lucy Marsden's gravestone nearby prompted Keynes, who knew the story of the Marsden sisters, to note: 'She was as unlucky with her parents and carers as Annie was lucky with hers.'[2]

The man Darwin once described as 'My beloved Dr Gully' died in Wandsworth less than a year later, on 27 March 1883. He was buried in London's Kensal Green Cemetery: 'The death is announced, in his 75th year, of Dr James Gully formerly of Great Malvern, whose name was prominently before the public five years ago in connection with the mysterious death of Mr Charles Bravo, at Balham.'³

On 8 August 1884, Sabina Welch changed her surname and that of her 5-year-old daughter to Marsden by deed poll, giving the impression that she and Dr Marsden had married. The doctor was planning to retire and it was his intention to spend his declining years living openly with Sabina and Ellen. Records show that by 1887 his permanent address had changed from Lower Grosvenor Street to Felix House, Brixton Rise. Dr Marsden's housekeeper, Miss Physick, also made the move across the river. The pretence of marriage may partly have been in deference to her respectability. Born in Devon, she was the daughter of a solicitor. Significantly, her title now changed to that of 'companion' to her employer's new 'wife', fulfilling the role of a female Professor Higgins to Sabina's Eliza Doolittle. At the time of the 1871 census, Miss Physick had been employed as a teacher, making her the ideal person to groom Sabina for a more public role in the doctor's life.

At some point, Mary Marsden and her daughters moved back to the mainland from the Isle of Wight. Emily and Alice were living at 14 Beacon Road, Exmouth, in January 1887 when 33-year-old Isabella, then living with her mother in north Somerset, fell seriously ill. What began with blinding headaches and stiffness of the neck was diagnosed as acute meningitis, an inflammation of the membranes covering the brain and spinal cord. For Mary, the news was devastating. Before the introduction of antibiotics in the twentieth century, meningitis was almost always fatal. All doctors could do for Isabella was to drain away the cerebrospinal fluid as her body convulsed with seizures and her sight and hearing began to fail. She died in hospital at Weston-super-Mare two months later, on 12 March. Emily had travelled from Devon to be at her half-sister's beside and, as with Rosa, it was she who organized the funeral and registered the death. Dr James Loftus Marsden was listed as Isabella's next-of-kin. Emily gave his address as Brixton Hill, London, but whether she was aware of the existence of her illegitimate half-sister Ellen is another mystery.

Isabella has received very little mention in this story and yet she was involved in and affected by the Célestine Doudet affair from the time of her conception. Dr Marsden used his new wife's pregnancy in 1853 as an excuse for failing to investigate the claims of cruelty against his older children. During her first, formative years Isabella's parents were dealing with the deaths of Marian and Lucy, the Paris trials, the family rift with the Rashdalls, and finally the birth of Mary's stillborn son in 1856. It is also likely that Isabella felt excluded from the close unit formed by her surviving half-sisters, and that she was resented by Alice in particular due to her special status as the youngest child, and Mary Marsden's birth daughter.

At the time of Isabella's death, Dr Marsden was about to leave south London, and Felix House. He retired to seaside Hastings with Sabina and Ellen. Miss Physick accompanied them. The doctor's experience with Mademoiselle Doudet had clearly not prejudiced him against her countrywomen, as a French governess was employed for Ellen. Dr Marsden wanted only the best for this child of his late years, but the little girl must have suffered terribly from loneliness. In an era of large families and close *extended* families, she was an only child, unaware of a single relation. She had been told that her birth father had died when she was a baby, which perhaps explained the absence of *his* connections, but what of her mother's family, and that of Dr Marsden? It is also unlikely that her parents socialized. Miss Physick may have smoothed some of Sabina's rough edges, but the nuances of Victorian society were so subtle and complex that people of Dr Marsden's class would have had little trouble in determining that the doctor's much younger wife was 'not quite a lady'.

The English winter of 1890/91 was one of the longest and harshest in living memory, with the temperature at freezing point from the end of November until the last week in January. In London, the well-to-do skated on the Serpentine in Hyde Park. Meanwhile, hot 'Robin' meals were served to the poor and William Booth, founder of the Salvation Army, pleaded for help for the homeless, who were freezing to death as they slept under the city's bridges. The weather also took its toll on Dr Marsden, who died at Hastings on 6 February 1891, aged seventy-six. Obituaries appeared in various homeopathic publications and a brief announcement was published in the *Hastings News*. Significantly, no relatives were mentioned.

Presumably prompted by the death of Isabella, the doctor had made a new will in December 1887. Unusually for the times, he made no bequests to charitable institutions nor made any provision for faithful family retainers such as Ellen Physick. In accordance with her marriage settlement, Mary

Marsden's life interest in Hardwicke House and Elmsdale was declared. Only after her death would Dr Marsden's beneficiaries take possession of the Great Malvern properties. Thus, measures taken by the doctor in 1852 to protect the interests of his legitimate children now hindered his desire to provide for Sabina and Ellen. Sabina had been left Elmsdale, with Hardwicke House and the Turkish baths bequeathed to Ellen. Anticipating opposition to the will, Dr Marsden cleverly left £1,000 to his niece Ellie Godfrey (his brother Frederick's daughter), on condition that neither she nor any other member of the Marsden family should dispute it. There were shades of the old Caroline Matthews affair, as effectively Mrs Godfrey would receive a bribe from her uncle rather than a bequest. In the ultimate repudiation by their father, Alice and Emily were not mentioned.

Mary Hartman, in her book *Victorian Murderesses*, can be forgiven for misinterpreting the will. Hartman assumed Emily and Alice had predeceased their father. The doctor's reference to 'Sabina Marsden (formerly Welch)' also left her under the mistaken impression that he had married a third time. She reasoned that his bequest to his niece may have been 'a kind of restitution' – belated acknowledgement of the misery he had caused his daughters. This conclusion, while understandable, provided Dr Marsden with a degree of absolution he did not deserve.

Following a service in the medieval All Saints Anglican Church on 12 February, the doctor's coffin was removed to Hastings Cemetery. There, in what can only be described as an act of sacrilege, he was interred within the same grave as Rosa – the daughter he cruelly referred to as 'a corpse' in 1853, when he saw her tied to her sister, Alice, in Mademoiselle Doudet's apartment. We must assume that in burying Dr Marsden beside his estranged daughter, Sabina was complying with his wishes, yet it cannot have been a comfortable situation for her. If Ellen were to visit the grave in the years ahead, the name Rosa Sidney Marsden would surely raise awkward questions.

Dr Marsden's death freed Mary Marsden from the uncomfortable status of a lady living apart from her husband. It also released the dowry she had brought to their marriage, prompting her to draw up her own will. With her daughter Isabella dead, Mary bequeathed the bulk of her estate to her nephew Colin Campbell, who had succeeded his father as Laird of Jura. By now her original £6,000 dowry had grown to a substantial £10,000. Her will included small bequests to other relatives, including her stepdaughters. Emily, who had been caring for Mary since Isabella's death, was also to receive an annuity.

As a relatively young and still handsome woman, the retirement haven of Hastings held little appeal for Sabina after the death of Dr Marsden. She moved back to London with Ellen, setting up home at 7 Leinster Square, Bayswater. On 26 November 1894 she married master mariner Lorenz Högstedt, in Bayswater's parish church of St Matthews. Having spent twenty years with a much older man, the 41-year-old now restored the balance by choosing a husband eleven years her junior. Captain Högstedt was twenty-nine, a fair-complexioned, blue-eyed Swede. The public affirmation of a church wedding was understandably important to Sabina after the years of secrecy surrounding her relationship with Dr Marsden. However, her marriage certificate reveals the extent of deception she was still forced to employ.

Not surprisingly, she gave her marital status as 'widow'. More bizarrely, and presumably inspired by the knowledge that her parents had worked as tea and coffee vendors at Malvern, Sabina stated that her father had been a tea planter! Was this the story she had told Ellen? Did she deflect awkward questions about her background by pretending her family had been wiped out in some tropical epidemic in India or Ceylon? Perhaps the strangest 'error' was that involving her father's name, which she recorded as James Marsden. Considering Dr Marsden had been old enough to be her father, this could be dismissed as a Freudian slip, but there is another possibility. Ellen was one of the witnesses at the ceremony, as was Sabina's solicitor, Charles Paice. If they were under the impression that young Ellen's father had been James Welch, Sabina could hardly claim the same man as her own father. Assuming she had forgotten giving her maiden name as Jones on Ellen's birth certificate, she may have panicked and written Marsden, hoping it would go unnoticed. This theory is substantiated by a handwritten amendment to the document made a full two months later, when Sabina's daughter and solicitor were *not* present. It reads: 'In entry No. 32 Col. 7 For "Marsden" read "Welch" corrected by me Edward A. Stuart Vicar. In the presence of Lorenz Edward Högstedt [and] Sabina Amanda Högstedt, the parties married.'[4] It is impossible to know who or what prompted the correction, or how much of her past Sabina revealed to her new husband.

The wedding breakfast was a seven-course meal at one of London's most fashionable and cosmopolitan restaurants, Frascati's, of Oxford Street. Its lavish interior was described in the book *Dinners and Diners*, published in 1889:

> There are gilt rails to the balcony, which runs, as in a circus, round the great octagonal building; the alcoves that stretch back seem to be all gold and mirrors and electric light. What is not gold or shining glass is either light buff or delicate grey, and electric globes in profusion, palms, bronze statuettes, and a great dome of green glass and gilding all go to make a gorgeous setting.[5]

The buff menu, printed with a spray of orchids and the names of the newlyweds, was carefully preserved by the bride, and subsequently by Ellen. It was a memorable occasion, although the anxiety involved in filling out the marriage certificate was a reminder for Sabina that the details of her previous life could be exposed at any time, and that her new world could collapse like the *soufflé au chocolat* they were served for dessert.

Sabina and Lorenz Högstedt's wedding breakfast menu, from Frascati's London restaurant

As a young woman Ellen was clearly confused about her identity. When she was seventeen she wrote her name in a book of poems as Nellie Marsden Högstedt. Sabina's constant evasiveness about 'family' created another issue. How was her daughter to cope with that perennial, snobbery-laden query, 'Who are your people?' Ellen was as ignorant on the subject as an orphaned foundling. In 1900, when she turned twenty-one, she assumed control of the trust fund set up for her under Dr Marsden's will. It was at this point she discovered she had been left Hardwicke House, increasing her suspicion that the doctor had been something more than an affectionate step-parent. On 15 October 1900, just weeks after her birthday, she went to the trouble of changing her name by deed poll from Welch to Högstedt, as if to dissociate herself from the James Welch she had been told was her biological father. Some months later, and presumably without her mother's knowledge, she wrote to the family solicitor Charles Paice, asking for information about Dr Marsden. Mr Paice replied, 'Upon reference to her papers [presumably Sabina's] I find that Dr Marsden was a son of Mr James Marsden of Cheltenham who died between the years 1835 and 1837, and it appears to have been a Gloucestershire family.'[6] This vague response was due either to the solicitor's genuine ignorance or to his loyalty to Sabina.

Sabina and Lorenz had been married for six years and were living in Addison Road in Kensington with Ellen and Miss Physick when the country prepared to celebrate the arrival of the twentieth century.

28. Bequests and Legacies

❧

It is not given to all to see a new century in, and there are many who are thinking how so considerable an occasion is to be celebrated. Great Britain especially has much cause to be grateful to the century which is dying…What wondrous gifts is the twentieth century bringing? Will man fly in a hundred years hence, will war be made impossible by science, will poverty be diminished to almost vanishing point, and will life be prolonged to unexpected lengths? If ever man had cause to be solemn it will be when the clock strikes twelve on the last night of 1900.[1]

The new century had barely begun when the nation was plunged into mourning for Queen Victoria, who died at Osborne House on the Isle of Wight on 22 January 1901. She had reigned for sixty-three years and seven months. Multicoloured bunting put up to celebrate New Year was replaced by the royal mourning colours of purple and white. The Victorian era has often been described as a paradox, in which extraordinary advances in science and technology took place within an environment of rigid class division, moral duplicity, and the sexual prudery and ignorance that blighted the lives of the Marsden sisters. What did Emily and Alice make of the old Queen's death? The feelings of loss they shared with the rest of the population were complicated by more personal reflections. Her Majesty's note recommending one of her departing wardrobe ladies had influenced Dr Marsden's decision to employ Célelestine Doudet as their governess. And on 24 May 1853 an outing to celebrate the Queen's birthday ended with their sister Marian lying on the floor at Cité Odiot, unconscious and paralyzed.

By the spring of 1901 Emily had left Exmouth and was living in Christchurch Road, Bournemouth, caring for a now 80-year-old Mary

Marsden. Alice was in lodgings at Brighton, although it is unclear whether this was a permanent arrangement or simply another 'change of air'. At the time of their half-sister Ellen's letter to the solicitor requesting information on Dr Marsden, his widow Mary had been preoccupied with the disposal of her estate. On 9 March 1901 she added a codicil to her will. The Campbell family properties on the Hebridean Isle of Jura were heavily in debt, and in an attempt to assist her nephew and principal beneficiary, Colin Campbell, she revoked all other legacies and bequests, including those to her siblings and to Alice Marsden. Mary's proud Highland heritage took precedence over everything – even a bequest to the hospital where her daughter Isabella died went by the wayside. Only Emily's annuity remained, a miniscule £40 from an estate now valued at around £16,000. Yet all the old lady's personal effects, including trinkets and jewellery, were entrusted to Emily to distribute as she saw fit, a demonstration of the implicit trust she had in her stepdaughter. Mary Lyon Marsden died at the Karrakatta private hotel in Christchurch on 16 February 1905, aged eighty-four.* For Sabina Högstedt, Mary Marsden's death opened the proverbial Pandora's box. With Mary's life-interest in the properties at Malvern extinguished, Hardwicke House and Elmsdale were conveyed to herself and Ellen according to the provisions under Dr Marsden's will.

The legal documentation revealed the secrets Sabina had been hiding for so long. Ellen discovered that her mother's long relationship with Dr Marsden had been adulterous. And if the doctor was her real father, as by now she suspected, then she was illegitimate. Her trust in her mother must have been completely shattered…what other lies had been told? There were also implications for Sabina's relationship with her husband. Did Lorenz Högstedt discover that his wife had misrepresented herself as a widow on their wedding day?

Following their stepmother's death, Alice and Emily moved to No. 11 Mount Ephraim Road, Royal Tunbridge Wells, another famous spa centre. Their neighbours would never have suspected that the two quiet maiden ladies had grown up knowing some of the Victorian era's most eminent

---

* Mary might just as well have hurled her fortune into the dreaded Corryvrecken whirlpool off Jura. In 1938 her great-nephew sold the debt-ridden family estates. In so doing, Charles Campbell, who had lost an eye in the First World War, fulfilled a strange prophecy: 'The last of the Campbells will be one-eyed and will leave Jura with his entire possessions in a cart drawn by a white horse.'

figures, or that they had been the victims in one of the mid-nineteenth century's most famous cases of child abuse.

John Rashdall's widow, Emily, had remained in touch with the Marsden sisters after her husband's death, and no doubt kept them informed concerning her son Hastings's academic successes. The child who had played at being a preacher as a 6-year-old fulfilled his destiny by becoming a highly respected theologian, historian and philosopher. When Hastings made a late marriage in July 1905,* he and his bride Constance received what he jocularly referred to as a 'congratulatory epistle' from his spinster cousins.

However, a letter to his elderly mother dated 15 November reveals he had very little contact with Emily and Alice: 'I want to be <u>quite</u> sure that I am right in supposing that "we" means herself [Emily] and Isobel, before I reply. Will you please let me have a line to say whether this is so. You know my haziness about people I only hear about.'[2]

In 1907 Rashdall published his most well-known work, *The Theory of Good and Evil; A Treatise on Moral Philosophy*. Through his father's diaries he was well aware of his cousins' tragic past, and perhaps Dr Marsden's treatment of his daughters influenced the theologian's views on forgiveness: 'Nor in private relations can we always be called upon to treat the man who has betrayed our trust – even after repentance and apology – as though he had not betrayed it.'[3]

Alice fell ill on 20 November 1910, aged sixty-five, and her physician Dr Thomas Elliott was called. Emily nursed her sister until she died four days later from heart failure. Her death certificate also noted that she was a chronic sufferer of asthma and insomnia. She was buried in the town's Borough Cemetery on 28 November after a service at Holy Trinity Church. In Alice's death, Emily not only lost her sister and closest companion but the person who had shared the misery and multiple bereavements of their childhood, followed by the equally troubling deaths of their siblings, James and Rosa.

Emily lived on alone for nearly six years. At some point she moved into lodgings at No. 34 Dudley Road, Tunbridge Wells. Happily she was not friendless. In the 1911 census (taken on the night of 12 April) she was

---

* In 1953 Hastings Rashdall's widow Constance donated the Reverend John Rashdall's unpublished diaries and notebooks to the Bodleian Library at Oxford University.

listed as a visitor at the home of another unmarried lady, Rosamund Foy, in Elham, a picturesque village in the Kentish Downs.

Given all that had happened in her life, it is doubtful whether Emily, now seventy-four years old, feared for her safety when war against Germany was declared on 4 August 1914. Nor would she have panicked when, on Christmas Eve that year, the first enemy bomb landed in a garden at Dover, just 45 miles away, knocking a startled holly gatherer from a tree. Three of Mary Marsden's Campbell great-nephews had enlisted and, like so many others, Emily would probably have responded immediately when Queen Mary appealed for women to knit socks and vests for the troops.

Men were still fighting in the trenches of northern France when Emily Frances Marsden died on 18 September 1916. The cause of her death was given as cerebral embolism, heart failure and convulsions. Acknowledged even by her father as spirited, intelligent and attractive, Emily had grown up burdened by responsibility and denied the opportunity to fulfil her potential. Nevertheless, her life could be described as heroic. She spent her middle and late years as a selfless carer: a comforting presence at the deathbed of Rosa, her half-sister Isabella, her stepmother Mary, and finally her sister Alice. Sadly, though perhaps inevitably, only a neighbour, Amelia Snell, was present at *her* death. Emily was buried on 21 September beside Alice. Their headstone, like that of Rosa and Dr Marsden at Hastings, has long since vanished.

The 1911 census records Emily's half-sister Ellen as being aged thirty-one. She was still single, but now living in her own home, Hemmet, at 22 Park Avenue, in London's leafy Hampstead. If the girl who enjoyed reading poetry at seventeen once dreamed of romance and marriage, she may have been inhibited by the knowledge that she was illegitimate, and by the ambiguity of her position within the English class system. Ellen could have lived comfortably on her inheritance from Dr Marsden. It is testament to her character that instead she chose to become a pioneer of vocational training. She was employed as a millinery instructress by the London County Council at one of their first training colleges. It is likely her needlework skills had been acquired from Miss Physick, now retired and eking out an existence on the old age pension of five shillings per week. A modest legacy under Dr Marsden's will would have made the old lady's life so much easier. Fortunately, Ellen demonstrated her affection for Miss Physick by offering her a home at Hemmet.

Soon, a third person joined the household, when Ellen informally adopted a little girl. Her name was Christina Dorothea, but Ellen acknowledged her late father by giving the child the additional middle name of Loftus. This may also have been an attempt by Ellen to establish some sort of familial bond. It is to be hoped Miss Physick had a sense of humour as she was affectionately known by Christina as Auntie Piggy! The details surrounding the child's birth in November 1911 are hazy, but like Ellen herself she was illegitimate. Her birth mother was in service in Kensington, where Christina dutifully visited her 'aunt' every week, completely unaware that this woman was her mother. It was only when 'Aunt Asta' died in 1927 that the 16-year-old was told the truth. Exactly how Ellen came into contact with Christina's mother is unclear, but having lived in Kensington for some years she may have known the young woman's employer.

Like her daughter Ellen, Sabina Högstedt owned a house in London's Hampstead, but in early 1911 she was living alone at a cottage in Haddenham, a village near Aylesbury in Buckinghamshire. On 16 April 1912 she made her will. The testament was witnessed by a local surgeon and a minister, suggesting Sabina was ill and feared she might not recover. It appears she was estranged from her husband, which may explain her move to Haddenham. Her estate had a gross value of £10,000, but Captain Högstedt was pointedly dismissed in one line: 'I bequeath to my said husband Lorenz Edward Hogstedt the sum of fifty pounds.'[4] Everything else, including Elmsdale at Malvern, was to go to Ellen.

By the beginning of 1916 a failing Sabina had moved next door to Ellen in Park Avenue, Hampstead. The then 5-year-old Christina had the habit of slipping in to sit by Sabina's bedside. Her childish prattle distracted the sick woman and she appreciated the little girl's company. On 15 February Sabina added a codicil, providing for the child who had stolen her heart. She died five months later, on 25 August 1916, aged sixty-three.

Following the death of her mother, Ellen decided that thereafter she would be known by the surname of Marsden, acknowledging her real father and marking the end of lifelong confusion over her identity. At the end of 1926 the elderly Miss Physick became ill with cancer of the bowel. She spent her last days in Manor House Hospital at Golders Green, where she died on 9 May 1927 at the age of ninety-five. Ellen was at her bedside. Miss Physick had been part of Ellen's life for more than forty years

– becoming more grandmother figure than family retainer. Touchingly, Ellen paid tribute to the old lady's status as a gentlewoman when registering the death, describing her previous occupation as 'lady housekeeper', and noting she had been born the daughter of a solicitor.

Thanks to Ellen and Sabina, Christina received a good education. In 1932 she married a lawyer and the couple went on to have five children. Ellen was regarded as the youngsters' maternal grandmother. She thus enjoyed the companionship and support of 'family' in her old age despite the fact that, like her seven half-siblings, she never married. Ellen Amy Marsden died at her home in Thurlow Road, Hampstead, on 22 May 1966, aged eighty-eight. Found among her papers was a document that would add a final twist to the story of Dr Marsden's daughters, turning it almost full circle.

The document was a blank Gretna Green marriage application with a cryptic note on the back in Dr Marsden's hand: 'To save time if in haste!' Had the naive Sabina followed her lover to London in the mistaken belief that he intended to divorce his wife? For the form to have been preserved by Sabina and subsequently by Ellen indicates its significance to them both: precious, if flimsy, evidence of Dr Marsden's commitment and good intentions. But close inspection of the document reveals it was printed in the 1840s, and that the women may have been entirely wrong in their assumptions.

The wording on the form states that having declared themselves single, the parties named would be duly:

Married after the manner of the Laws of the Church of England, and agreeable to the Laws of Scotland: as witness our Hands;

GRETNA HALL, this ………. day of ………… 184…[5]

It is feasible that forms intended for the 1840s remained in use beyond that date, but they would certainly not have been in use when Dr Marsden began his relationship with Sabina Welch a full thirty years later.

Nor, due to a change in Scottish law, would the doctor's exclamatory 'To save time if in haste!' have made any sense in the 1870s. Gretna Green became a popular venue for 'shotgun' weddings in the eighteenth century because religious ceremonies were not mandatory in Scotland and hence there was no requirement for the usual reading of banns on three successive Sundays prior to the marriage – a relief for a woman with a swelling stomach. However, in 1856 a bill was enacted requiring that, from 1 January 1857, either the bride or groom had to have been resident in Scotland for the preceding twenty-one days, effectively cancelling Gretna's twin advantages of time and convenience. Since Dr Marsden had married his first wife Lucy in the 1830s, the woman he thought he might have to marry in haste can only have been Mary Campbell, prior to their eventual, very proper, Edinburgh wedding in December 1852.

It might be remembered that when Célestine Doudet was prosecuted for cruelty against the Marsden sisters she hit back by claiming Mary had lived with Dr Marsden for two years before her marriage, that she was '...a light woman, hiding her past under the veil of an honourable union' and that her marriage had only taken place because she fell pregnant. The governess had a habit of exaggerating or twisting information to her own advantage, but there was always a kernel of truth to her charges. Mary Campbell *was* living in Dr Marsden's home as early as October 1851 and it is also possible the governess had got wind of the old scandal in which Mary was accused of having an affair with her brother-in-law, Lachlan Macquarie Jr. Immediately before joining Dr Marsden's household, Mademoiselle Doudet was living in Scotland, where the court case over the dissolute Macquarie's will was creating a good deal of gossip.

Could it be that Mary fell pregnant to Dr Marsden and that the couple contemplated an irregular Gretna Green wedding until abortion or miscarriage saved the day? If so, the blank marriage application reveals the complete hypocrisy of a man who judged his own young daughters as morally corrupt. Of the many ironies in this story, perhaps the greatest is that the document may have been preserved by Dr Marsden's lover, and subsequently by his illegitimate daughter, on a totally false premise.

Epilogue

Malvern

Although Great Malvern prospered due to the purity and efficacy of its spring waters, it was deadly *impurities* in the water supply that brought a final end to the town's reputation as a spa centre. By 1900 Dr John Fergusson was one of Malvern's last water-cure practitioners. In the spring of 1905 a widow from Eton, Mrs Alice Merton, went to stay at the doctor's Abbey Road clinic with her two sons. Regrettably, typhoid fever broke out and the infection was traced to a well used to fill Dr Fergusson's tanks. Hugh Merton, aged seventeen, was one of three people who died and his mother successfully sued the doctor, as did several others.[1] The epidemic and its aftermath badly affected Fergusson's practice and in 1913 he was declared bankrupt. The town survived because many of the grand medical establishments and boarding houses became schools and colleges.

In October 2010 it was announced that after more than 150 years, production of bottled Malvern water would cease and that the plant would be sold as a development site – a sad end after the glory days when Malvern spring water flowed from the crystal fountain at the Great Exhibition. However, visitors can still fill their own containers from several of the town's springs or, alternatively, buy a bottle or two of Dr Gully's Winter Ale from the Malvern Hills Brewery.

During the 1960s Dr Marsden's Hardwicke House was replaced by what is quite possibly the ugliest block of flats ever constructed. Happily the separate, Gothic-inspired bath house still stands, as does Elmsdale House. In 1908 Elmsdale was being advertised as 'A Home School for little Boys. Preparatory for the Public Schools and Navy'. Now divided into flats, its turreted tower and stepped gables provide a glimpse of Hardwicke House's past splendour. In Worcester Road, Cotswold House has resumed its original name of Abberley House. The rear garden terrace, where the Marsden children built their playhouses, is unchanged. Like Elmsdale, and in common with many of Malvern's old homes, both Abberley House and Abbotsfield have been converted to residential apartments.

In the Priory churchyard the grave Lucy Marsden shares with her mother carries a poignant reminder of the young girl's struggle with her schoolwork. A well-intentioned person has retraced the weathered inscription in silver paint, mistakenly transforming the word 'also' into 'alos'.

Within the church is a brass plate in memory of John Rashdall. Located in the ambulatory it pays tribute to his six-year ministry: '…during which time the Tower was restored and the district church of Holy Trinity of Malvern was built'. There are also memorials to Queen Victoria. Three bells were added to St Mary's tower in celebration of Her Majesty's golden jubilee in 1887. And at the eastern end of St Anne's chapel is the Queen Victoria diamond jubilee window, dedicated by the women of the parish. The fine Georgian vicarage in Abbey Road where John Rashdall lived during his incumbency was demolished many years ago. In 1936 Great Malvern's post office was erected on the site.

Lady Emily Foley, Great Malvern's own 'royal personage', died as the clock struck midnight on 1 January 1900, aged ninety-four. There is a signed portrait of her in the foyer of the recently refurbished Foley Arms Hotel. The old lady's private waiting room at the railway station has been transformed into Lady Foley's Tearooms.

Paris

In the spring of 2010 my partner Rob and I visited the site of Mademoiselle Doudet's old school at Cité Odiot. The historically significant private *allée* leading off Rue Washington is often included in 'secret' walking tours of the city. Having purposely arrived on a weekday when we had been told the electronic security gates are left open for visitors, I was dismayed to find them locked. My French is not fluent, but walking away was impossible. Miraculously, as I was summoning the courage to press a random intercom button, the gates swung open and a departing resident smilingly waved us through.

Inside, I was almost overwhelmed by the spirit of Emily and her siblings. Judging from old photographs, the exterior of the terraces, with their shuttered windows and tiny wrought iron balconies, is unaltered. Adjacent to No. 1 stood the old porter's lodge. It was easy to imagine the increasingly malnourished girls looking on longingly as Monsieur and Madame Tassin enjoyed their simple, al fresco meals. Célestine Doudet's first floor apartment was undergoing renovation and it occurred to me that the workmen may have been removing the last vestiges of its nineteenth-century interior. Perhaps the overflowing skip held fragments of wallpaper imprinted with the marks of children's hairnets! Despite all the evidence at the trials, exactly what occurred in those rooms will never be known, but certainly it was where Marian lay dying for many weeks without a single visit from her father.

One bonus of the building work was that the front door of No. 1 had been propped open, revealing the communal staircase Lucy had been forced to trudge up and down until Madame Espert's cook feared she would collapse. The closed shutters of the ground floor apartment were a reminder of Monsieur Rapelli, the reclusive doctor of theology who claimed to have neither seen nor heard anything amiss with the young Marsdens, and who testified in favour of the governess.

Before leaving we walked the length of the cobbled *allée*. It was here the sisters rolled their hoops and skipped and jumped with their little French friends until sickness and psychological damage robbed them of the capacity to play. I found it difficult to control my emotions.

From Cité Odiot we went to visit the Bureau de la Conservation at Montmartre Cemetery. I was hoping to find Marian's grave, or at least to locate the official record of her burial. '*Est elle célèbre?*' ('Is she famous?') was the first question I was asked. Most visitors to the cemetery are making pilgrimages to the graves of luminaries such as Vaslav Nijinsky, Edgar Degas and Jacques Offenbach. 'Not *really*,' I replied, explaining the story as best I could. Wide-eyed with horror, the three female staff members dropped what they were doing and joined forces in poring over old record books. Eventually they found the entry: 'July 1853, MARSDEN, Marian Theodosia, aged twelve and a half'.

The girl's grave was described as 'full', meaning that the bodies of other, unnamed people had been buried below Marian. One of the ladies explained that this was often the case within families, although it seemed unlikely that other Marsden family members had been buried in Montmartre. We all agreed that, given the circumstances of the little girl's death, a sympathetic friend may have offered the space. But we were to discover an even bigger mystery. The date of Marian's exhumation was recorded as 18 November 1854, but no mention could be found of her reburial. Later records listed someone else as occupying her original space. 'She was perhaps taken home to England?' the French ladies suggested, but I am almost certain this was not the case.

Wherever the unfortunate and blameless Marian rests, I hope this book will serve as a memorial to her and her siblings, who were so badly let down by their carers.

Notes

❧

ABBREVIATIONS USED IN THE NOTES

- Fouquier, Armand, *Causes Célèbres de Tous Les Peuples* (Lebrun, Paris, 1860) – *Causes Célèbres*
- Marsden, James Loftus, *Notes on Homeopathy* (Leath, 1849) – *NOH*
- Papers of the Reverend John Rashdall (Diaries 1827–69) – JRD

CHAPTER 1

1 Hutton, Catherine, *Reminiscences of a gentlewoman of the last century: Letters of Catherine Hutton* (Birmingham, 1891), p. 134.
2 *New Monthly Magazine and Humorist*, 1842, p. 432.
3 *Provincial Medical Journal*, vol. 6, September 1843, p. 541.
4 *Provincial Medical and Surgical Journal*, November 1842, p. 149.
5 Wilson, James, and Gully, James Manby, *The Dangers of the Water Cure and its Efficacy Examined and Compared with those of the Drug Treatments of Diseases* (London, 1843).

CHAPTER 2

1 Baillie, John, *Memoir of the Revd W.H. Hewitson* (James Nisbet & Co., 1853), p. 22.
2 *Gentleman's Magazine*, April 1812, p. 394.
3 *Provincial Medical Journal*, 10 July 1844, p. 224.
4 Holmes, Oliver Wendell, *Homeopathy and its kindred delusions; two lectures delivered before the Boston Society for the Diffusion of Useful Knowledge* (Ticknor, Boston, 1842).
5 JRD, 2 October 1844.
6 *NOH*, p. 27.
7 Ibid., p. 24.
8 *Provincial Medical Journal*, 3 February 1844, p. 350.
9 *NOH*, p. 164.

CHAPTER 3

1 Hall, Radclyffe, *The Well of Loneliness* (Jonathan Cape, 1928), p. 6.
2 Davies, H., *Visitor's Handbook for Cheltenham* (Longman, 1840), p. 9.
3 Lee, Edwin, *Homeopathy and Hydropathy Impartially Appreciated* (Churchill, 1859), p. 68.

4 Nichols, Thomas Low, and Nichols, Mary Sargeant Gove, *Marriage: Its History, Character, and Results* (Nichols, New York, 1854).

5 Benson, A.C. and Esther, R.B.B. Viscount (eds), *The Letters of Queen Victoria*, vol. III (Murray, 1908)

6 *Monthly Homeopathic Review*, vol. 1, 1857, p. 291.

7 Lot 130A 3pp., 8vo, St James Square, Cheltenham, 2 August [c. 1845]. www.liveauctioners.com/item/2061540, date viewed 1 July 2010.

8 Bostridge, Mark, *Florence Nightingale: The Woman and Her Legend* (Viking, 2008), pp. 124, 125.

9 Darwin, Charles (ed. by Francis Darwin), *The Life and Letters of Charles Darwin*, vol. 1 (Murray, 1887), p. 373.

10 JRD, 14 June 1849.

11 Leech, Joseph, *Three Weeks in Wet Sheets: Being the Diary and Doings of a Moist Visit to Malvern* (Hamilton, Adam & Co., 1851), pp. 94–5.

12 Severn Burrow, C. F., *A Little City Set on a Hill: the Story of Malvern* (Priory Press, 1948), p. 73.

13 Marsden, James Loftus, *The Action of the Mind on the Body* (H.W. Lamb, 1859), p. 36.

14 Darwin, Charles, *The Descent of Man and Selection in Relation to Sex* (Murray, 1871), pp. 99–100.

15 Leech, Joseph, *Three Weeks in Wet Sheets: Being the Diary and Doings of a Moist Visit to Malvern* (Hamilton, Adam & Co., 1851), p. 16.

16 Gully, James, *The Water Cure in Chronic Disease* (Churchill, 1846), p. 379.

CHAPTER 4

1 JRD, 10 March 1834.

2 Simpson, Helen J., *The Day the Trains Came* (Gracewing Fowler Wright Books, 1997), p. 101.

3 McMenemy, William H., *Life and Times of Sir Charles Hastings* (Livingstone, 1959), p. 286.

4 Keynes, Randal, *Annie's Box: Charles Darwin, his Daughter and Human Evolution* (Fourth Estate, 2001), p. 166.

5 Ibid., p. 198.

6 Tennyson, Alfred, *The Letters of Alfred Tennyson*, vol. II, ed. by Cecil Y. Lang and Edgar F. Shannon (Oxford University Press, 1987), p. 15.

CHAPTER 5

1 Benson, A.C. and Esther, R.B.B. Viscount (eds), *The Letters of Queen Victoria*, vol. II (Murray, 1908), pp. 317–18.

2 JRD, 8 May 1851.

3 www.online-literature.com/tennyson/the-early-poems/2, viewed 6 August 2012.

4 Smith, Brian, *A History of Malvern* (Leicester University Press, 1964), p. 201.

5 Forster, John, *The Life of Charles Dickens* (Chapman and Hall, 1872–3).

6 JRD, 17 November 1851.

7 Tennyson, Hallam, Baron, *Alfred Lord Tennyson: A Memoir by His Son*, vol. I (Macmillan, 1897), p. 355.

8 Ibid., p. 156.

9 Ibid., vol. II, pp. 21–2.

CHAPTER 6

1 *The Naval Chronicle*, vol. 13 (Jan.–July 1805), p. 405.

2 Bouchardon, Pierre, *Célestine Doudet, institutrice* (A. Michel, Paris, 1928), p. 10.

3 Ibid.

4 Ibid.

5 Thomas, Frédéric, *Petites Causes Célèbres Du Jour* (Gustave Harvard, Paris, 1855), vol. 3.

6 Ross, Miss, *The Governess, or Politics in Private Life* (Smith, Elder & Co., 1836), p. 16.

7 Hughes, Kathryn, *The Victorian Governess* (Hambledon Press, 1993), p. 106.

8 Le Fanu, J. Sheridan, *Uncle Silas* (Richard Bentley, 1864), pp. 41–2.

CHAPTER 7

1 *The Carlyle Letters Online* [CLO] 2007, http://carlyleletters.org, date viewed 10 October 2010.

2 Bouchardon, Pierre, *Célestine Doudet, institutrice* (A. Michel, Paris, 1928), p. 22.

3 *Medical Times and Gazette*, 11 April 1863.

4 *British Medical Journal*, 9 May 1863.

5 *National Archives of Scotland* GD174/1731 (Draft letter from Lachlan Macquarie to Colin Campbell of Jura, 14 January 1842).

6 *Memoire Pour Mademoiselle Célestine Doudet contre Le Ministère Public et M. Marsden, partie civile* (Cour Imperiale, Paris, 1855), p. 17.

CHAPTER 8

1 JRD, 25 June 1852.

2 Nichols, Thomas Low and Nichols, Mary Sargeant Gove, *Marriage: Its History, Character and Results* (Nichols, New York, 1854), pp. 223–4.

3 Arago, François, *Meteorological Essays* (Longman, Brown, Green and Longmans, 1855), p. 37.

4 Ritchie, Anne Thackeray, *Anne Thackeray Ritchie: Journals and Letters*, biographical commentary and notes by Lillian F. Shankman, ed. by Abigail Burnham Bloom & John Maynard (Ohio State University Press, 1994), p. 38.

5 *Causes Célèbres*, p. 13.

6 JRD, 12 September 1852.

7 Williamson, William Henry, *Annals of Crime; Some Extraordinary Women* (Routledge, 1930), p. 245.

8 *Causes Célèbres*, p. 13.

9 Thackeray, William, *The Letters and Private Papers of William Makepiece Thackeray*, vol. III, ed. by Gordon Norton Ray (Harvard University Press, Cambridge, 1946) p. 106.
10 Hartman, Mary S., *Victorian Murderesses: The True History of Thirteen Respectable French and English Women Accused of Unspeakable Crimes* (Schocken, New York, 1977) p. 284, note 56.
11 Ibid., p. 103.
12 JRD, 8 December 1852.
13 Ibid., 14 February 1853.

CHAPTER 9

1 *Causes Célèbres*, p. 13.
2 JRD, 15 June 1853.
3 Ibid., 21 June 1853.
4 Smith, Mary, *The Autobiography of Mary Smith, Schoolmistress and Nonconformist* (Bemrose, 1892), pp. 38–9.
5 JRD, 24 June 1853.
6 carlyleletters.dukejournals.org. Viewed 3 May 2010.
7 Chopin, Frédérick, *Chopin's Letters*, collected by Henry Opienski (Dover, New York, 1988), p. 391.
8 Thackeray, William, *The Letters and Private Papers of William Makepiece Thackeray*, vol. III, ed. by Gordon Norton Ray (Harvard University Press, Cambridge, 1946), p. 93.
9 *Causes Célèbres*, p. 4.

CHAPTER 10

1 JRD, 11 August 1853.
2 *Causes Célèbres*, p. 14.
3 Leakey, Caroline W., *Lyra Australis; or, Attempts to Sing in a Strange Land* (Bickers & Bush, 1854).
4 JRD, 11 August 1853.
5 Smyth, Ethel, *Little Innocents: Childhood Reminiscences* (Oxford University Press, 1986), p. 81.
6 *La Tribune Judiciaire. Process de Mademoiselle Célestine Doudet devant la Cour Imperiale de Paris, chambre des appels correctionnels* (Paris, 1855), p. 63.
7 JRD, 16 September 1853.
8 Ibid., 18 September 1853.
9 Ibid., 20 September 1853.
10 *Causes Célèbres*, p. 8.
11 JRD, 20 December 1853.
12 Ibid., 31 December 1853.

CHAPTER 11

1 JRD, 8 May 1854.
2 Ibid., 12 May 1854.
3 Williamson, William Henry, *Annals of Crime; Some Extraordinary Women* (Routledge, 1930), p. 258.
4 *Berrow's Worcester Journal*, 31 March 1855.
5 *The Century Illustrated Monthly Magazine*, vol. 67 (1904), p. 503.
6 *Causes Célèbres*, p. 11.
7 *Berrow's Worcester Journal*, 31 March 1855.

CHAPTER 12

1 *Memoire Pour Mademoiselle Célestine Doudet contre Le Ministère Public et M. Marsden, partie civile* (Cour Imperiale, Paris, 1855), pp. 5–7.
2 *La Tribune Judiciaire. Process de Mademoiselle Célestine Doudet devant la Cour Imperiale de Paris, chambre des appels correctionnels* (Paris, 1855), p. 148.
3 *Memoire Pour Mademoiselle Célestine Doudet contre Le Ministère Public et M. Marsden, partie civile* (Cour Imperiale, Paris, 1855), p. 9.
4 Ibid.
5 Ibid., p. 10.
6 Ibid., p. 13.
7 Ibid., p. 15.
8 Ibid., p. 22.
9 Ibid.
10 Ibid., p. 23.
11 Ibid., p. 24.

CHAPTER 13

1 *London Daily News*, 13 December 1854.
2 JRD, 15 December 1854.
3 Ibid., 22 December 1854.
4 *London Daily News*, 23 February 1855.
5 *Petites Causes Célèbres du Jour*, vol. 3, March 1855.
6 Benson, A.C. and Esther, R.B.B. Viscount (eds), *The Letters of Queen Victoria*, vol. I – 1837–1843 (Murray, 1908), p. 392.
7 *Berrow's Worcester Journal*, 3 March 1855.
8 *Causes Célèbres*, p. 16.
9 Thomas, Frédéric, *Petites Causes Célèbres Du Jour* (Gustave Harvard, Paris, 1855), vol. 3, p. 53.
10 Williamson, William Henry, *Annals of Crime; Some Extraordinary Women* (Routledge, 1930), pp. 244–5.
11 *Causes Célèbres*, p. 24.
12 *Berrow's Worcester Journal*, 31 May 1855.

13 *Causes Célèbres*, p. 18.

14 Ibid., p. 10.

15 Ibid., p. 19.

CHAPTER 14

1 *Causes Célèbres*, p. 15.

2 Ibid.

3 Ibid., p. 24.

4 Ibid., p. 48.

5 Williamson, William Henry, *Annals of Crime; Some Extraordinary Women* (Routledge, 1930), p. 256.

6 *Petites Causes Célèbres du Jour*, vol. 3, March 1855.

7 *Causes Célèbres*, p. 20.

8 *Berrow's Worcester Journal*, 31 March 1855.

9 *Memoire Pour Mademoiselle Célestine Doudet contre Le Ministère Public et M. Marsden, partie civile* (Cour Imperiale, Paris, 1855), p. 12.

10 JRD, 21 February 1855.

11 *Petites Causes Célèbres du Jour*, vol. 4, April 1855.

12 Ibid.

13 *Berrow's Worcester Journal*, 31 March 1855.

CHAPTER 15

1 *Causes Célèbres*, p. 15.

2 *Berrow's Worcester Journal*, 3 March 1855.

3 *Causes Célèbres*, p. 14.

4 Ibid., p. 5.

5 *Reynold's Newspaper*, 4 March 1855.

6 *Berrow's Worcester Journal*, 24 March 1855.

7 *Petites Causes Célèbres du Jour*, vol. 3, March 1855.

8 *Morning Chronicle*, 1 March 1855.

9 *Petites Causes Célèbres du Jour*, vol. 3, March 1855.

10 Williamson, William Henry, *Annals of Crime; Some Extraordinary Women* (Routledge, 1930), p. 261.

11 *Berrow's Worcester Journal*, 3 March 1855.

12 *Petites Causes Célèbres du Jour*, vol. 3, March 1855.

13 JRD, 28 February 1855.

14 Ritchie, Anne Thackeray, *Anne Thackeray Ritchie: Journals and Letters*, biographical commentary and notes by Lillian F. Shankman, ed. by Abigail Burnham Bloom and John Maynard (Ohio State University Press, 1994), p. 41.

15 Thackeray, William, *The Letters and Private Papers of William Makepiece Thackeray*, vol. III, ed. by Gordon Norton Ray (Harvard University Press, Cambridge, 1946), p. 439.

16 *Harper's New Monthly Magazine*, May 1855, vol. X, pp. 844–5.
17 *The Lancet*, 1 February 1855, vol. 1, p. 249.

CHAPTER 16

1 *Petites Causes Célèbres du Jour*, vol. 4, April 1855.
2 Marsden, James Loftus, *The Action of the Mind on the Body* (Lamb, 1859), p. 40.
3 *Berrow's Worcester Journal*, 31 March 1855.
4 *Causes Célèbres*, p. 42.
5 Ibid.
6 Ibid., p. 41.
7 Ibid., p. 42.

CHAPTER 17

1 *New York Times*, 16 April 1855.
2 *Petites Causes Célèbres du Jour*, vol. 4, April 1855.
3 *Berrow's Worcester Journal*, 31 March 1855.
4 *Morning Chronicle*, 15 March 1855.
5 *Lloyd's Weekly*, 1 April 1855.
6 *The Examiner*, 24 March 1855.
7 *London Daily News*, 3 April 1855.
8 Ibid.
9 *Household Words*, vol. 15, May 1858, pp. 477–8.
10 Rose, Kenneth, *Superior Person: a Portrait of Curzon and his Circle in Late Victorian England* (Weidenfeld & Nicolson, 1969), p. 20.

CHAPTER 18

1 *New York Times*, 23 March 1913.
2 *Petites Causes Célèbres du Jour*, vol. 5, May 1855.
3 *Causes Célèbres*, p. 29.
4 Ibid., p. 34.
5 Ibid., p. 32.
6 Ibid., p. 22.
7 Ibid., p. 33.
8 Ibid., p. 23.
9 Hughes, Kathryn, *The Victorian Governess* (Hambledon, 2001), p. 143.
10 *Causes Célèbres*, p. 45.
11 Ibid., pp. 45-6.
12 Ibid., p. 29.
13 Ibid p. 55.
14 Vandam, Albert Dresdon, *An Englishman in Paris* (Appleton, New York, 1892), p. 170.
15 *The Letters of Charles Dickens*, ed. by Madeline House, Graham Storey, Kathleen Tillotson, and Angus Easson (Clarendon Press, 1993), vol. 7, 1853–5.

16 *Causes Célèbres*, p. 56.
17 *New York Times*, 25 February 1885.
18 *Appleton's Journal*, 11 September 1875, p. 346.
19 *Western Daily Press*, 12 July 1858.
20 *Household Words*, vol. XIV, 1856.
21 Axelrad, Jacob, *Anatole France: A Life Without Illusion* (Harper & Brothers, 1944), p. 19.
22 www.sueyounghistories.com.

CHAPTER 19

1 JRD, 1 May 1855.
2 Wohl, Anthony, *The Victorian Family: Structure and Stresses* (Croom Helm, 1978), p. 73.
3 JRD, 30 September 1855.
4 *Monthly Homeopathic Review*, vol. 1, 1857, p. 291.
5 *The British Friend*, December 1856.
6 www.ncbi.nlm.nih.gov/pmc/articles/.../pdf/medhistsuppl00033-0480.pdf, viewed 3 September 2011.
7 JRD, 15 December 1856.
8 JRD, 15 June 1856.

CHAPTER 20

1 www.grosvenorprints.com, viewed 20 May 2011.
2 JRD, 28 October 1862.
3 *Hampshire Telegraph & Sussex Chronicle*, 1 November 1862.
4 *London Daily News*, 20 March 1964.
5 JRD, 23 November 1864.
6 Matheson, Percy Ewing, *The Life of Hastings Rashdall* (OUP, 1928), p. 5.
7 JRD, 20 December 1868.
8 *England & Wales National Probate Calendar.*
9 Reclus, Elisée, *The Earth and Its Inhabitants...Amazonia and La Planta* (Appleton, New York, 1895), p. 443.

CHAPTER 21

1 James, Henry, *The Complete Letters of Henry James*, vol. 2, 1855–72, ed. by Pierre Walker and Greg Zacharias (University of Nebraska Press, 2006).
2 Curzon, Jane, *Diary of Jane Curzon*, 1870 (unpublished).
3 *New York Times*, 23 September 1871.
4 *Malvern Advertiser*, 20 June 1874.
5 *Return of Owners of Land, Worcestershire*, 1873, p. 20.

CHAPTER 22

1 *Monthly Homeopathic Review*, 1 November 1864, pp. 702–3.
2 *The Graphic*, 18 December 1875.

3 *The Times*, 3 August 1876.

4 Ibid., 21 July 1876.

5 *New York Times*, 20 August 1876.

6 *Worcestershire Chronicle*, 12 August 1876.

7 *National Archives*, CMY to MY 308-208.

8 Fraude, James Anthony, *Thomas Carlyle: A History of his Life in London, 1834–1881*, vol. 2 (Longmans, Green, 1884), p. 445.

9 Barlow, Nora (ed.) *The Autobiography of Charles Darwin, 1809-1882* (W.W. Norton, New York, 1958).

CHAPTER 23

1 *Evangelical Christendom*, vol. 15, 1874, p. 263.

2 Trollope, Anthony, *He Knew He Was Right* (Penguin, 1994), p. 254.

3 *London Society of Light and Amusing Literature for the Hours of Relaxation*, 1863, p. 136.

4 *New York Times*, 30 December 1877.

5 *Hastings & St Leonards Observer*, 22 December 1877.

CHAPTER 24

1 *Hastings & St Leonards Observer*, 29 December 1877.

CHAPTER 25

1 Dickens, Charles, *Bleak House* (Bradbury & Evans, 1853), p. 102.

2 *Hastings & St Leonards Observer*, 29 December 1877.

3 Ibid.

4 Ibid.

5 Ibid.

6 *London Medical Gazette*, 1848, vol. 7, pp. 590–4.

7 *Hastings & St Leonards Observer*, 29 December 1877.

8 *Medical Times & Gazette*, 17 October 1868, p. 441.

9 *Hastings & St Leonards Observer*, 29 December 1877.

10 *Hastings News*, 28 December 1877.

11 *Hastings & St Leonards Observer*, 29 December 1877.

12 Ibid.

13 Ibid.

14 Ibid.

15 Ibid.

16 *British Medical Journal*, 25 November 1876, pp. 678–9.

17 *General Register Office*.

CHAPTER 26

1 Ashfield, Andrew (ed.), *Romantic Women Poets: 1770–1838* (Manchester University Press, 1997), p. 257.

2 *British Homeopathic Review*, vol. 21, 1877.

3 *Portsmouth Times and Naval Gazette*, 24 September 1878.

CHAPTER 27

1 Darwin, Charles (ed. by Francis Darwin), *The Life and Letters of Charles Darwin* (Murray, 1887).

2 Keynes, Randal, *Annie's Box: Charles Darwin, his Daughter and Human Evolution* (Fourth Estate, 2001), p. 267.

3 *Liverpool Mercury*, 5 April 1883.

4 General Register Office.

5 Newnham-Davis, *Dinners and Diners: Where and How to Dine in London* (Grant Richards, 1901), pp. 264–5.

6 Personal Correspondence – Timothy Stunt.

CHAPTER 28

1 *The Graphic*, 15 December 1900.

2 *Papers of the Rev. Hastings Rashdall (1858–1924)*, New College Archives, Oxford.

3 Rashdall, Hastings, *The Theory of Good and Evil: A Treatise on Moral Philosophy* (Clarendon Press, 1907), p. 309.

4 General Register Office.

5 From original document in the possession of Timothy Stunt.

EPILOGUE

1 *British Medical Journal*, 22 December 1906, p. 1854.

Further Reading

Bailey, Victor, *This Rash Act: Suicide Across the Life Cycle in the Victorian City* (Stanford University Press, Stanford, 1998).

Euringer, Fred, *Night Noises* (Oberon Press, Toronto, 2001).

Frost, Ginger Suzanne, *Victorian Childhoods* (Praeger Publishers, Westport, 2009).

Garrard, Rose, *Donkey's Years on the Malvern Hills: A History of the Famous Hill Donkeys at Malvern's Springs, Spouts and Holy Wells* (Aspect Design, 2008).

Hembry, Phyllis, *British Spas from 1815 to the Present: A Social History* (Athlone Press, 1997).

Jalland, Patricia, *Death in the Victorian Family* (Oxford University Press, 1996).

Jenkins, Elizabeth, *Tennyson and Dr Gully* (Tennyson Research Centre, 1974).

Jones, Robert, *The History of the French Bar: Ancient and Modern; comprising a notice of the French courts, their officers, practitioners etc., and of the system of legal education in France* (Johnson & Co., 1886).

Marsden, the Revd Benjamin A., Marsden, James A. and Marsden, Robert S., *Genealogical Memoirs of the Family Marsden: their ancestors and descent traced from public records, wills and other documents, and from private sources hitherto unrecorded* (Griffith & Sons, 1914).

Matheson, P.E., *The Life of Hastings Rashdall. D.D.* (Oxford University Press, 1928).

Moriarty, Gerald Patrick, *The Paris Law Courts: Sketches of Men and Manners* (Seeley, 1894).

Ruddick, James, *Death at the Priory: Love, Sex, and Murder in Victorian England* (Grove Press, 2002).

Shaw, Arthur, *Forty Years in the Argentine Republic* (Mathews, 1907).

Smith, Brian S., *A History of Malvern* (Leicester Press, 1864).

Index

Abberley House *see also* Cotswold House, 27–8, 129, 255
Abbotsfield, 78
ABC Liniment, 222, 224, 232 (*footnote*)
Albert, Prince, 45, 116, 186
Antrim, Lady Louisa, 89
appel de minima, 164, 168, 172
Argentina, 191
autopsy, 108, 136, 137, 223, 237
Axelrad, Jacob, 173

Bailie, Monsieur, 171
Bailleux, Léocadie, 123–4, 133–4
Baker, Frederick Parker, 66, 99, 125, 173
Bedford Chapel, 21
Belgravia, 25
Bell, James Alfred, 255–8
belladonna, 22, 221–9 *passim,* 232, 233
Bélot, Adolphe, 171
Bennet, Miss, 89
Berryer, Antoine, 161, *162*
Binnie, Adelaide (*née* Burnell), 52, 56, 57, 63–4, 100, 105
Black, Dr, 90, 99
Bonher, Mademoiselle, 79
Bonnet, Dr, 139, 164
Bournemouth, 214, 215
Bravo, Charles, 206, 208–10 *passim*
Bravo, Florence, 198–9, 201–2, 205–6, 208, 210, 237
Brighton, 176, 178
Bulwer-Lytton, Sir Edward, 32
Burdett, Sir Francis, 24–5
Burford, Fanny, 103–4
Burnell, Adelaide, *see* Binnie, Adelaide
Burnell, Eliza, 52, 100
Burrows, Charles, 100, 104

Campbell, Mary Lyon, *see also* Marsden, Mary, 59–60, 62–3, 71, 253
Campeney, Selina, 216, 228–9
Candler, Hester, 105–7 *passim,* 128, 155, 156
Candler, William, 28, 105, 128
Carlyle, Jane, 59
Carlyle, Thomas, 84, 212
Carmichael-Smyth, Mrs, 68, 85, 140–1, 178
Chabaud-Latour de, Madame, 54
Chabaud-Latour de, Mademoiselle, 54, 114
Chaillot, Rue de, 147–51 *passim*
Chaix-d'Est-Ange, Gustave , 115, 116, *117*
Cheltenham, 20, 26–7 *passim, 26,* 102, 111
child abuse, 77, 81, 82–3, 86, 89, 93, 96–7, 118–20, 124, 133, 136 (*footnote*), 138, 140, 143–4, 146–7, 154, 157, 158–9, 173, 249
Christina Dorothea Loftus, 251
Cité Odiot, 67–8, *67,* 255–6
Claremont Cottage, 21, 27
Claridge, R.T., 15
Clark, Sir James, 49
Clermont, 170–1
Collomp, Monsieur, 81, 121
Conciergerie, 112
Cotswold House *see also* Abberley House, *27,* 28, 49
Cowley, Lord, 110, 158
Cox, Jane, 202, 209, 210
crystal fountain, *see* Great Exhibition
Crystal Palace, see Great Exhibition
Curzon, Lord, 159

Darwin, Anne (Annie) Elizabeth, 10, 41–3, grave, *43*

Darwin, Charles, 11, 30, 41–2, 240
Darwin, Emma, 42, 212
Darwin, Etty, 30, 41
Darwin, Francis, 240
Dauglish, Dr John, 181
Davenport-Jones, Mr, 229–30
Dawlish, 189
Dessiter, Félicité, 130, 131
Dickens, Charles, 47, 169–70, 172, 223
Dix's Field, 21, 21
douche
  ascending, 15
  descending, 18
Doudet
  Captain Antoine, 53–4
  Flore-Marguerite-Célestine (Célestine),
    52–7, 66, 68, 82, 83, 87, 93–3, 95–6,
    99, 110
      appeal, 161–8 passim, 172, 173, 255
      first trial, 112–42 passim
      second trial, 143–57 passim
  Louise, 54, 95, 113–14, 149, 173
  Madame, 54, 63
  Zéphyrine, 54, 77, 83, 85, 120, 150–2
Dowmann, Miss, 63, 116, 177
Dunkerque, 37, 105
Dyson, Charlotte, 184, 211

Earls Colne, 190
Eaton Chapel, 25, 179, 181
Edinburgh University, 16, 19
Elliott, Admiral, 98
Elmsdale, House, 78, 78, 92
English Enquiry, 100
ennui, 19, 81
Erskine, Katherine, 84, 84, 141
Espert, Madame, 68, 118–20, 165
Exeter, 21
Exmouth, 241

Felix House, 239
Fergusson, Dr John, 254
Fergusson, Mr William, 181–2
Fleishmann, Dr, 23
Foley Arms Hotel, 255
Foley, Lady Emily, 40, 41, 255
Fouquier, Armond, 170
Fox, Caroline, 103, 167
Frascati's restaurant, 245, 245

Frayle Muerto, 191, 192
Fry, Elizabeth, 160

Gabriel, Monsieur, 93
Gaudinot, Dr Gaston, 79–80
Gaujal, Monsieur de, 168
Gavelle, Madame, 76
Glenister, William, 229
Godfrey, Ellen (Ellie) (née Marsden), 191,
  243
Governesses' Benevolent Society, 55
Great Exhibition, 45–6, 46
Great Malvern see Malvern
Gretna Green, 252–3
Griffith, George, 209
Gully, Anne, 16
Gully, Helen, 16
Gully, Dr James Manby, 16, 198–200, 199,
  201–2, 205–6, 208–9, 211–12, 237,
  240–1

Haguenau prison, 171–2
Haisell, James, 223, 226, 227–8
Hall, Radclyffe, 26
Hampstead, 250
Hankey, Emily see Rashdall, Emily
Hardwicke House, 46–7, 47, 254
Hastings, 216, 242
Hastings Cemetery, 235, 243
Hastings, Dr Charles, 17
Hatton, Monsieur, (President Hatton),
  112
Hayne, Maria, 25, 28, 145–6
Heath, Dr, 221, 222, 224
Hemmet, 250
Hewitson, William, 19
Hind, Mary, 30, 129
Högstedt, Lorenz Edward, 244, 248, 251
Högstedt, (née Welch) Sabina Amanda,
  44, 201, 206, 211, 238–9, 241, 243, 244,
  252
Holmes, Oliver Wendall, 22
homeopathy, 11, 22, 24, 28, 29, 33, 66, 80,
  180, 204
Hooper, Mrs, 92–3
Hotel Windsor, 75, 162
Hughes, Sidney Jane, see Marsden, Sidney
  Jane
Hutton, Catherine, 14

hydropathy, *see* water-cure
hysteria, 60, 61

Isle of Wight, 191, 238

James, Henry, 198

Kempsey, 19
Kensal Green Cemetery, 240
Kensington, 183, 246
Kerry, Mary, 220, 229
Keynes, Randal, 240
Kissingen, 201, 209

Lansdowne Terrace, *26*, 27
Leakey, James, 38–9
Leech, Joseph, 31, 34, 42

Macquarie, Isabella (*née* Campbell), 62
Macquarie, Lachlan Jr, 62–3, 74, 96, 253
Maitrejean, Madam, 160
Malta, 23, 94, 189
Malvern 11, 14, 18, 45–8, 184–5, 197, 198, 200
Malvern Hills, 13, 26–7
Marsden
　Alice, 23, 89, 92–3, 99, 123, 143–4, 203, 215–16, 220, 224, 228–9, 230, 231–2, 238, 248, 249
　Emily Frances, 20, 52, 71–3, 82, 93, 94, 122–3, 132–3, 147, 150–2, 175, 184, 193, 219–22, 224–5, 231, 234, 238, 241, 248, 249–50
　Frederick, 19, 177, 184, 190, 213–14
　Frederick Jr, 190, 214
　Harriet, 19, 102, 116, 191
　Isabella, 92, 202, 241–2
　Captain James, 19, 20
　James Jr (Jimmy), 21, 29, 177, 184, 187–8, 189–92, 195–6
　Dr James Loftus, 11, 19, 20–5, 31–6, *35,* 51–2, 58, 61–2, 72–3, 74–6, 78, 80, 92, 93, 95, 135, 144, 145, 149–50, 156, 163, 175, 180–1, 197, 200, 202–4, 206, 213, 236–7, 238–9, 241–3, 246, 252–3
　John, 19
　Lucy Frances *née* Rashdall, 20, 23, 26, 28, 29, 66, 91

Lucy Harriet, 11, 20, 69, 79, 89–91
　grave, *91,* 97, 119, 121, 148, 150, 255
Marian Theodosia (Mary Ann, Poppy), 20, 79–80, 86, 87–80, 86, 87–8, 132–9 *passim,* 256–7
Mary Lyon (*née* Campbell), 59–60, 62–3, 71, 74–7 *passim,* 96–7, 175–6, 178–9, 181–2, 200, 213–14, 241, 247–8, 253
Rosa Sidney, 21, 57, 64–5, 102, 130–1, 148, 175, 215–16, 219, 220–3, 224–5, 229–36 *passim*
　death certificate, *233*
Sidney (*née* Hughes), 20, 190, 191
Theodosia, 21
Dr William, 142
Martel, President, 143
Martin, Madame, 86, 133
masturbation (self-abuse, moral sin etc.), 52, 57, 62, 63, 66–7, 72, 76, 81–2, 87, 90, 93, 106, 113, 116–18, 137–8, 140, 175, 191, 198, 203, 213
Mathilde, Princess, 155
Matthews, Caroline, 100–3, 104, 107, 163, 167
Mayfair, 204, 205
Melcombe Regis, 20
mesmerism, 51, 60, 191
misericords, 13, 41, 155
Montmartre Cemetery, 87, 108, 256–7

Napoleon III, Emperor, 169, 172
Netley House, 193, 198
Nichols, Mary Gove, 28, 66
Nightingale, Florence, 30, 126
Nogent-Saint-Laurens, Henri, 112, 113–14, *114,* 137–8, 154
Norman Hotel, 223
Notes on Homeopathy, 33, 180

Orwell Lodge, 205

Pacault, Désirée, 68, 121
Paice, Charles, 244
Palace, The, 19
Paris, 20, 52, 53, 64, 70, *70,* 74–5, 81, 95, 157, 173, 214–15
Peachfield, 180–1
Phipps, Colonel Charles Beaument, 96
Physick, Ellen Elizabeth, 239